SENTINEL

SALVAGE

STORY: SEAN McKEEVER
ART: UDON
PENCILS AND INKS: VRIENS, HELIG, HEPBURN & VEDDER
COLORS: HOU, YAN & YEUNG
UDON CHIEF: ERIK KO
LETTERS: CORY PETIT & DAVE SHARPE
ASSISTANT EDITOR: ANDY SCHMIDT
EDITOR: MARC SUMERAK

COLLECTIONS EDITOR: JEFF YOUNGQUIST
ASSISTANT EDITOR: JENNIFER GRÜNWALD
BOOK DESIGNER: JEOF VITA

EDITOR IN CHIEF: JOE QUESADA
PUBLISHER: DAN BUCKLEY

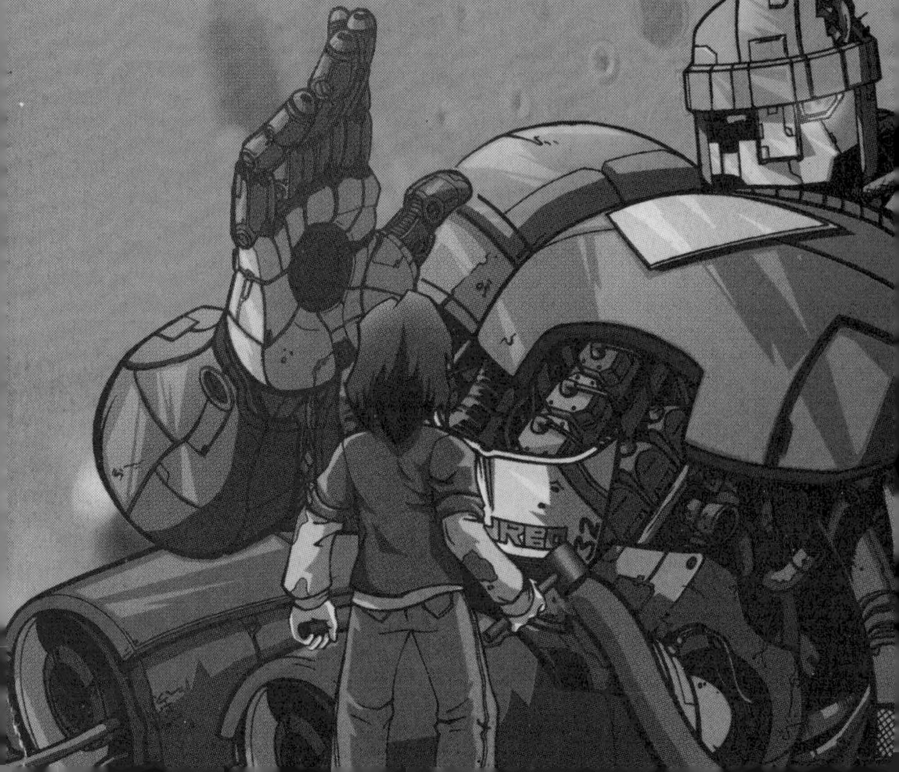

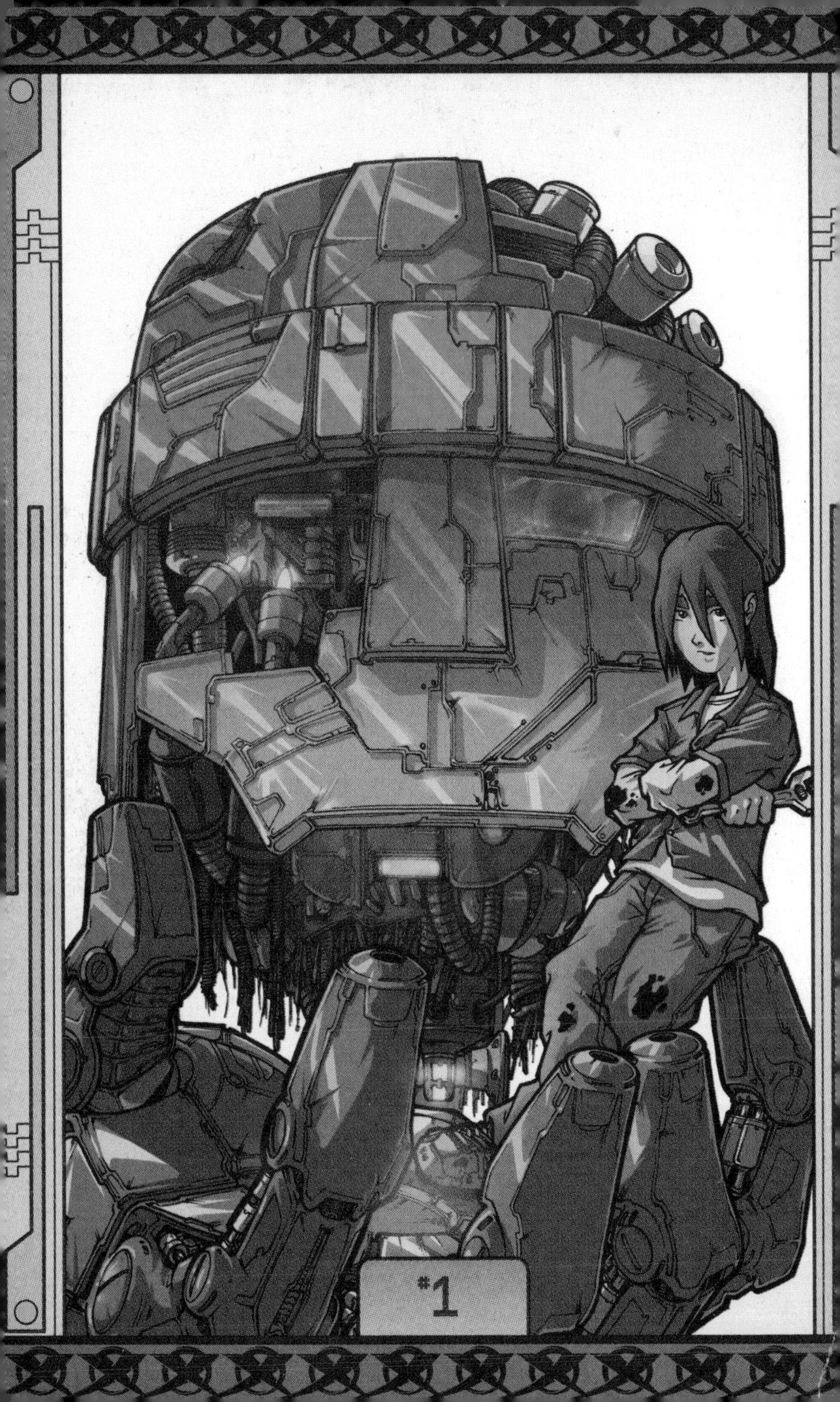
#1

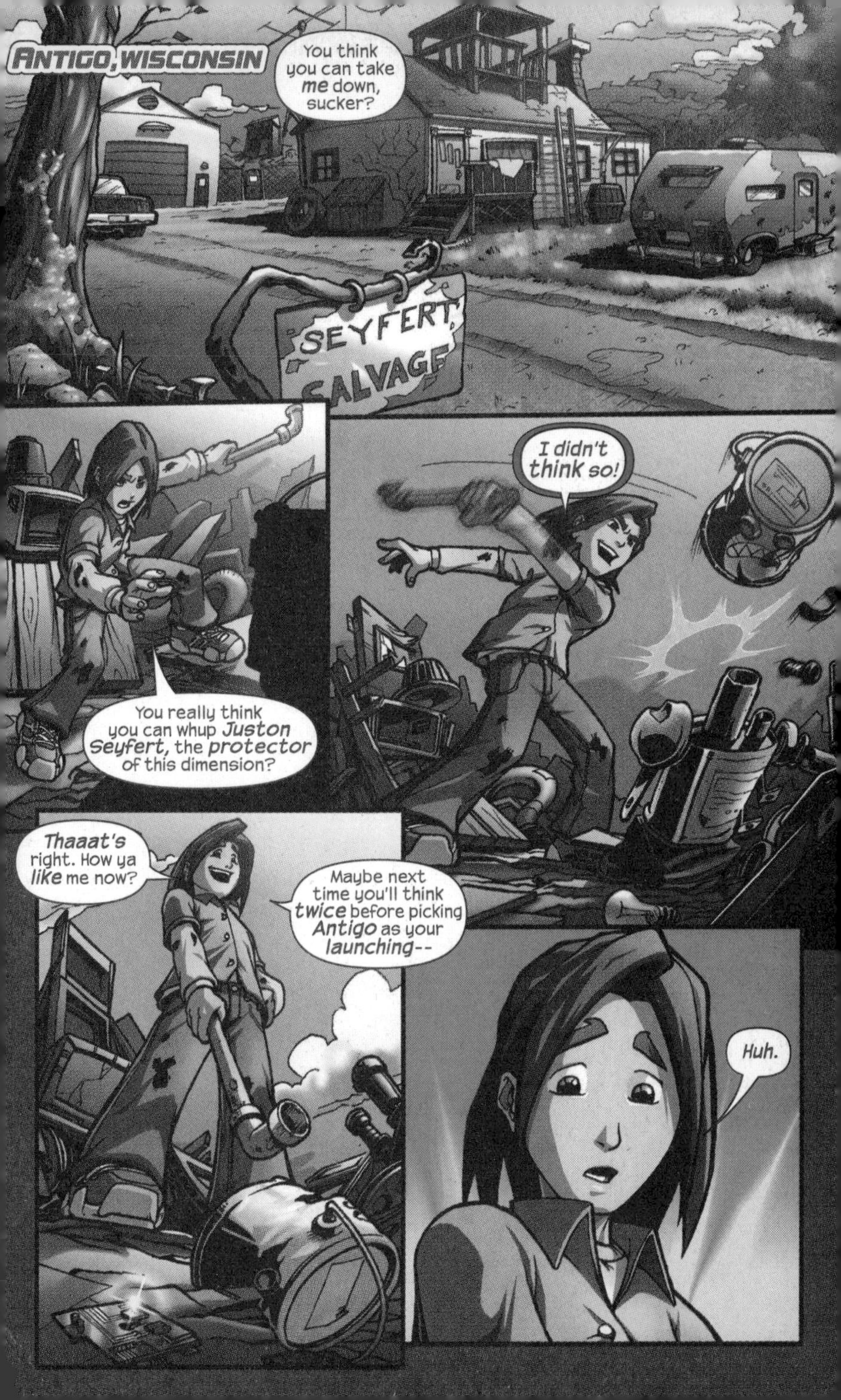
ANTIGO, WISCONSIN
You think you can take me down, sucker?
SEYFERT SALVAGE
You really think you can whup Juston Seyfert, the protector of this dimension?
I didn't think so!
Thaaat's right. How ya like me now?
Maybe next time you'll think twice before picking Antigo as your launching--
Huh.

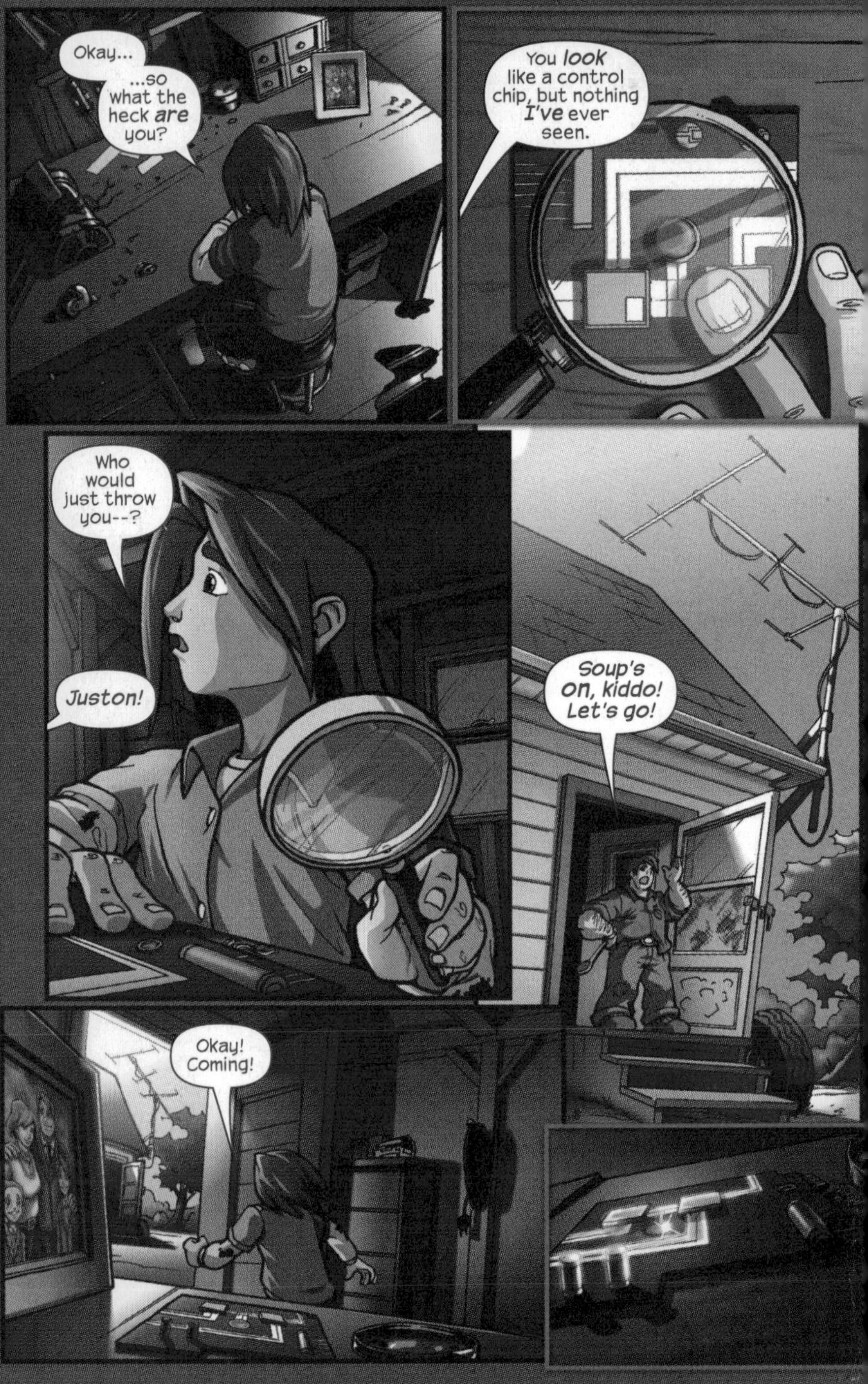
Okay...
...so what the heck *are* you?
You *look* like a control chip, but nothing *I've* ever seen.
Who would just throw you--?
Juston!
Soup's on, kiddo! Let's go!
Okay! Coming!

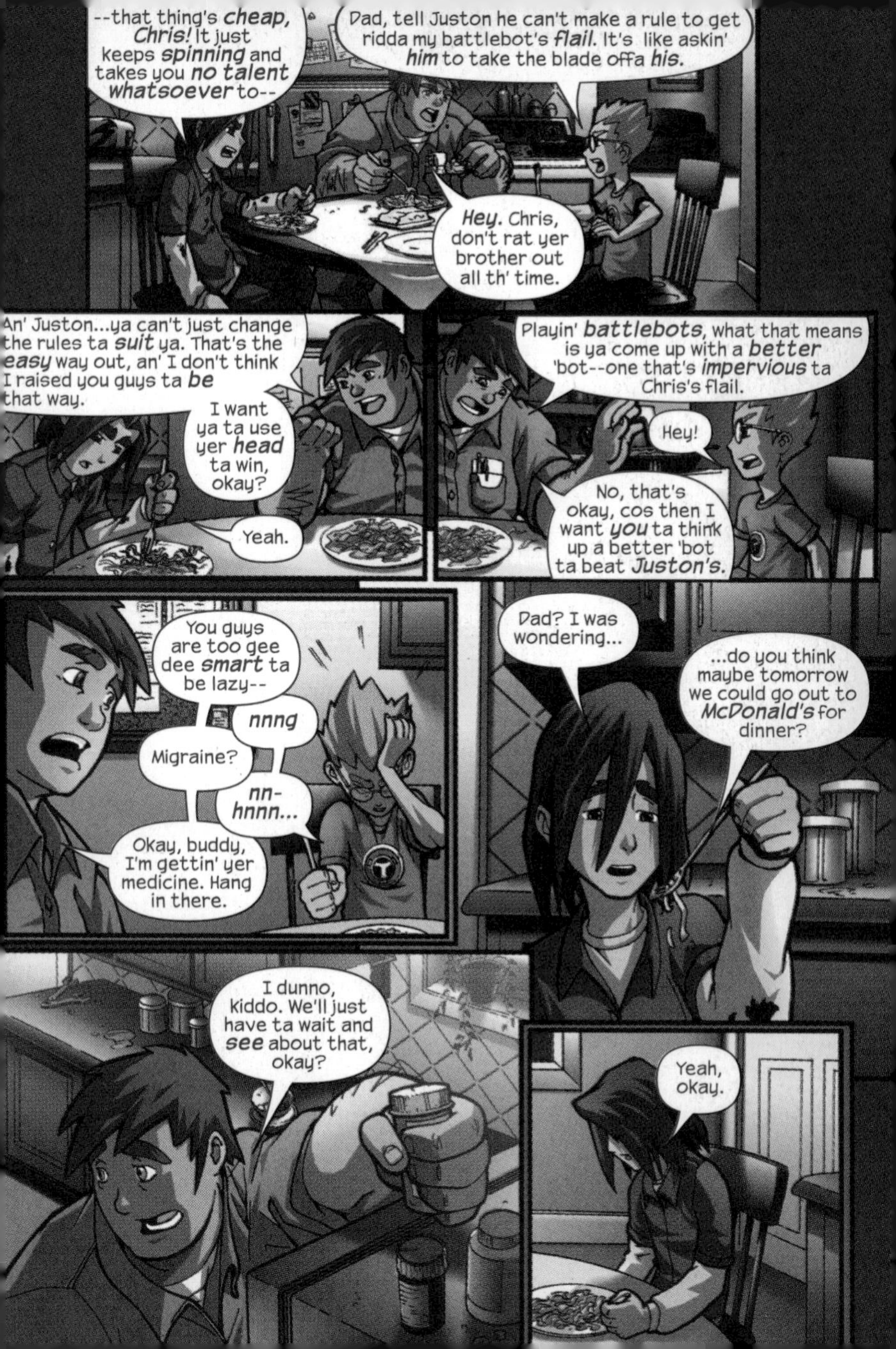
--that thing's *cheap, Chris!* It just keeps *spinning* and takes you *no talent whatsoever* to--
Dad, tell Juston he can't make a rule to get ridda my battlebot's *flail*. It's like askin' *him* to take the blade offa *his*.
Hey. Chris, don't rat yer brother out all th' time.
An' Juston...ya can't just change the rules ta *suit* ya. That's the *easy* way out, an' I don't think I raised you guys ta *be* that way.
I want ya ta use yer *head* ta win, okay?
Yeah.
Playin' *battlebots*, what that means is ya come up with a *better* 'bot--one that's *impervious* ta Chris's flail.
Hey!
No, that's okay, cos then I want *you* ta think up a better 'bot ta beat *Juston's*.
You guys are too gee dee *smart* ta be lazy--
nnng
Migraine?
nn-hnnn...
Okay, buddy, I'm gettin' yer medicine. Hang in there.
Dad? I was wondering...
...do you think maybe tomorrow we could go out to *McDonald's* for dinner?
I dunno, kiddo. We'll just have ta wait and *see* about that, okay?
Yeah, okay.

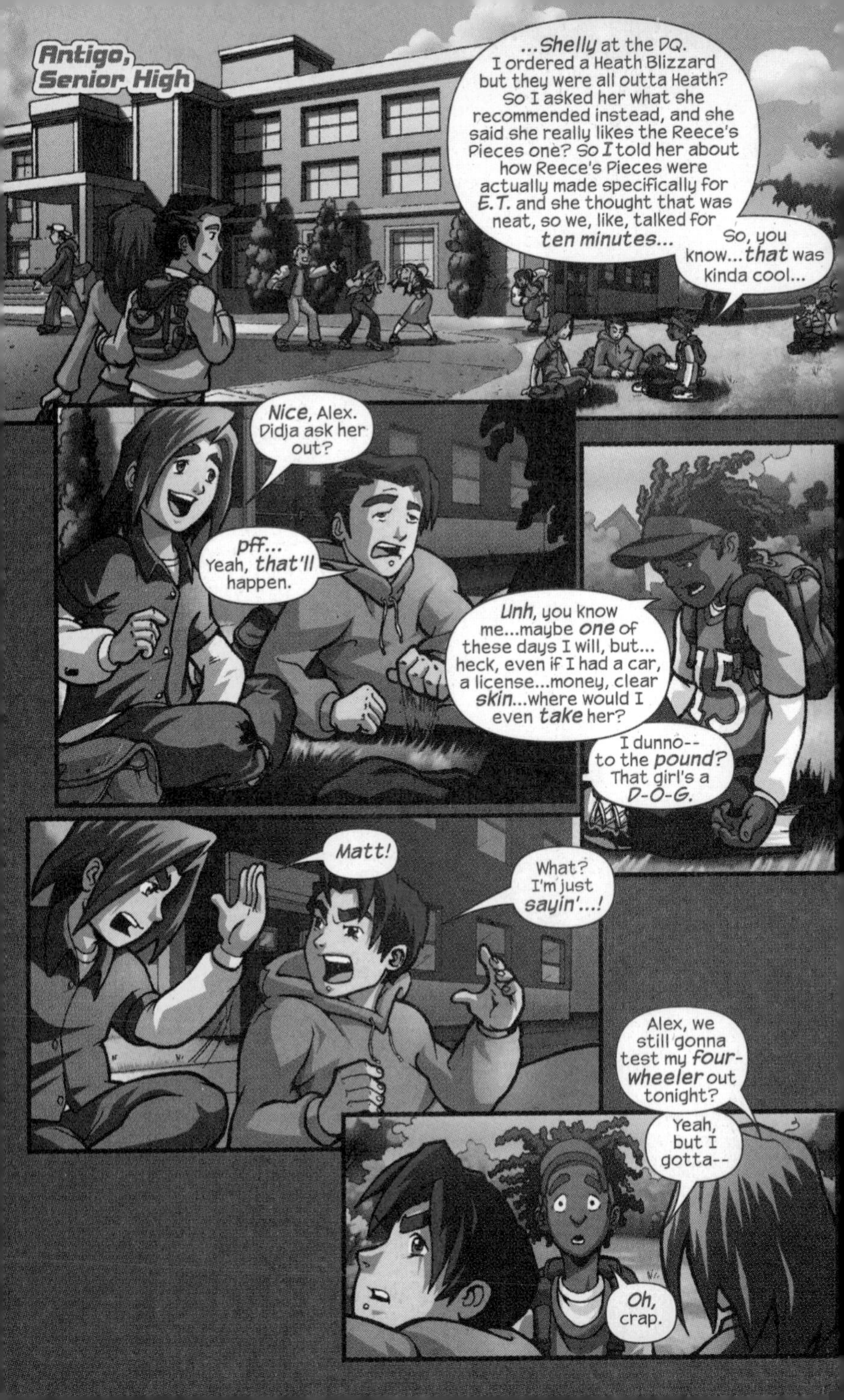
Antigo, Senior High
...Shelly at the DQ. I ordered a Heath Blizzard but they were all outta Heath? So I asked her what she recommended instead, and she said she really likes the Reece's Pieces one? So I told her about how Reece's Pieces were actually made specifically for E.T. and she thought that was neat, so we, like, talked for ten minutes...
So, you know...that was kinda cool...
Nice, Alex. Didja ask her out?
pff... Yeah, that'll happen.
Unh, you know me...maybe one of these days I will, but... heck, even if I had a car, a license...money, clear skin...where would I even take her?
I dunno-- to the pound? That girl's a D-O-G.
Matt!
What? I'm just sayin'...!
Alex, we still gonna test my four-wheeler out tonight?
Yeah, but I gotta--
Oh, crap.

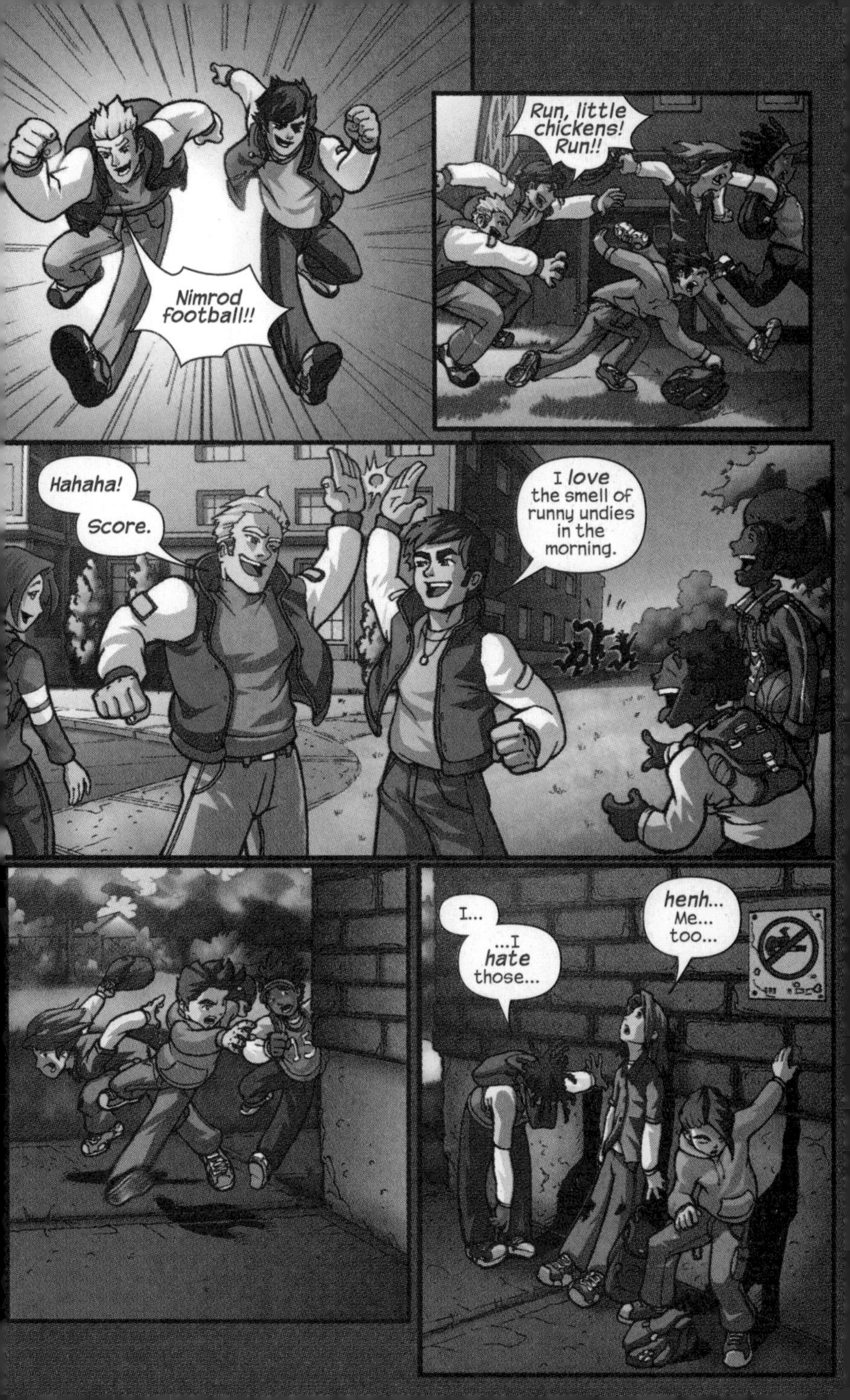
Nimrod football!!
Run, little chickens! Run!!
Hahaha!
Score.
I love the smell of runny undies in the morning.
I...
...I hate those...
henh... Me... too...

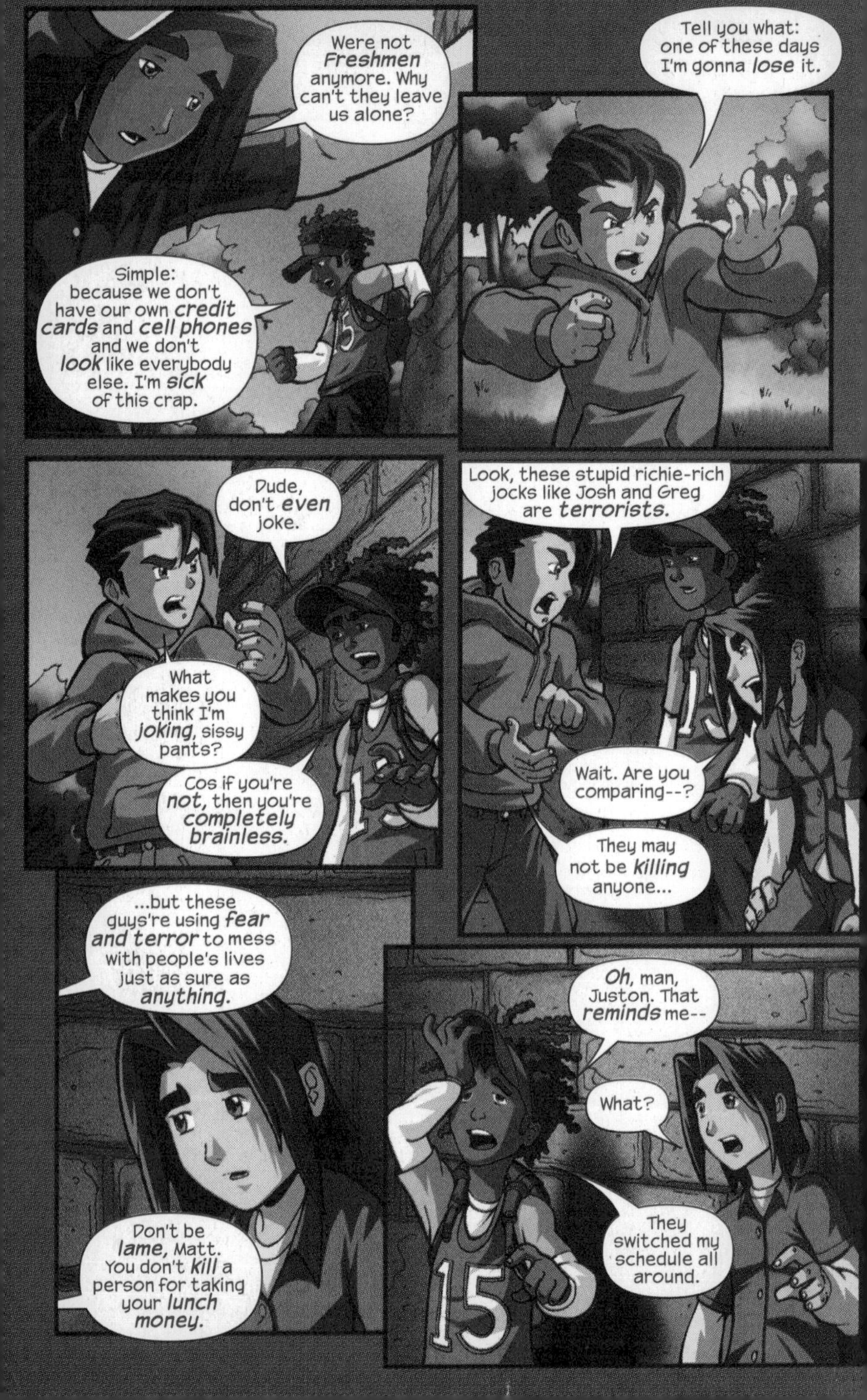

Were not Freshmen anymore. Why can't they leave us alone?
Simple: because we don't have our own credit cards and cell phones and we don't look like everybody else. I'm sick of this crap.
Tell you what: one of these days I'm gonna lose it.
Dude, don't even joke.
What makes you think I'm joking, sissy pants?
Cos if you're not, then you're completely brainless.
Look, these stupid richie-rich jocks like Josh and Greg are terrorists.
Wait. Are you comparing--?
They may not be killing anyone...
...but these guys're using fear and terror to mess with people's lives just as sure as anything.
Don't be lame, Matt. You don't kill a person for taking your lunch money.
Oh, man, Juston. That reminds me--
What?
They switched my schedule all around.

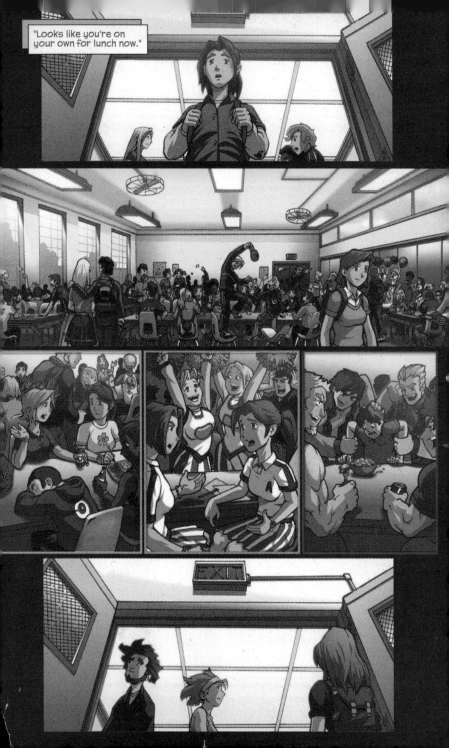

"Looks like you're on your own for lunch now."

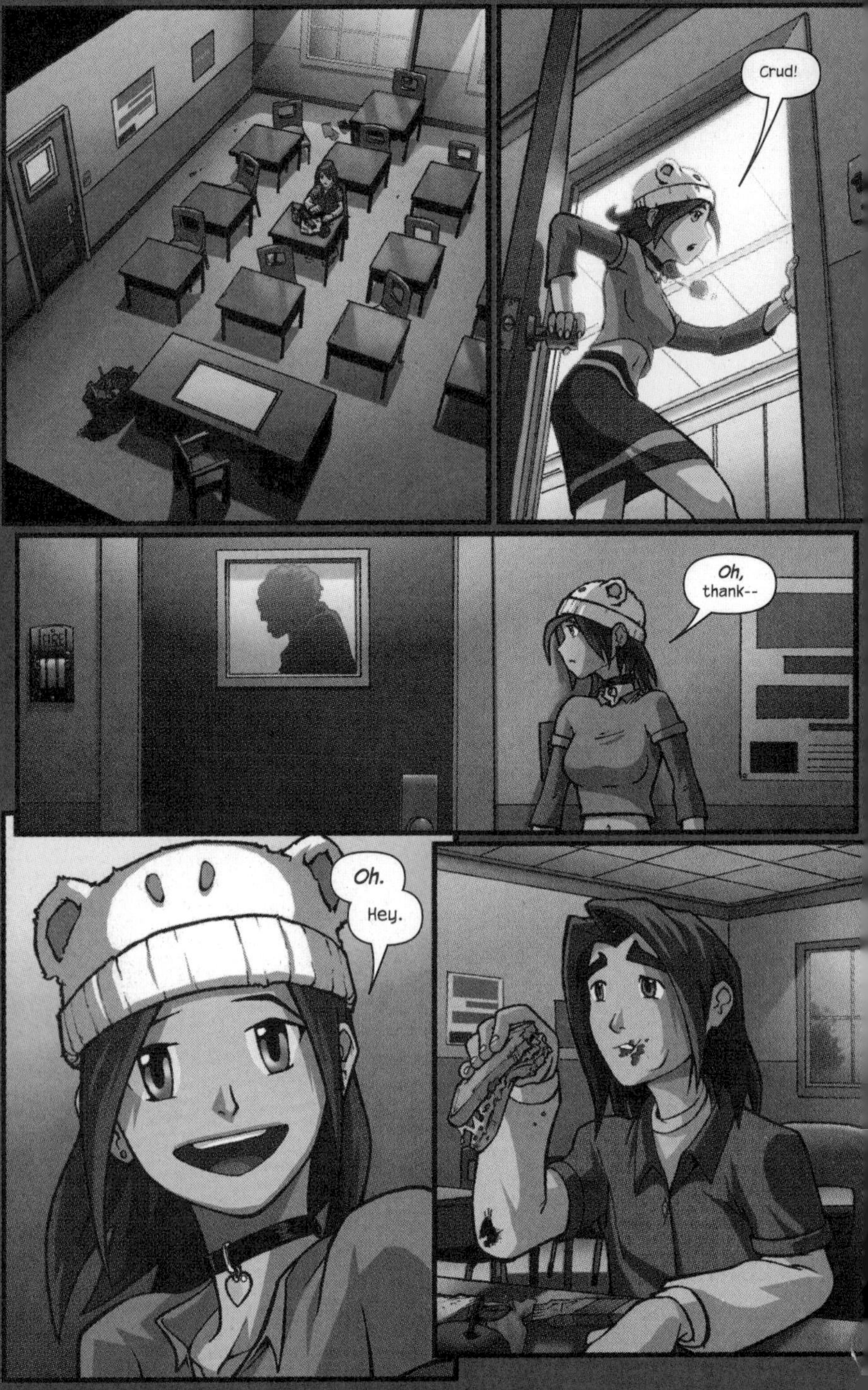
Crud!
Oh, thank--
Oh.
Hey.

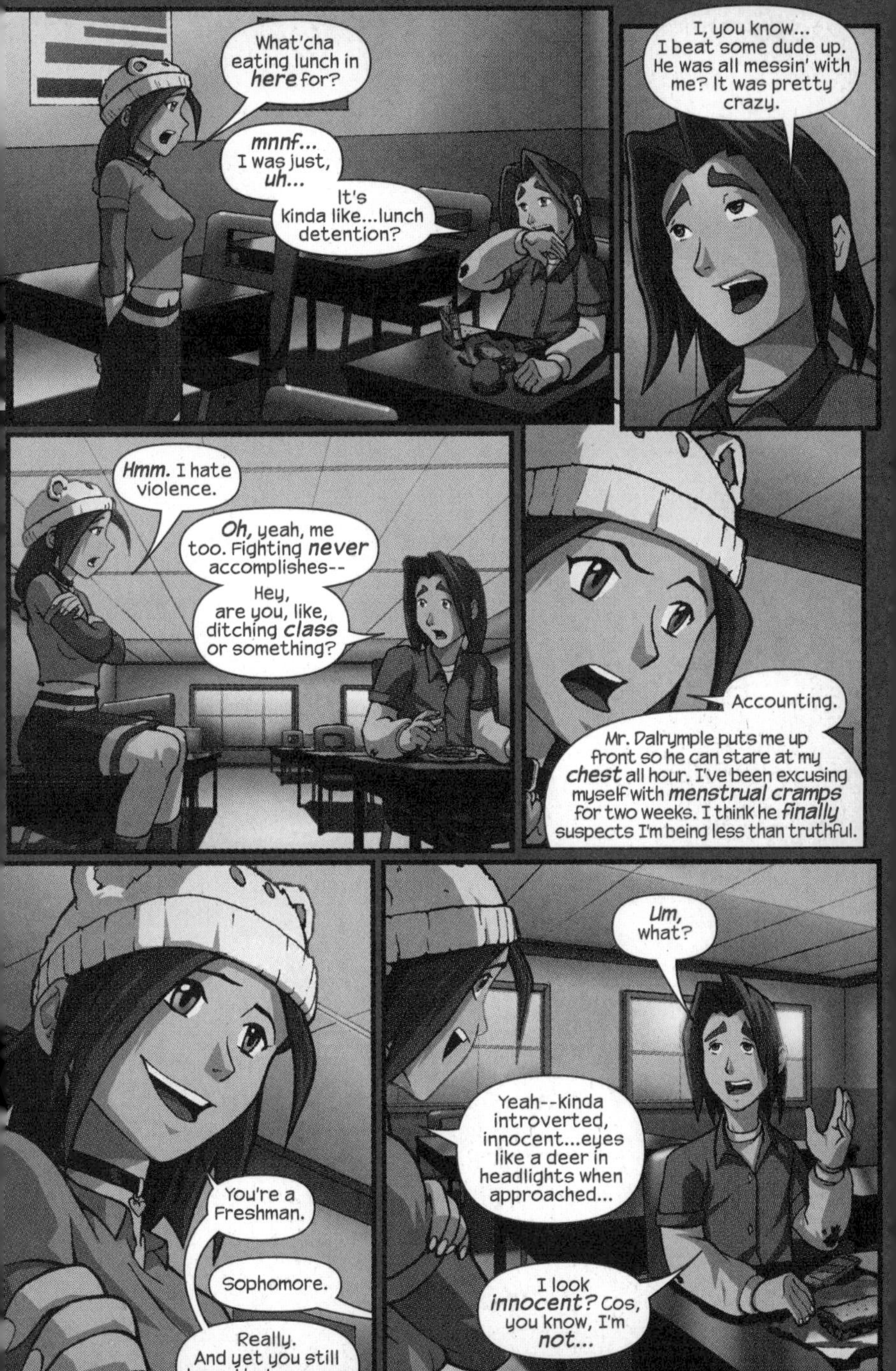
What'cha eating lunch in here for?
mnnf... I was just, uh...
It's kinda like...lunch detention?
I, you know... I beat some dude up. He was all messin' with me? It was pretty crazy.
Hmm. I hate violence.
Oh, yeah, me too. Fighting never accomplishes--
Hey, are you, like, ditching class or something?
Accounting.
Mr. Dalrymple puts me up front so he can stare at my chest all hour. I've been excusing myself with menstrual cramps for two weeks. I think he finally suspects I'm being less than truthful.
You're a Freshman.
Sophomore.
Really. And yet you still have that new car smell.
Um, what?
Yeah--kinda introverted, innocent...eyes like a deer in headlights when approached...
I look innocent? Cos, you know, I'm not...

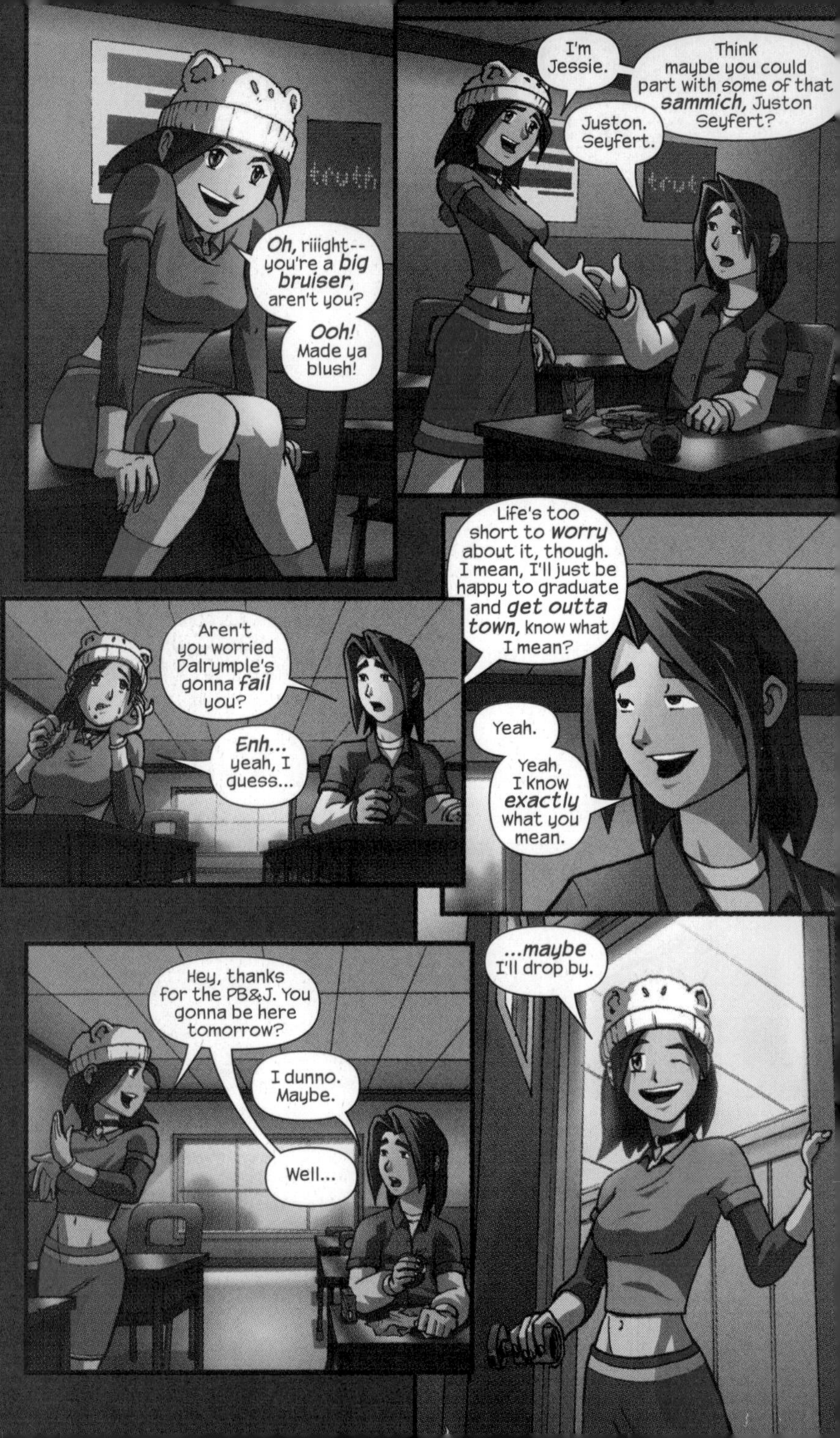

Oh, riiight--
you're a big
bruiser,
aren't you?
Ooh!
Made ya
blush!
I'm
Jessie.
Think
maybe you could
part with some of that
sammich, Juston
Seyfert?
Juston.
Seyfert.
Aren't
you worried
Dalrymple's
gonna fail
you?
Enh...
yeah, I
guess...
Life's too
short to worry
about it, though.
I mean, I'll just be
happy to graduate
and get outta
town, know what
I mean?
Yeah.
Yeah,
I know
exactly
what you
mean.
Hey, thanks
for the PB&J. You
gonna be here
tomorrow?
I dunno.
Maybe.
Well...
...maybe
I'll drop by.

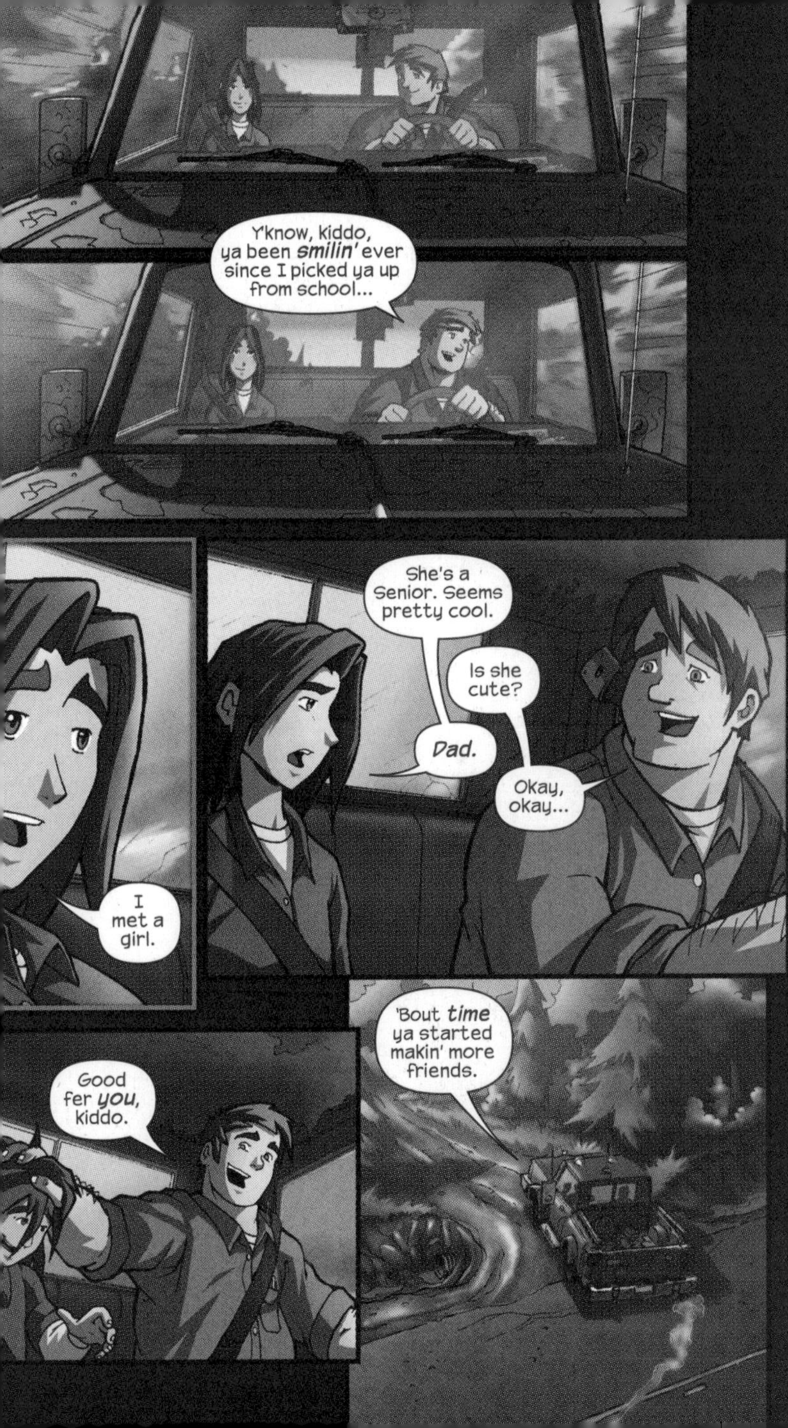
Y'know, kiddo, ya been smilin' ever since I picked ya up from school...
I met a girl.
She's a Senior. Seems pretty cool.
Is she cute?
Dad.
Okay, okay...
Good fer you, kiddo.
'Bout time ya started makin' more friends.

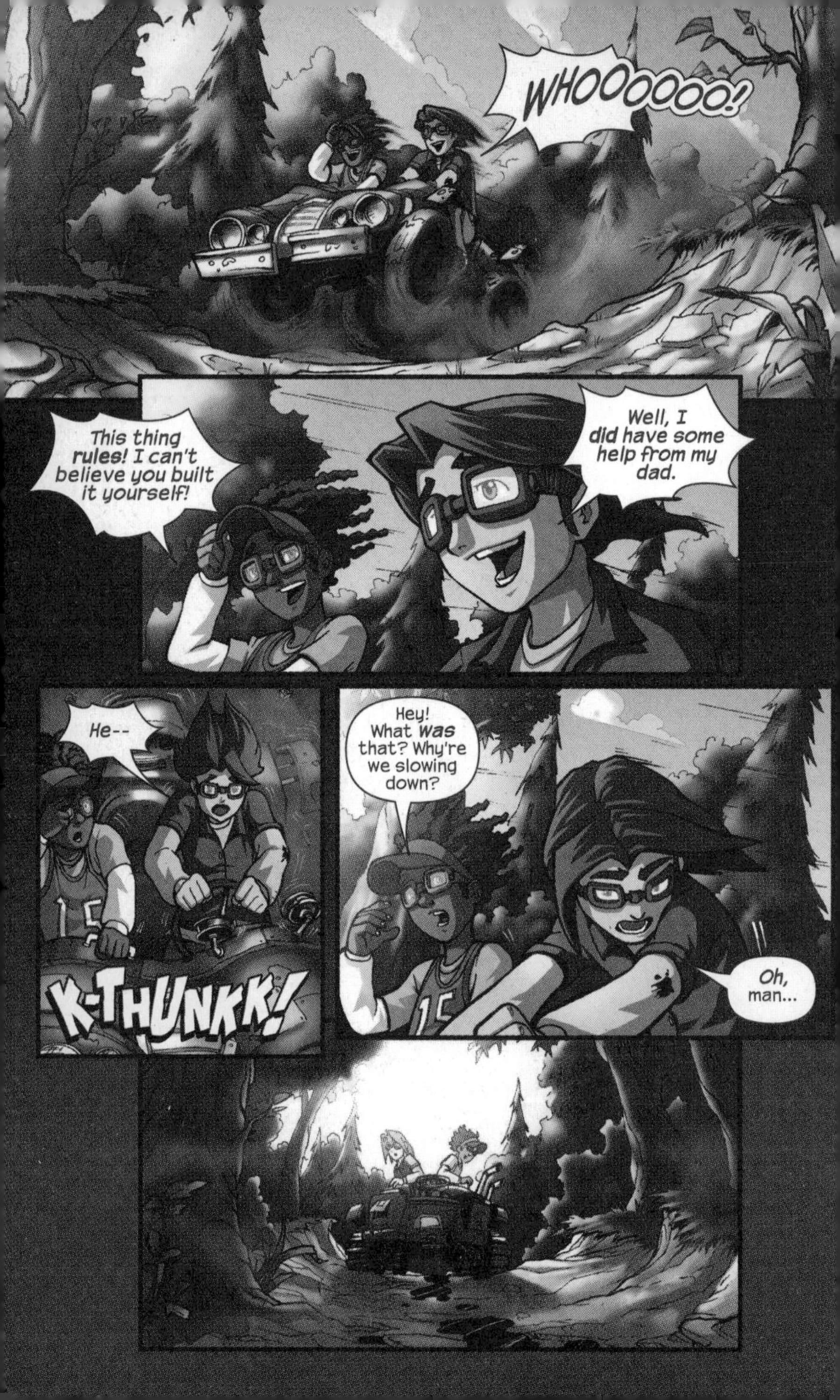
WHOOOOOOO!
This thing rules! I can't believe you built it yourself!
Well, I did have some help from my dad.
He--
K-THUNKK!
Hey! What was that? Why're we slowing down?
Oh, man...

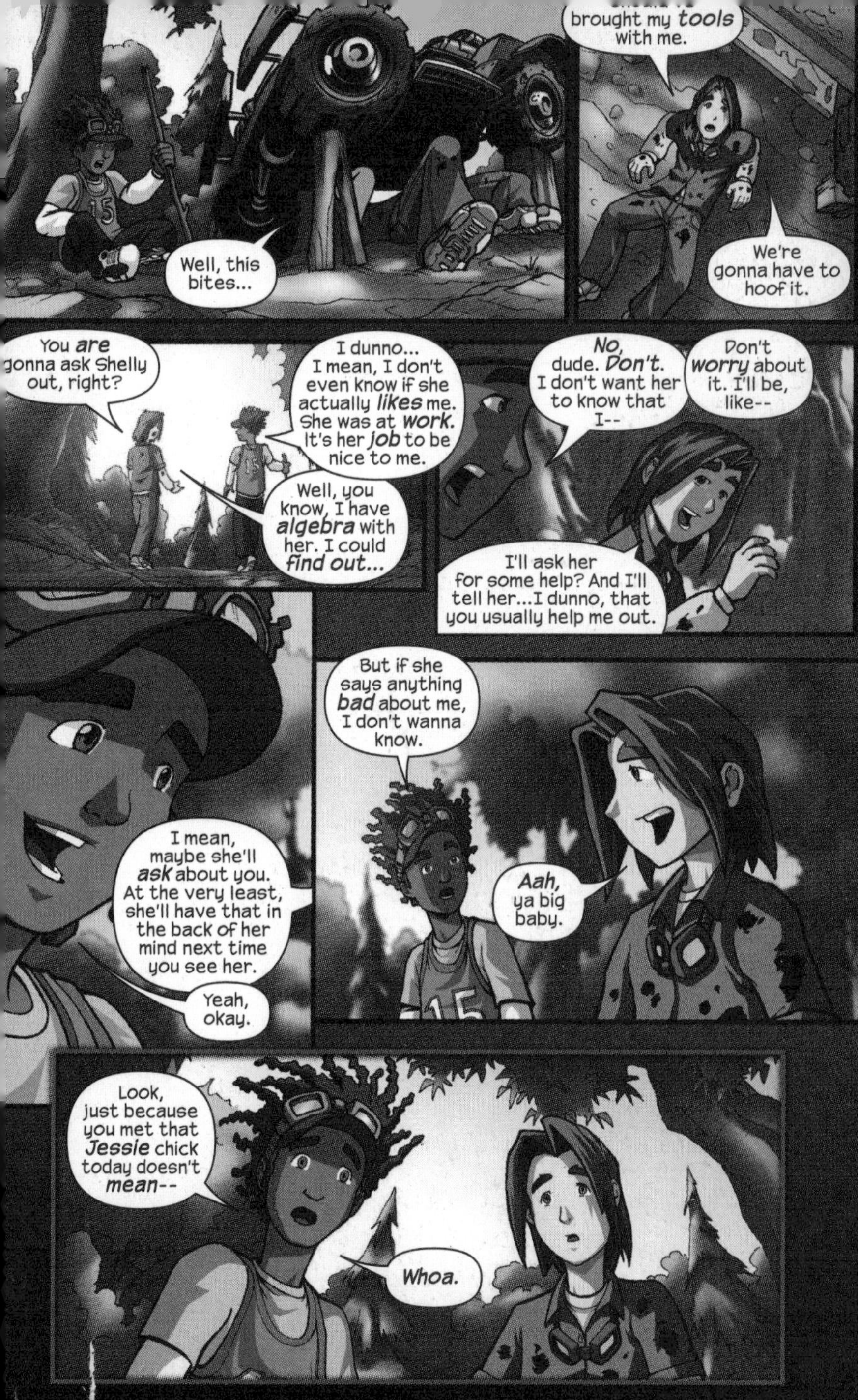
Well, this bites...
brought my tools with me.
We're gonna have to hoof it.
You are gonna ask Shelly out, right?
I dunno... I mean, I don't even know if she actually likes me. She was at work. It's her job to be nice to me.
Well, you know, I have algebra with her. I could find out...
No, dude. Don't. I don't want her to know that I--
Don't worry about it. I'll be, like--
I'll ask her for some help? And I'll tell her...I dunno, that you usually help me out.
I mean, maybe she'll ask about you. At the very least, she'll have that in the back of her mind next time you see her.
Yeah, okay.
But if she says anything bad about me, I don't wanna know.
Aah, ya big baby.
Look, just because you met that Jessie chick today doesn't mean--
Whoa.

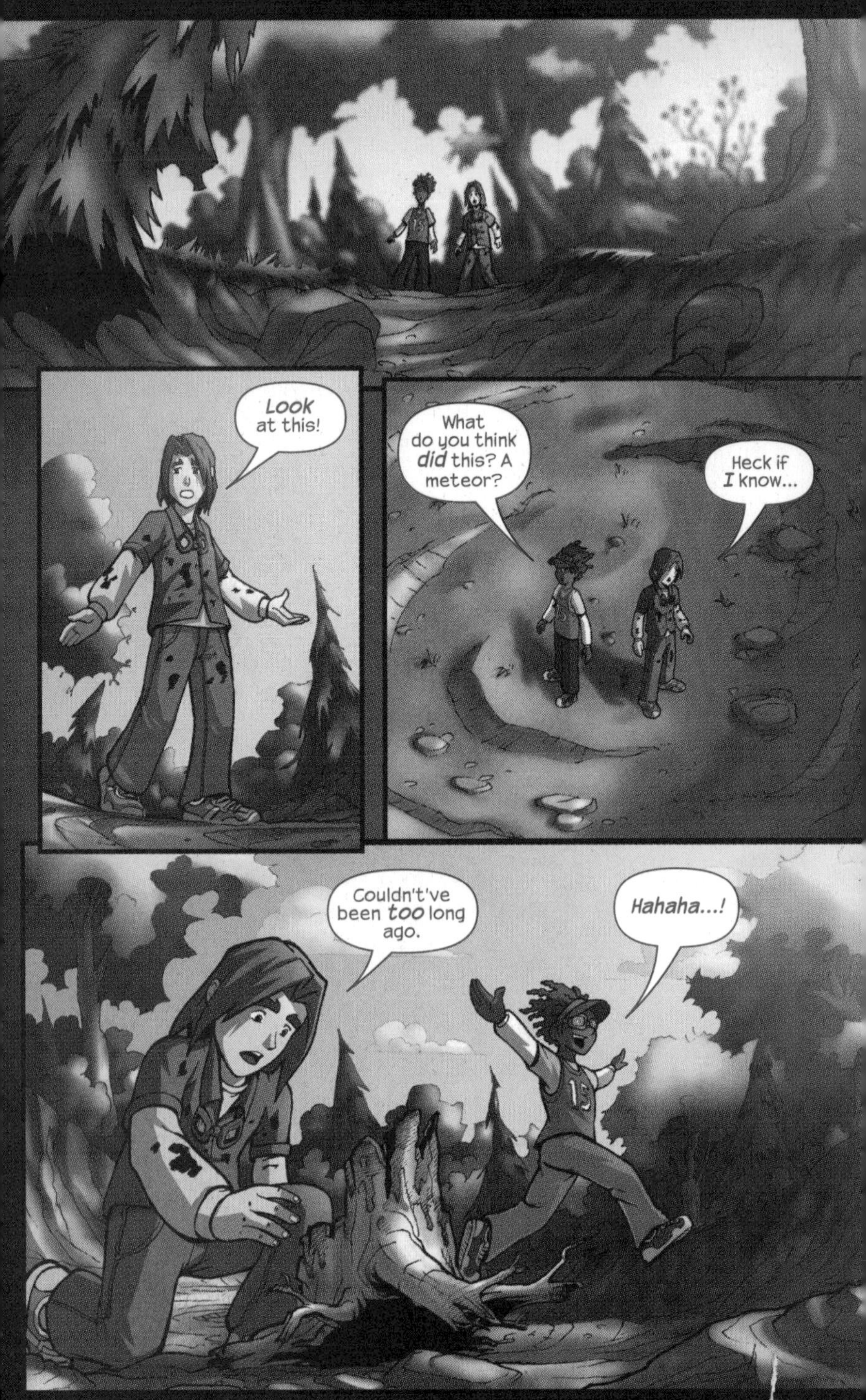
Look at this!
What do you think *did* this? A meteor?
Heck if *I* know...
Couldn't've been *too* long ago.
Hahaha...!

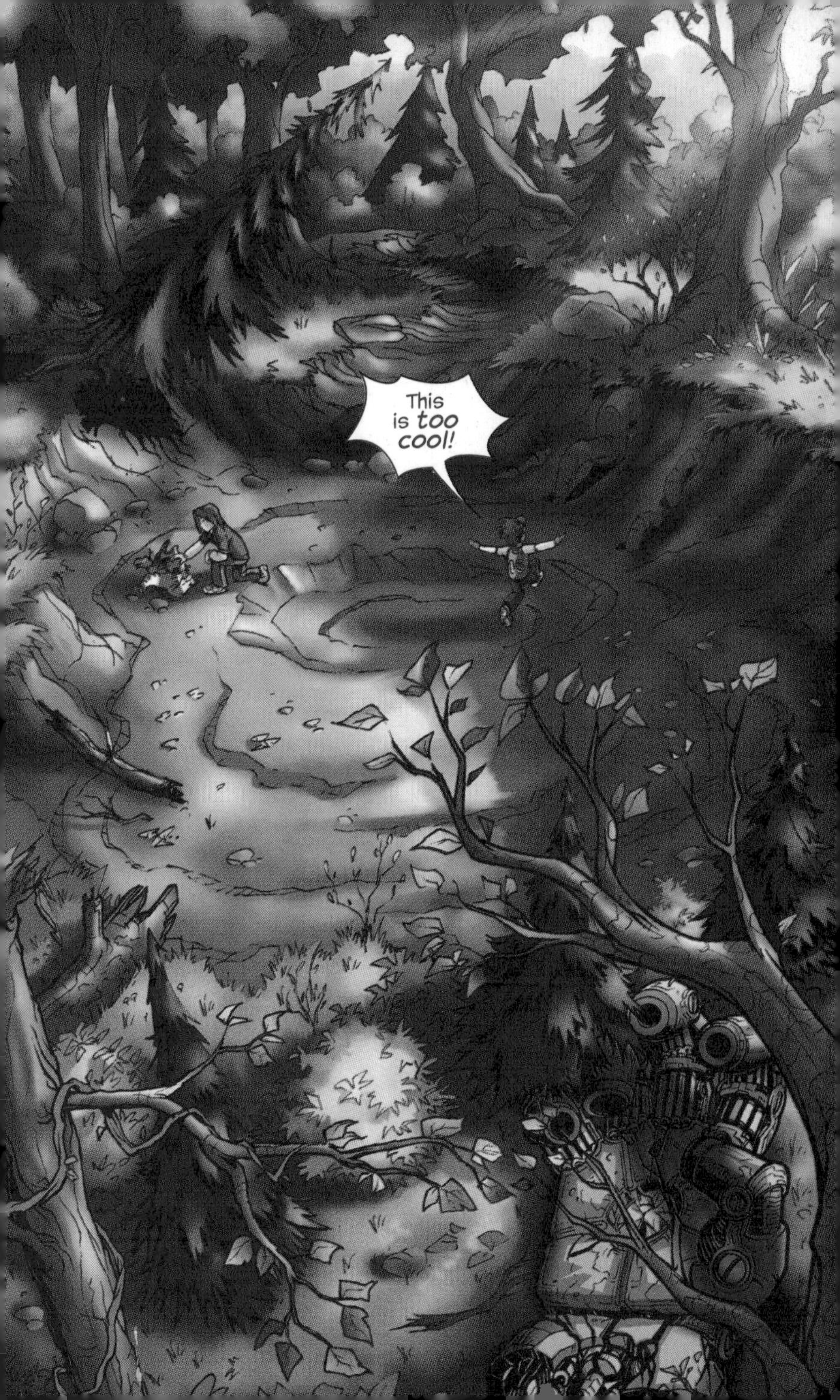
This is too cool!

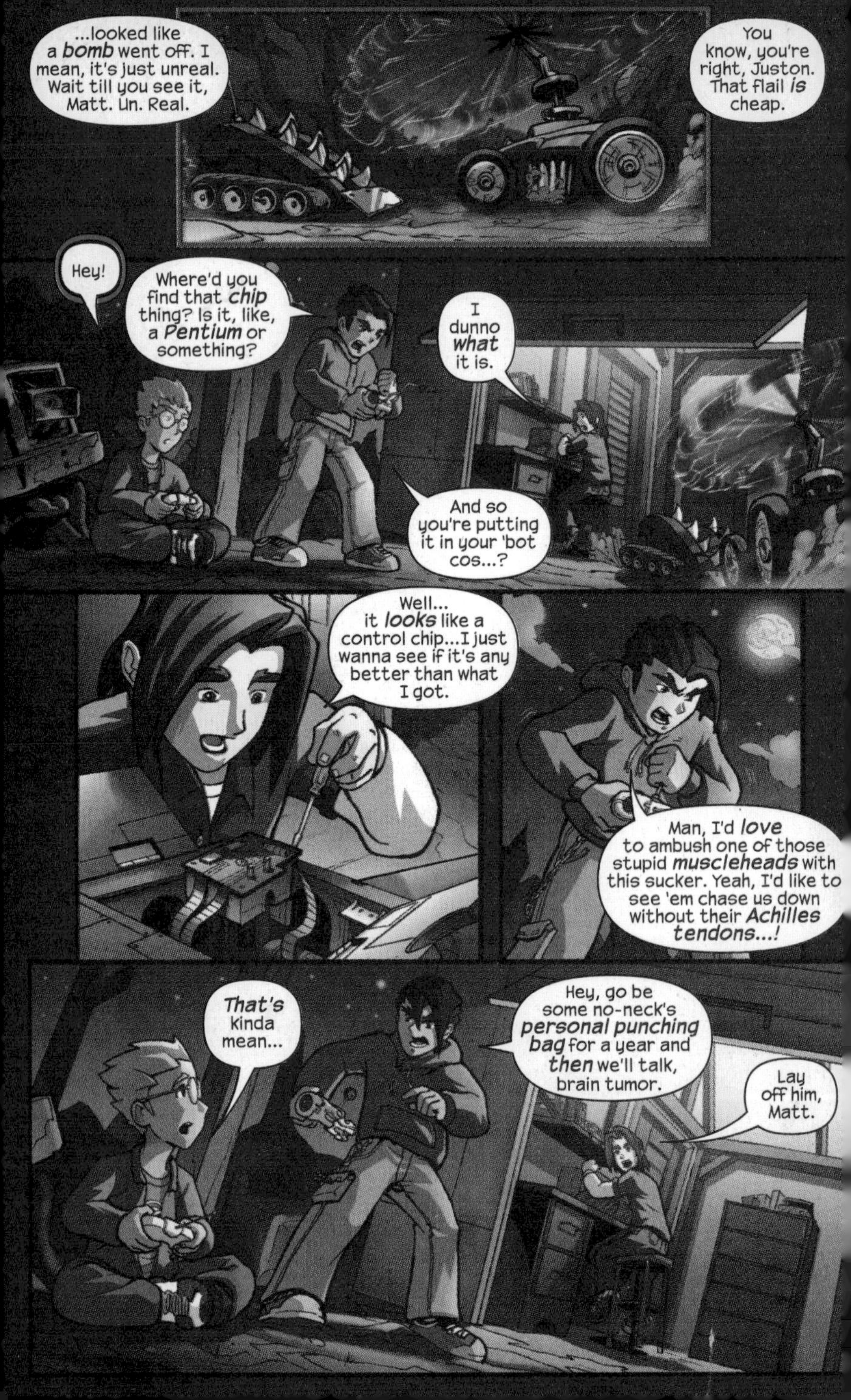
...looked like a *bomb* went off. I mean, it's just unreal. Wait till you see it, Matt. Un. Real.
You know, you're right, Juston. That flail *is* cheap.
Hey!
Where'd you find that *chip* thing? Is it, like, a *Pentium* or something?
I dunno *what* it is.
And so you're putting it in your 'bot cos...?
Well... it *looks* like a control chip...I just wanna see if it's any better than what I got.
Man, I'd *love* to ambush one of those stupid *muscleheads* with this sucker. Yeah, I'd like to see 'em chase us down without their *Achilles tendons...!*
That's kinda mean...
Hey, go be some no-neck's *personal punching bag* for a year and *then* we'll talk, brain tumor.
Lay off him, Matt.

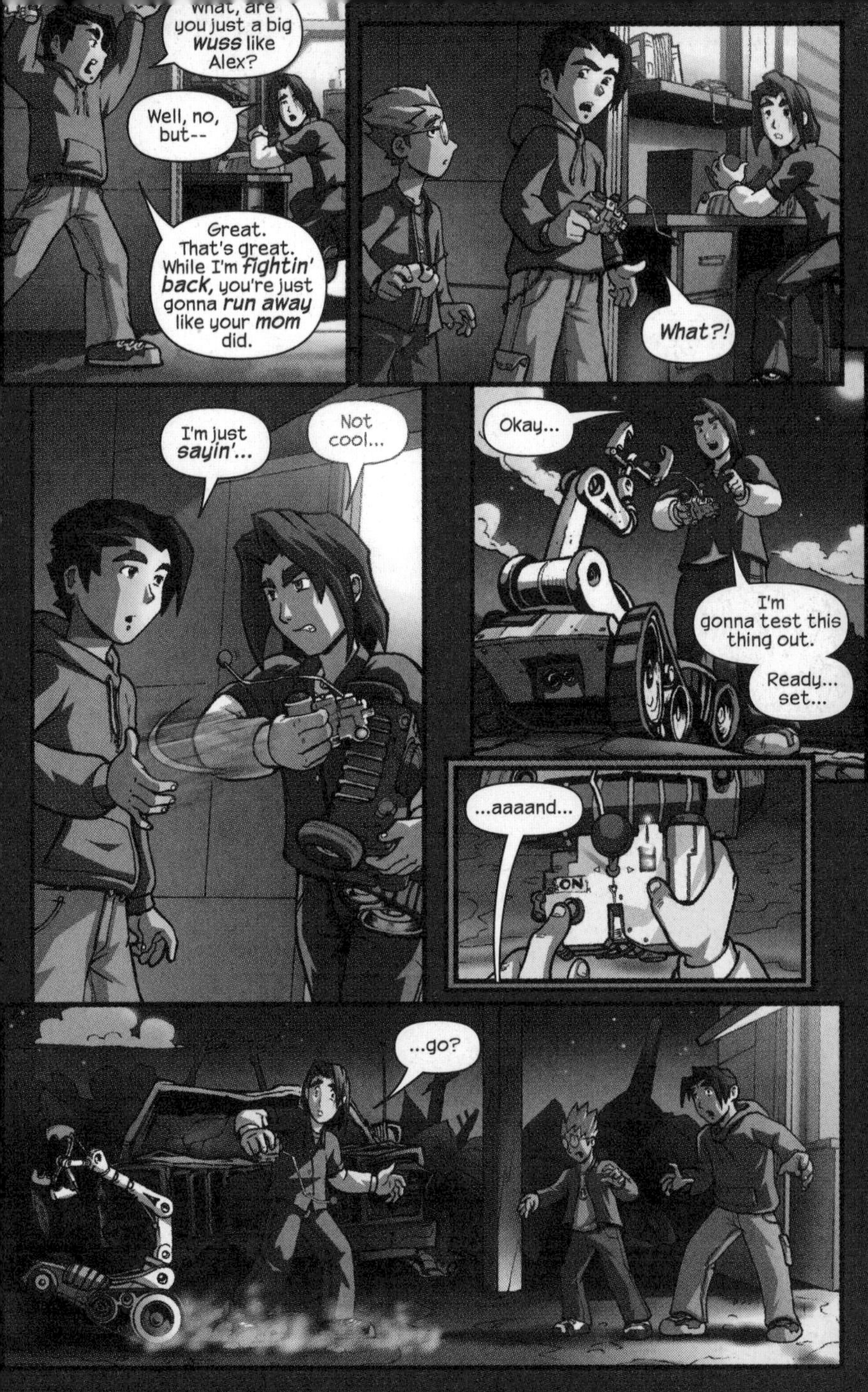
What, are you just a big *wuss* like Alex?
Well, no, but--
Great. That's great. While I'm *fightin' back,* you're just gonna *run away* like your *mom* did.
What?!
I'm just *sayin'...*
Not cool...
Okay...
I'm gonna test this thing out.
Ready... set...
...aaaand...
ON
...go?

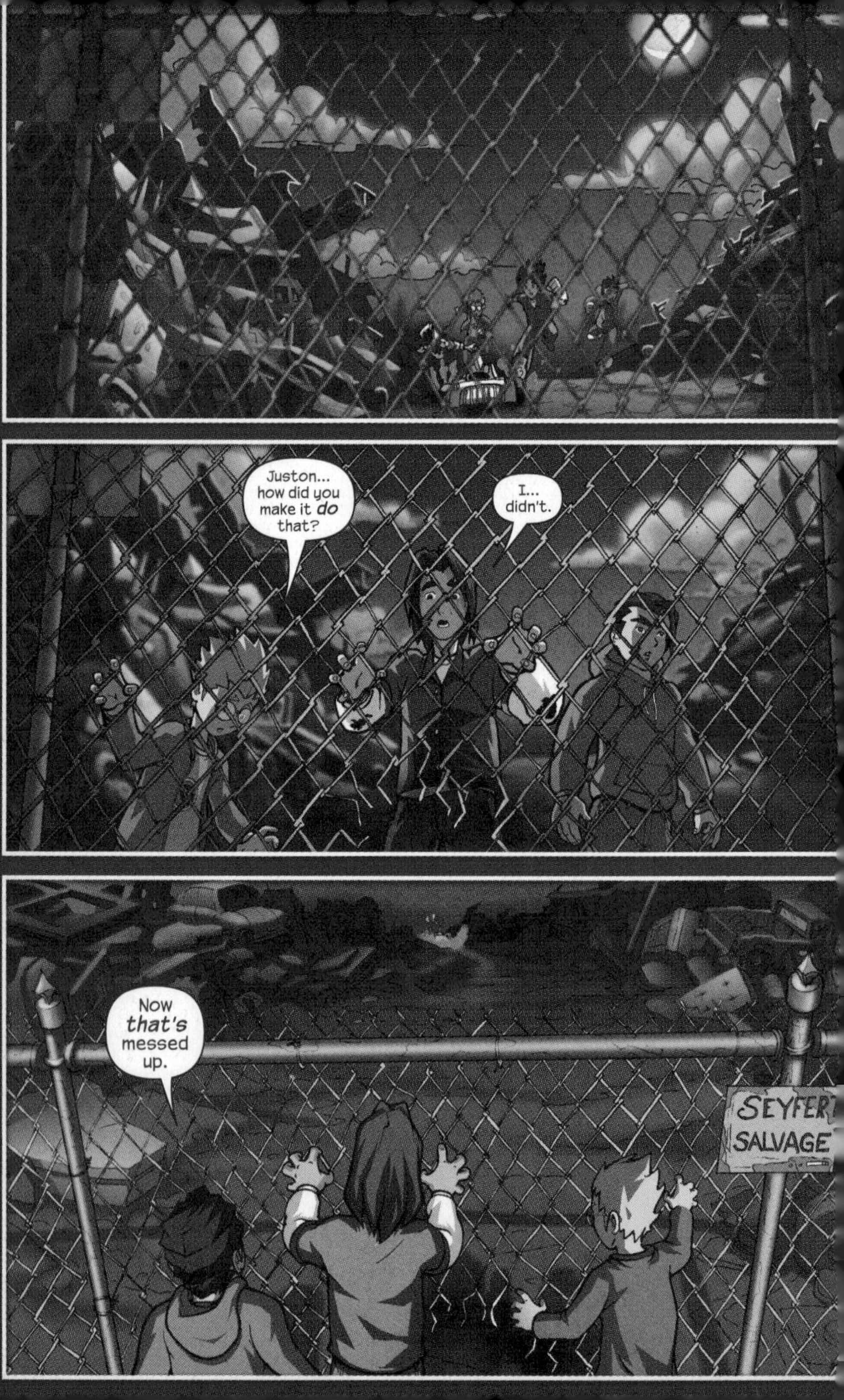
Juston... how did you make it *do* that?
I... didn't.
Now *that's* messed up.
SEYFERT SALVAGE

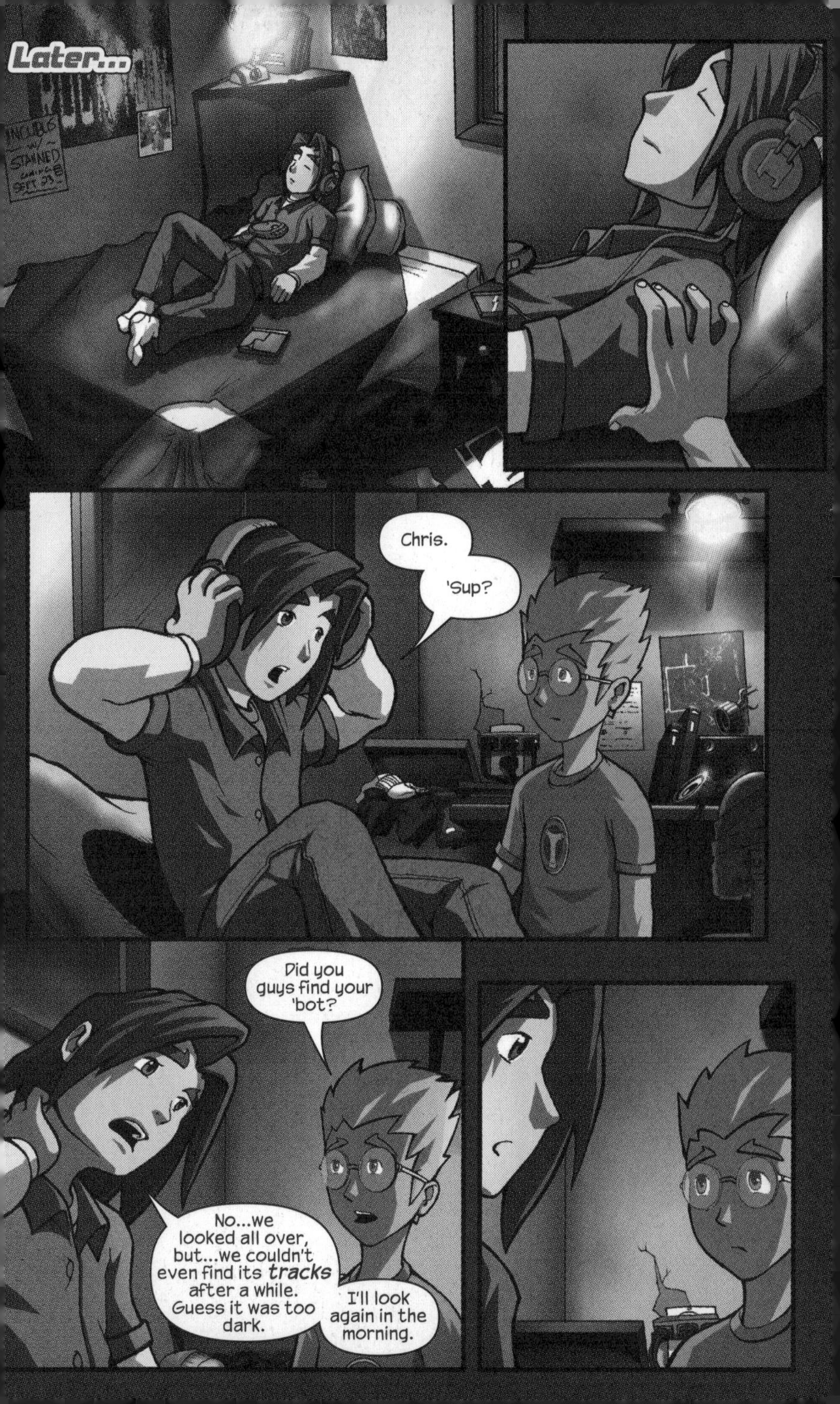
Later...
INCUBUS W/ STAINED
SEPT. 23
Chris.
'Sup?
Did you guys find your 'bot?
No...we looked all over, but...we couldn't even find its *tracks* after a while. Guess it was too dark.
I'll look again in the morning.

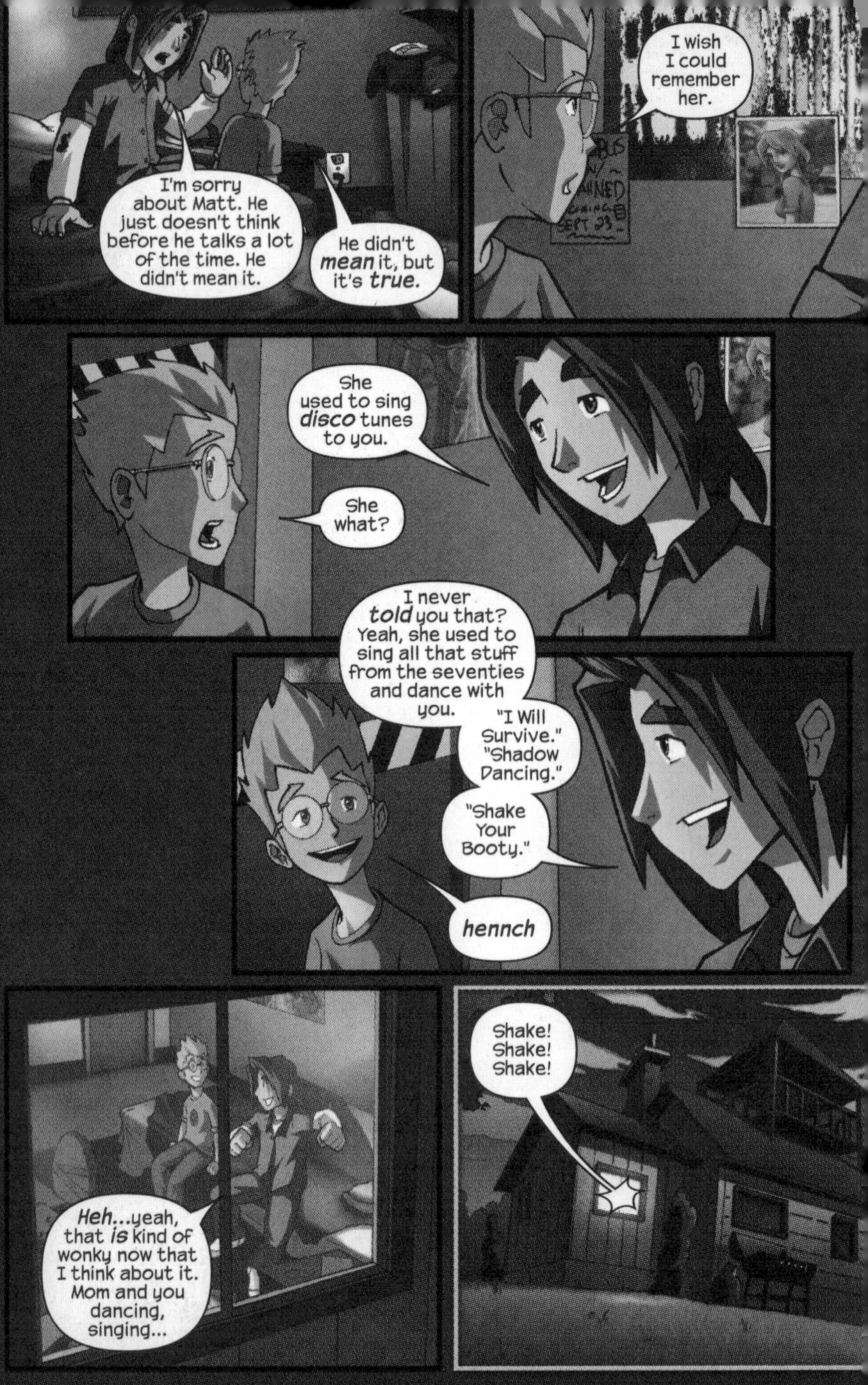
I'm sorry about Matt. He just doesn't think before he talks a lot of the time. He didn't mean it.
He didn't *mean* it, but it's *true*.
I wish I could remember her.
She used to sing *disco* tunes to you.
She what?
I never *told* you that? Yeah, she used to sing all that stuff from the seventies and dance with you.
"I Will Survive." "Shadow Dancing."
"Shake Your Booty."
hennch
Heh...yeah, that *is* kind of wonky now that I think about it. Mom and you dancing, singing...
Shake! Shake! Shake!

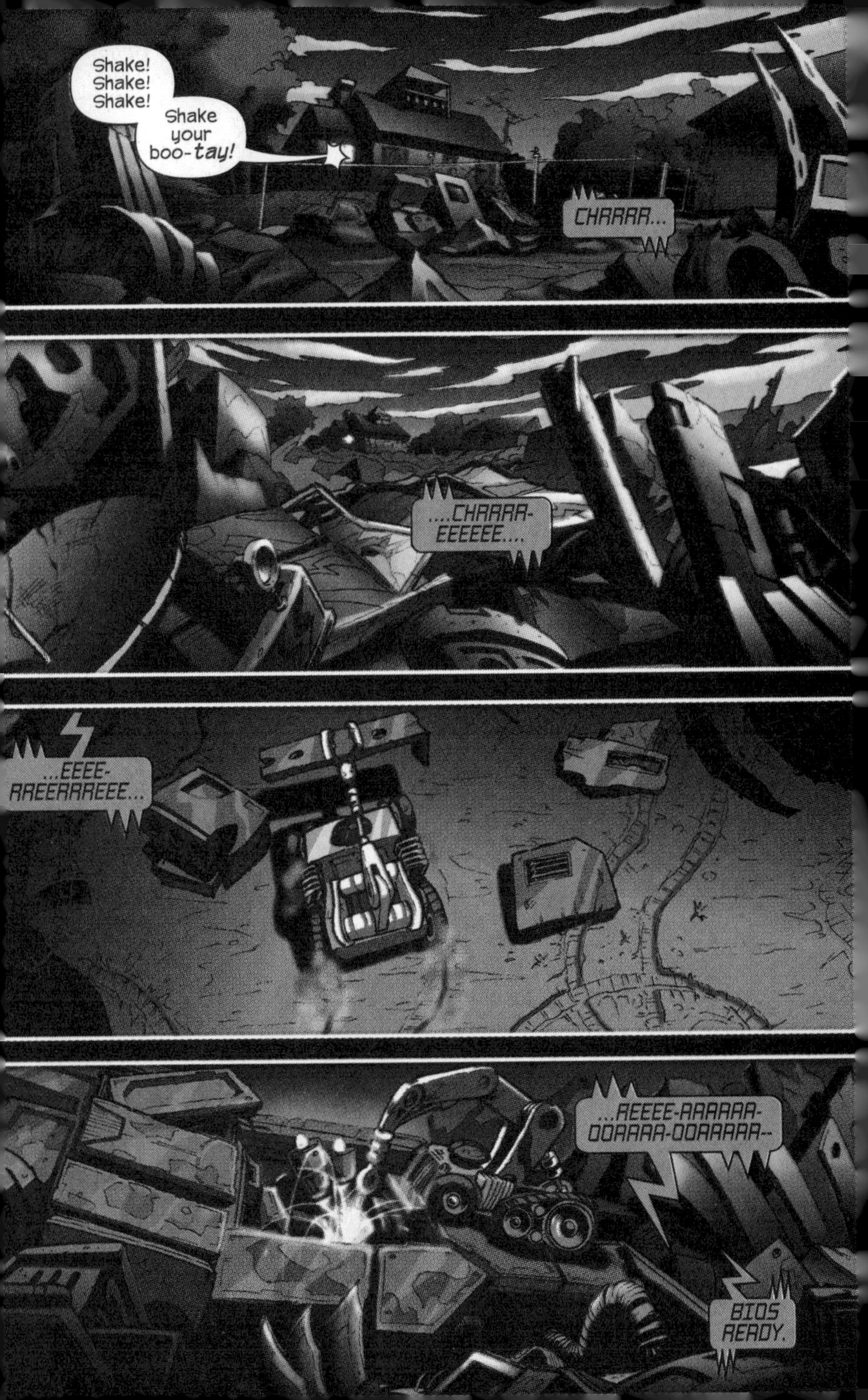
Shake! Shake! Shake!
Shake your boo-tay!
CHRRRR...
....CHRRRR-EEEEEE....
...EEEE-RREERRREEE...
...REEEE-RRRRRR-OORRRR-OORRRRR--
BIOS READY.

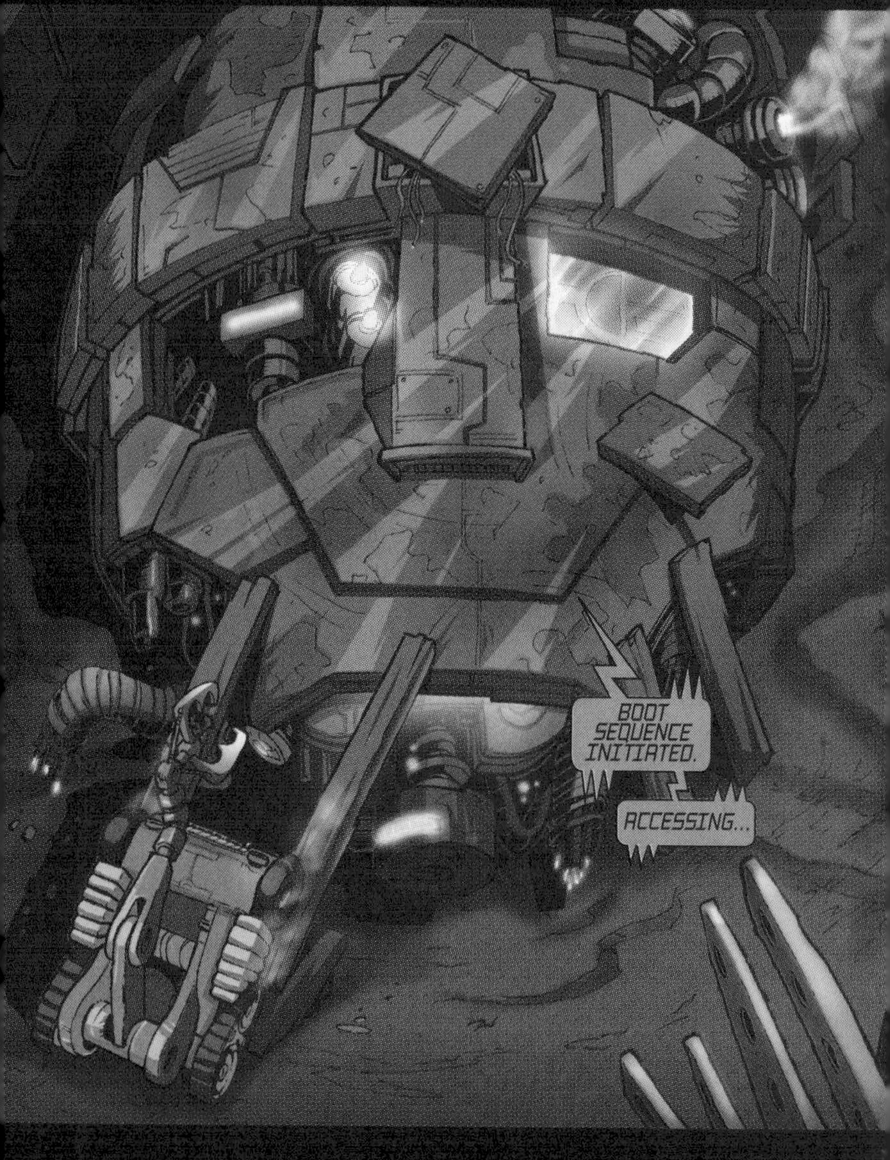
BOOT SEQUENCE INITIATED.
ACCESSING...

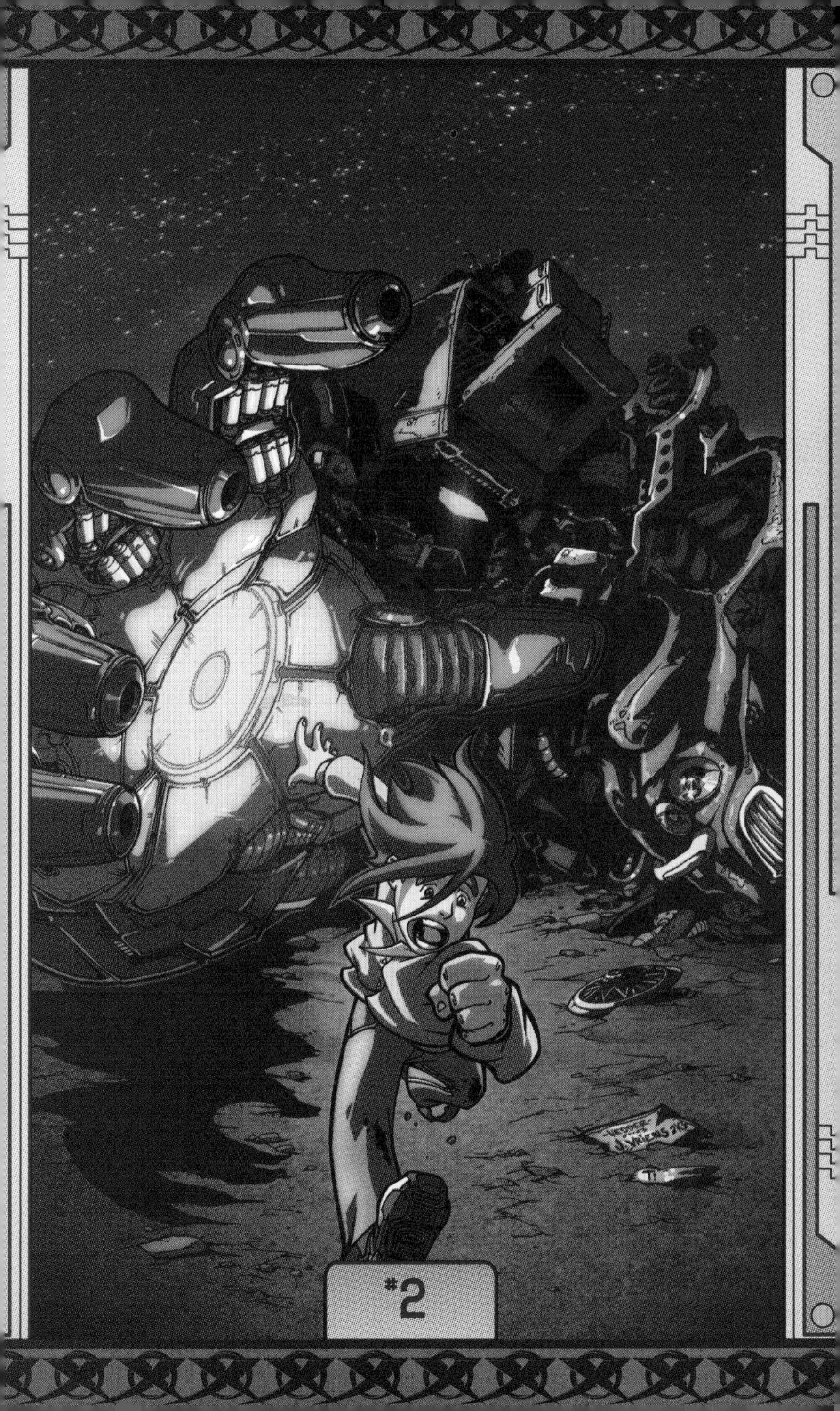
#2

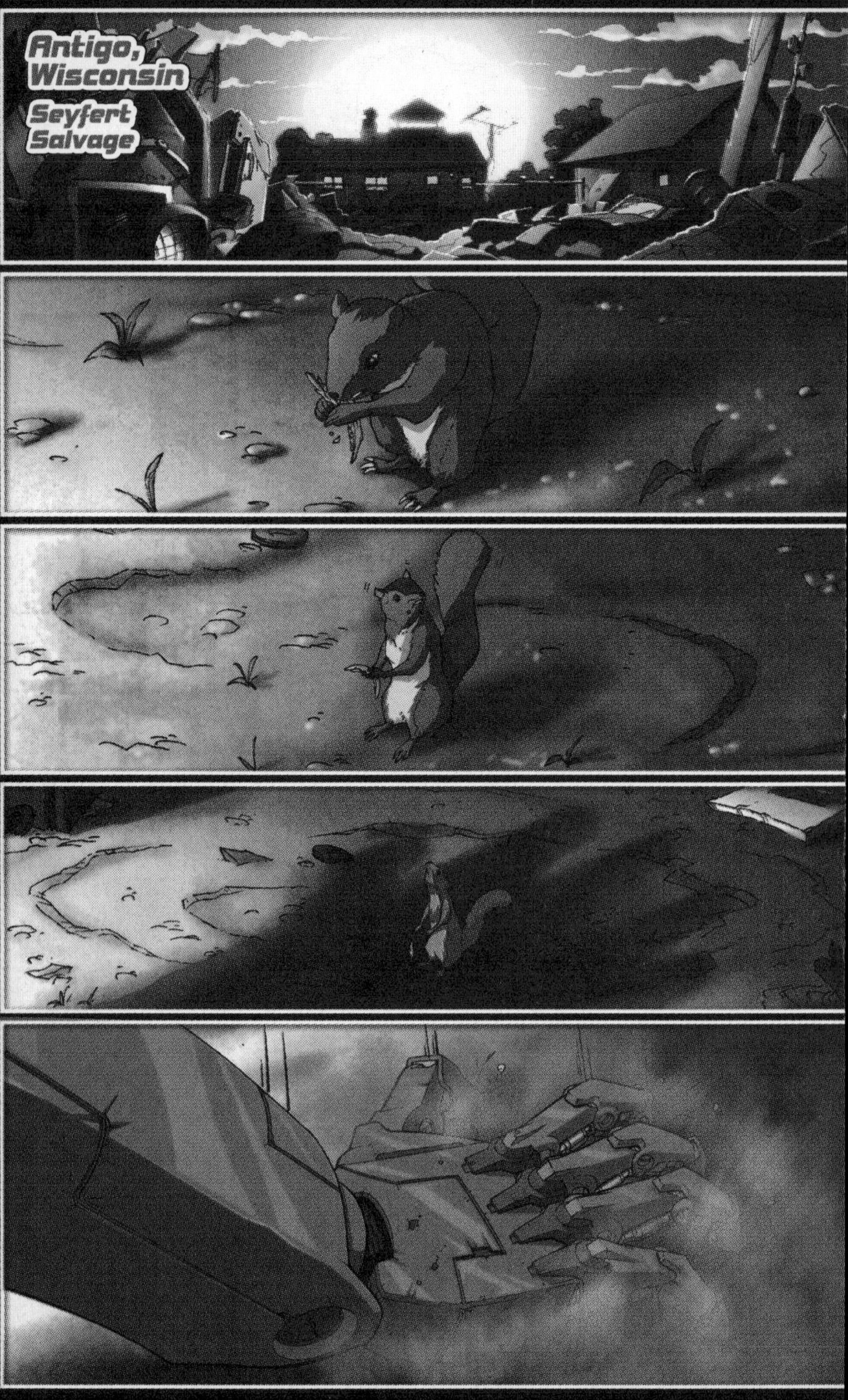
Antigo, Wisconsin
Seyfert Salvage

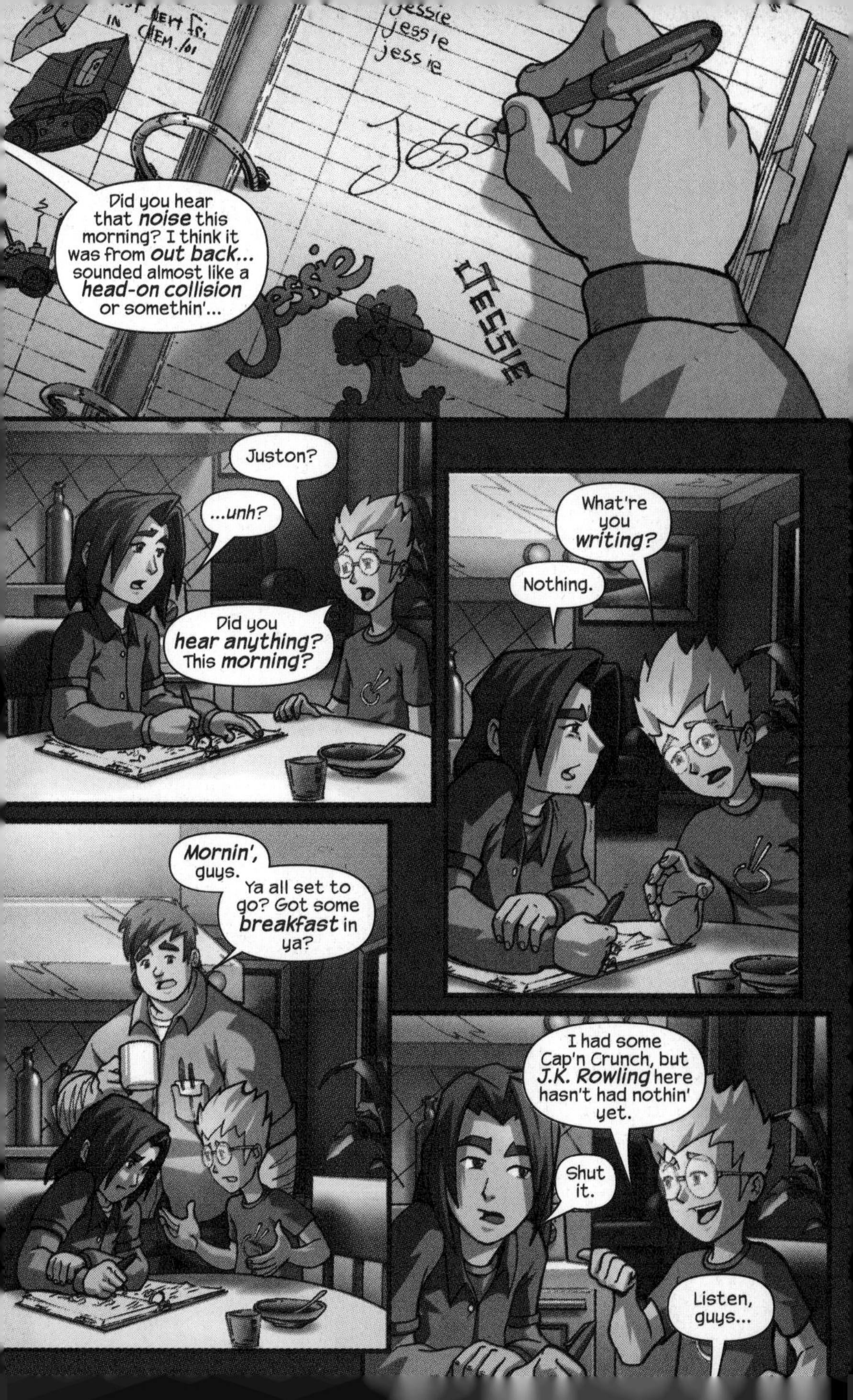
jessie
jessie
jessie
Jessie
JESSIE
Did you hear that noise this morning? I think it was from out back... sounded almost like a head-on collision or somethin'...
Juston?
...unh?
Did you hear anything? This morning?
What're you writing?
Nothing.
Mornin', guys.
Ya all set to go? Got some breakfast in ya?
I had some Cap'n Crunch, but J.K. Rowling here hasn't had nothin' yet.
Shut it.
Listen, guys...

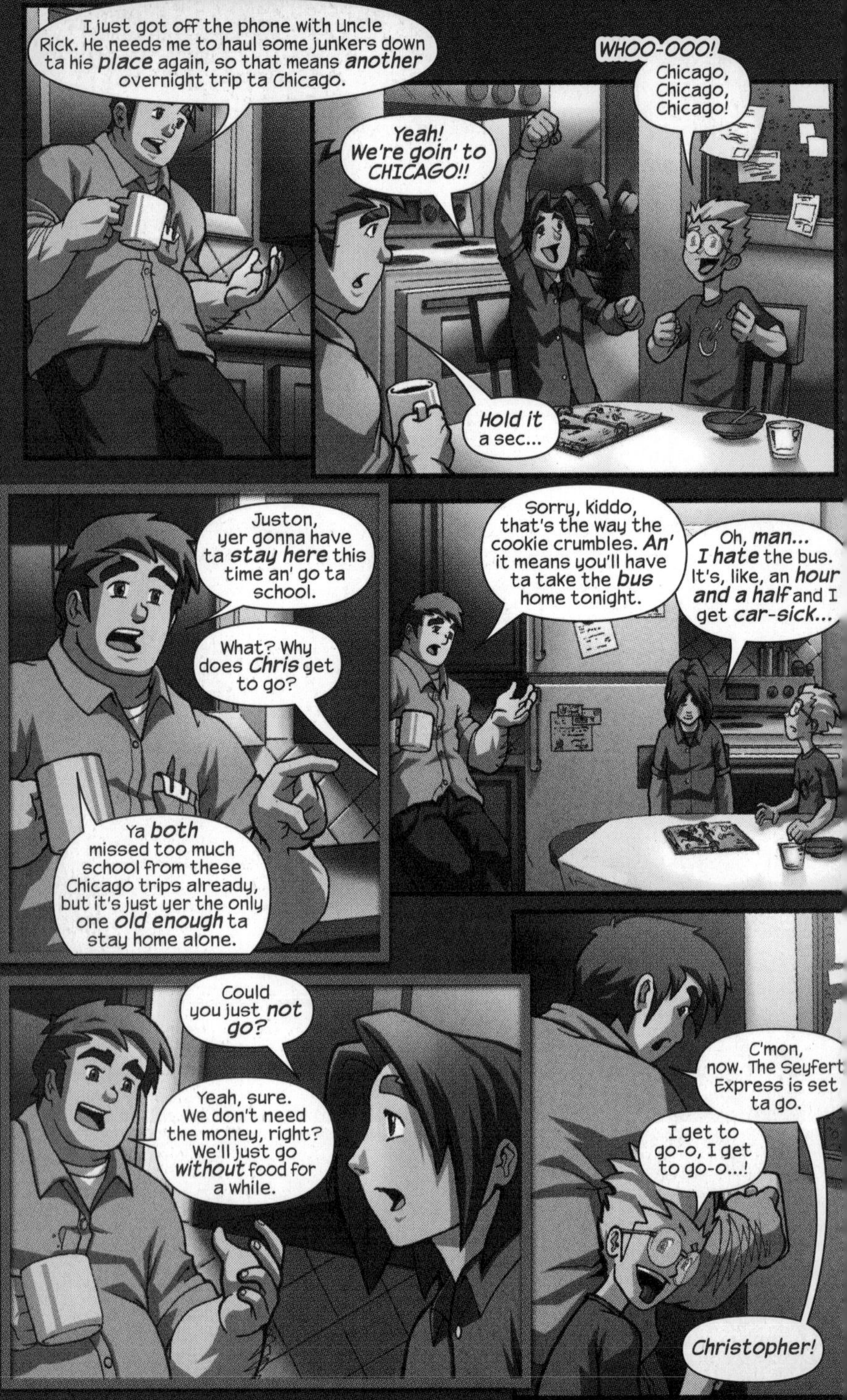

I just got off the phone with Uncle Rick. He needs me to haul some junkers down ta his *place* again, so that means *another* overnight trip ta Chicago.
Yeah! We're goin' to CHICAGO!!
WHOO-OOO!
Chicago, Chicago, Chicago!
Hold it a sec...
Juston, yer gonna have ta *stay here* this time an' go ta school.
What? Why does *Chris* get to go?
Ya *both* missed too much school from these Chicago trips already, but it's just yer the only one *old enough* ta stay home alone.
Sorry, kiddo, that's the way the cookie crumbles. *An'* it means you'll have ta take the *bus* home tonight.
Oh, *man...* *I hate* the bus. It's, like, an *hour and a half* and I get *car-sick...*
Could you just *not go?*
Yeah, sure. We don't need the money, right? We'll just go *without* food for a while.
C'mon, now. The Seyfert Express is set ta go.
I get to go-o, I get to go-o...!
Christopher!

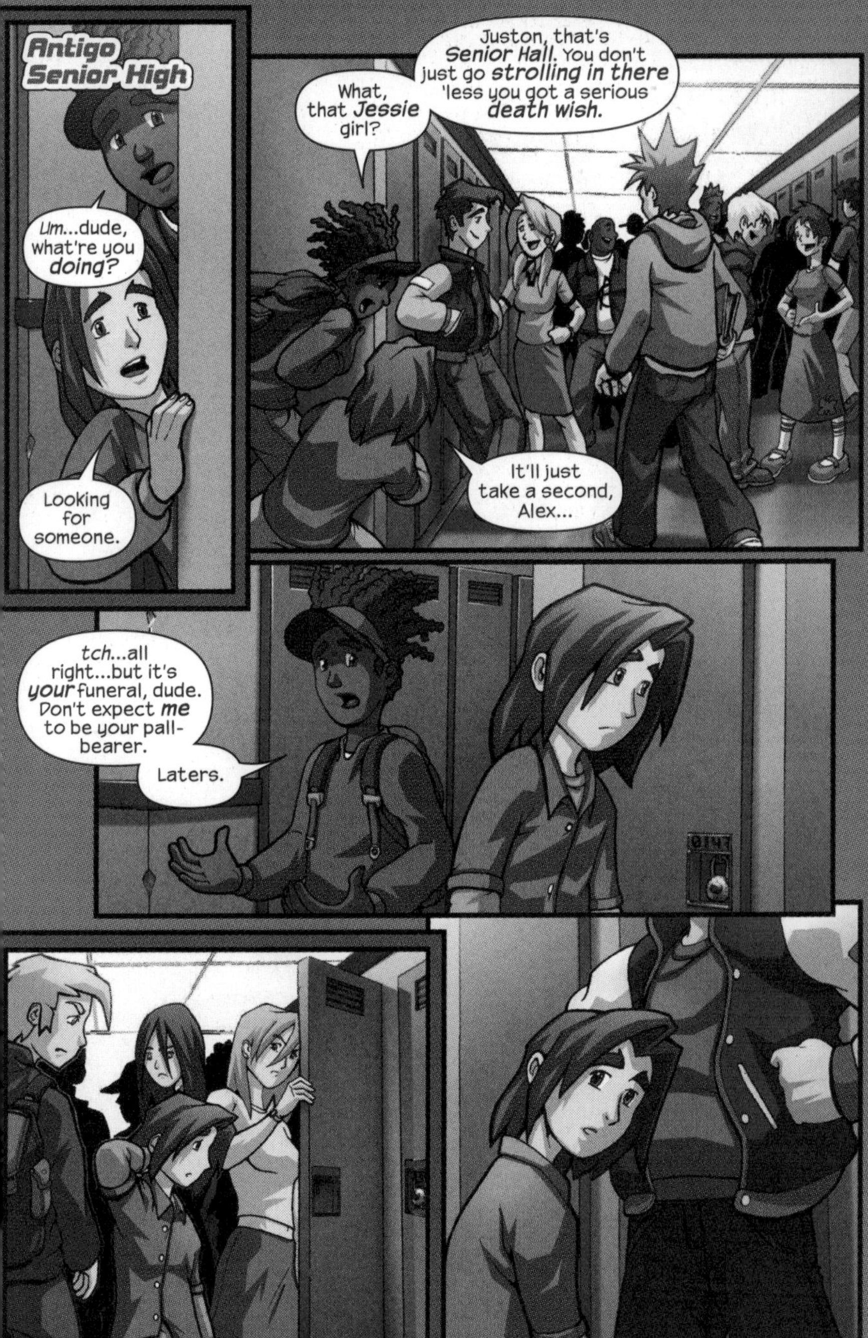
Antigo Senior High
Um...dude, what're you doing?
Looking for someone.
What, that Jessie girl?
Juston, that's Senior Hall. You don't just go strolling in there 'less you got a serious death wish.
It'll just take a second, Alex...
tch...all right...but it's your funeral, dude. Don't expect me to be your pall-bearer.
Laters.

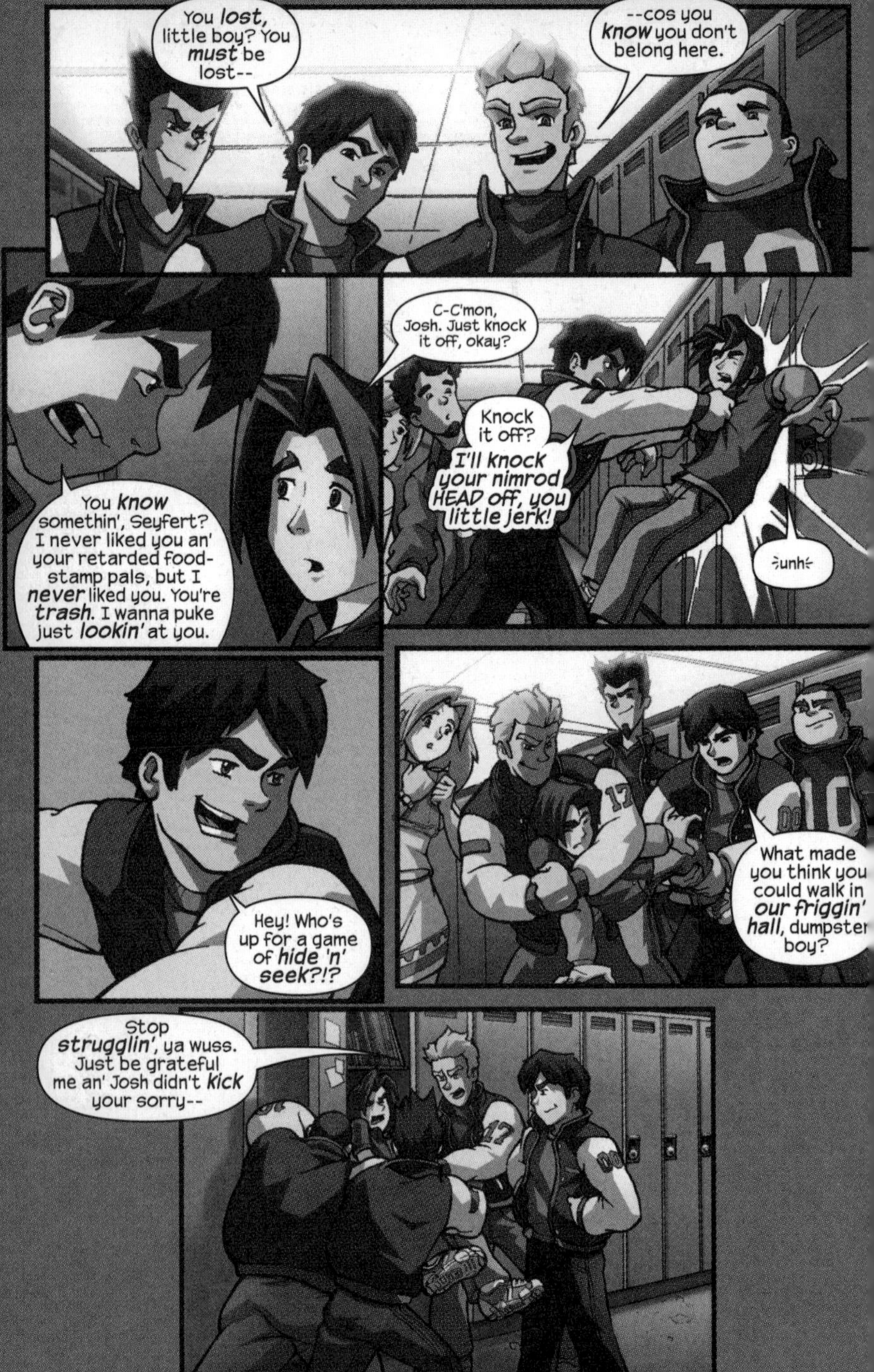

You lost, little boy? You must be lost--
--cos you know you don't belong here.
You know somethin', Seyfert? I never liked you an' your retarded food-stamp pals, but I never liked you. You're trash. I wanna puke just lookin' at you.
C-C'mon, Josh. Just knock it off, okay?
Knock it off? I'll knock your nimrod HEAD off, you little jerk!
unh
Hey! Who's up for a game of hide 'n' seek?!?
What made you think you could walk in our friggin' hall, dumpster boy?
Stop strugglin', ya wuss. Just be grateful me an' Josh didn't kick your sorry--

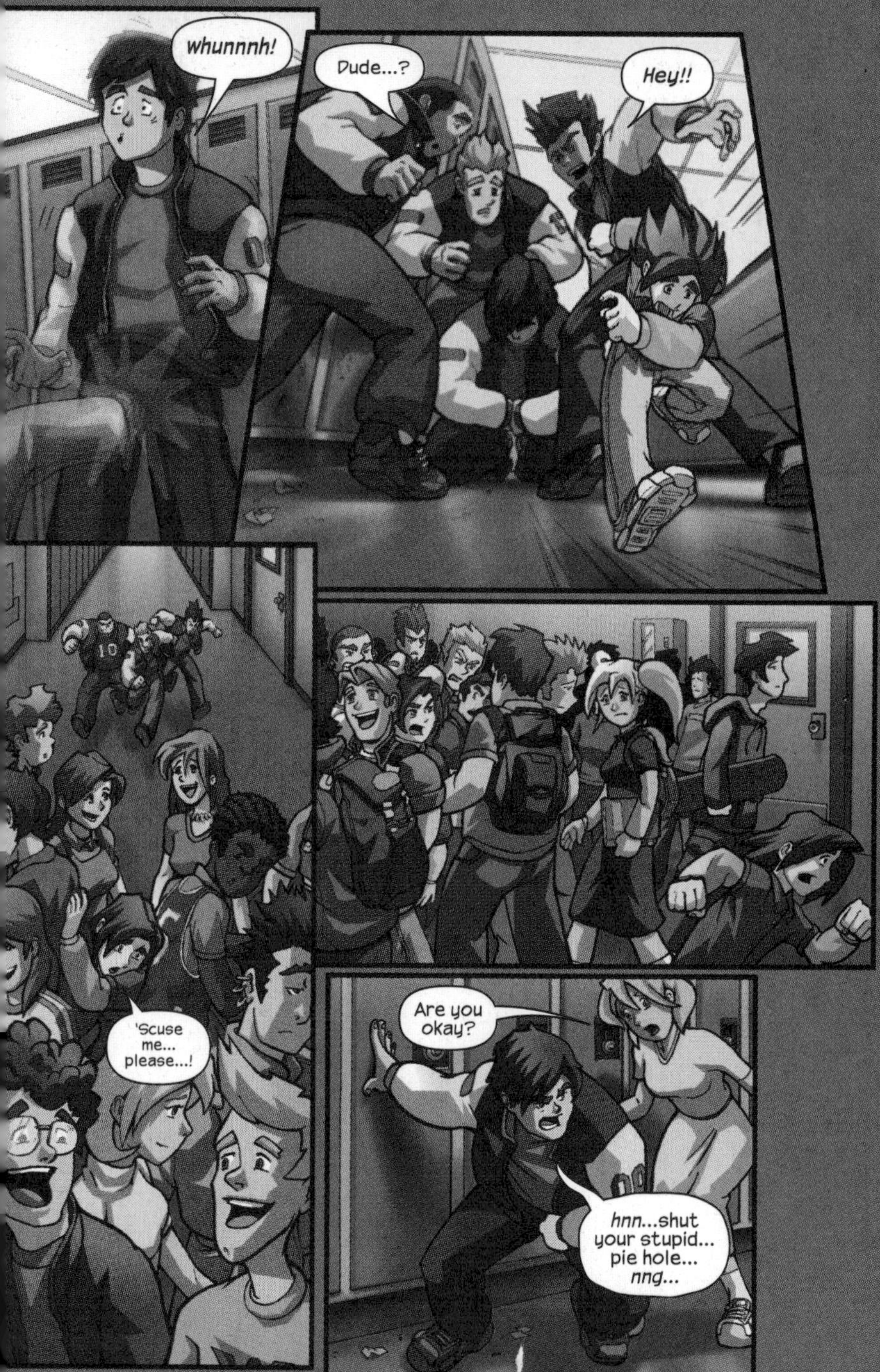
whunnnh!
Dude...?
Hey!!
'Scuse me... please...!
Are you okay?
hnn...shut your stupid... pie hole... nng...

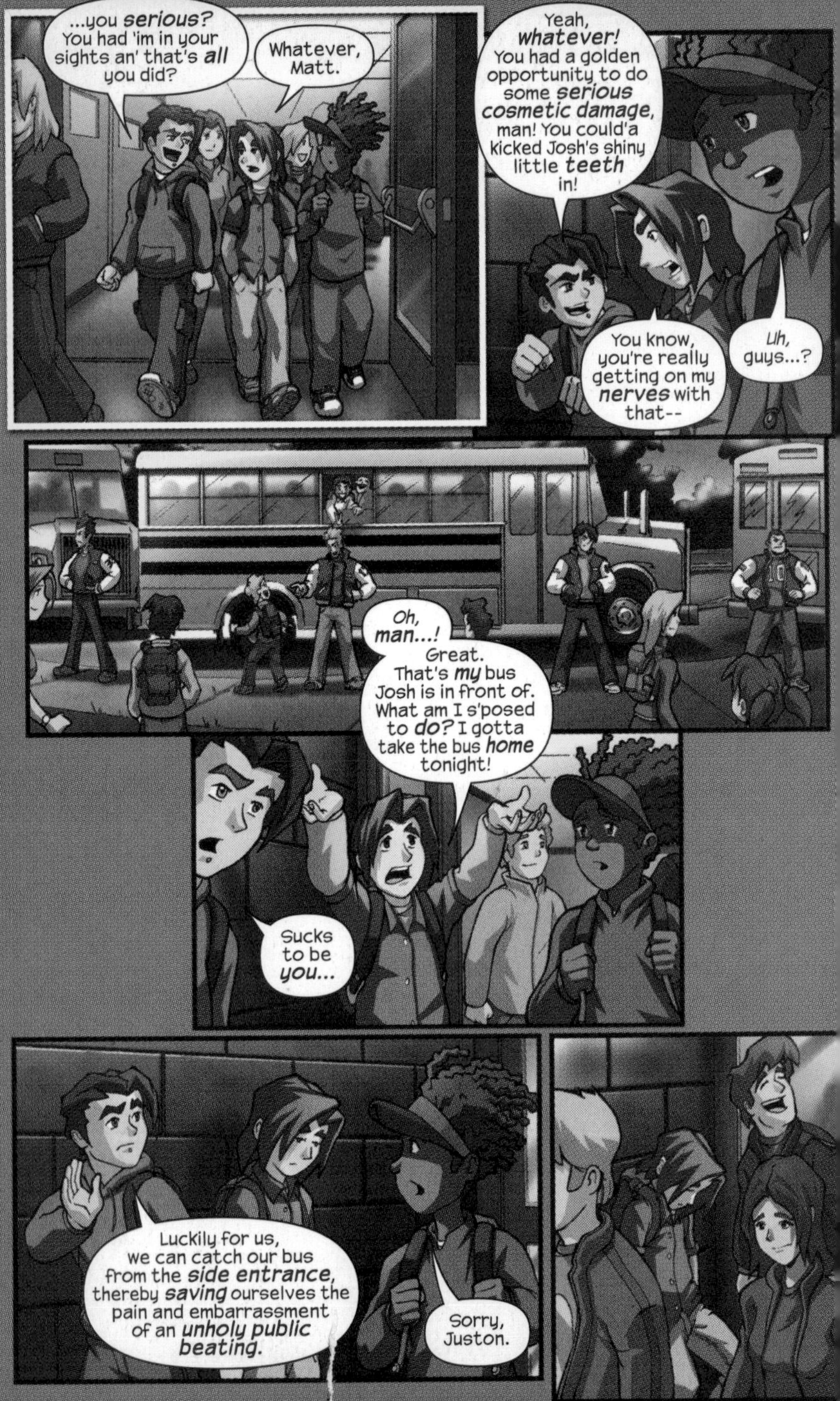
...you serious? You had 'im in your sights an' that's all you did?
Whatever, Matt.
Yeah, whatever! You had a golden opportunity to do some serious cosmetic damage, man! You could'a kicked Josh's shiny little teeth in!
You know, you're really getting on my nerves with that--
Uh, guys...?
Oh, man...! Great. That's my bus Josh is in front of. What am I s'posed to do? I gotta take the bus home tonight!
Sucks to be you...
Luckily for us, we can catch our bus from the side entrance, thereby saving ourselves the pain and embarrassment of an unholy public beating.
Sorry, Juston.

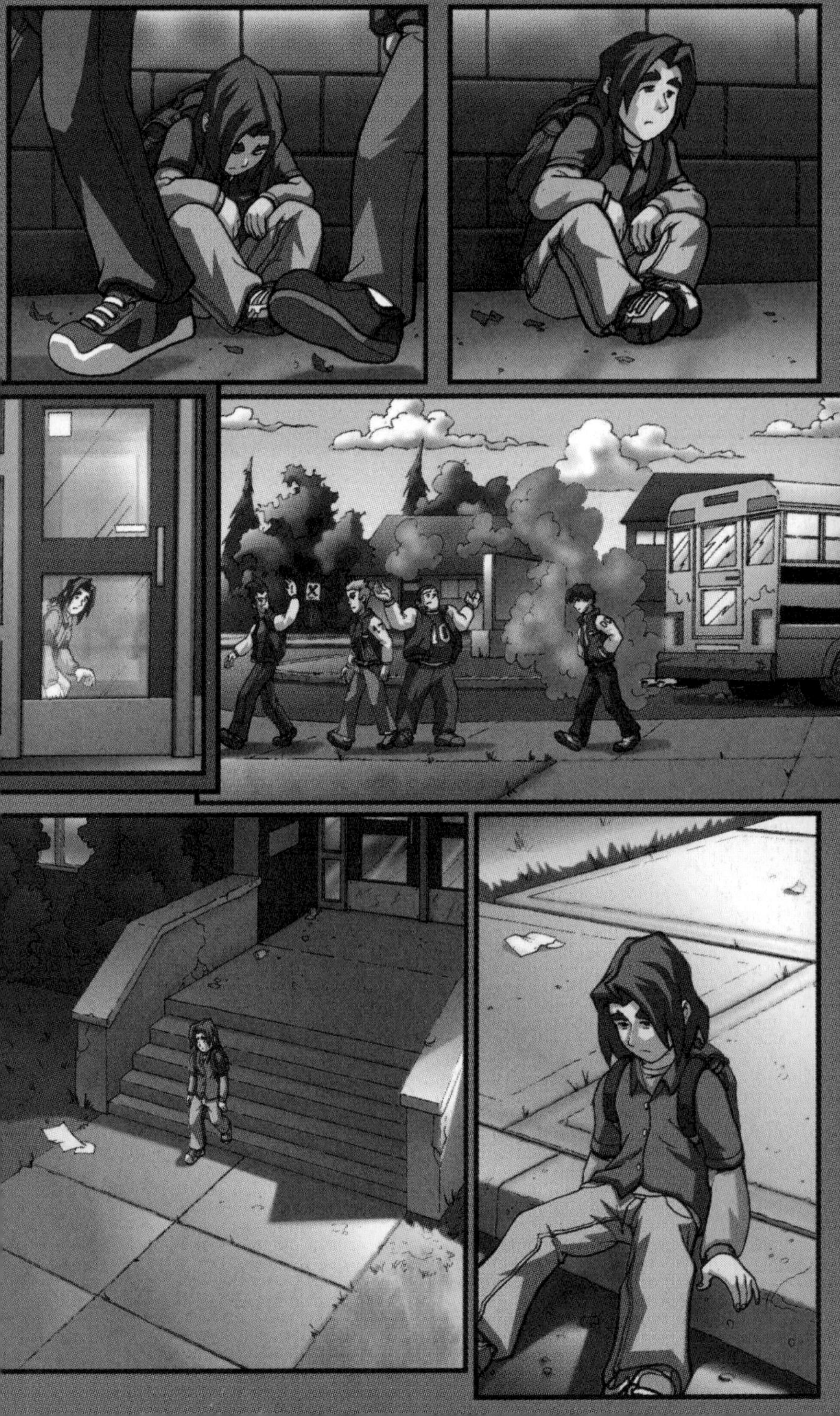

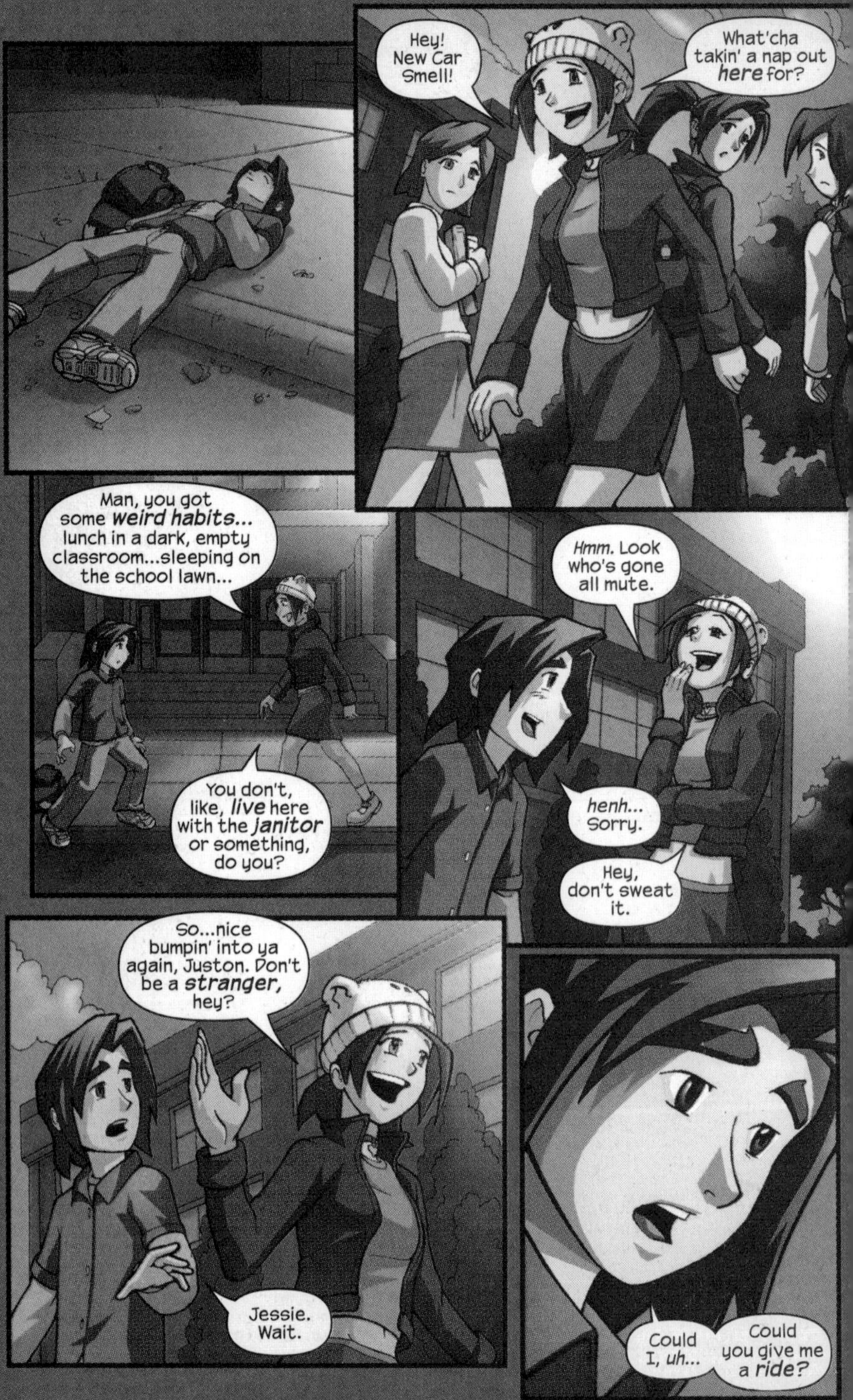
Hey!
New Car
Smell!
What'cha
takin' a nap out
here for?
Man, you got
some weird habits...
lunch in a dark, empty
classroom...sleeping on
the school lawn...
You don't,
like, live here
with the janitor
or something,
do you?
Hmm. Look
who's gone
all mute.
henh...
Sorry.
Hey,
don't sweat
it.
So...nice
bumpin' into ya
again, Juston. Don't
be a stranger,
hey?
Jessie.
Wait.
Could
I, uh...
Could
you give me
a ride?

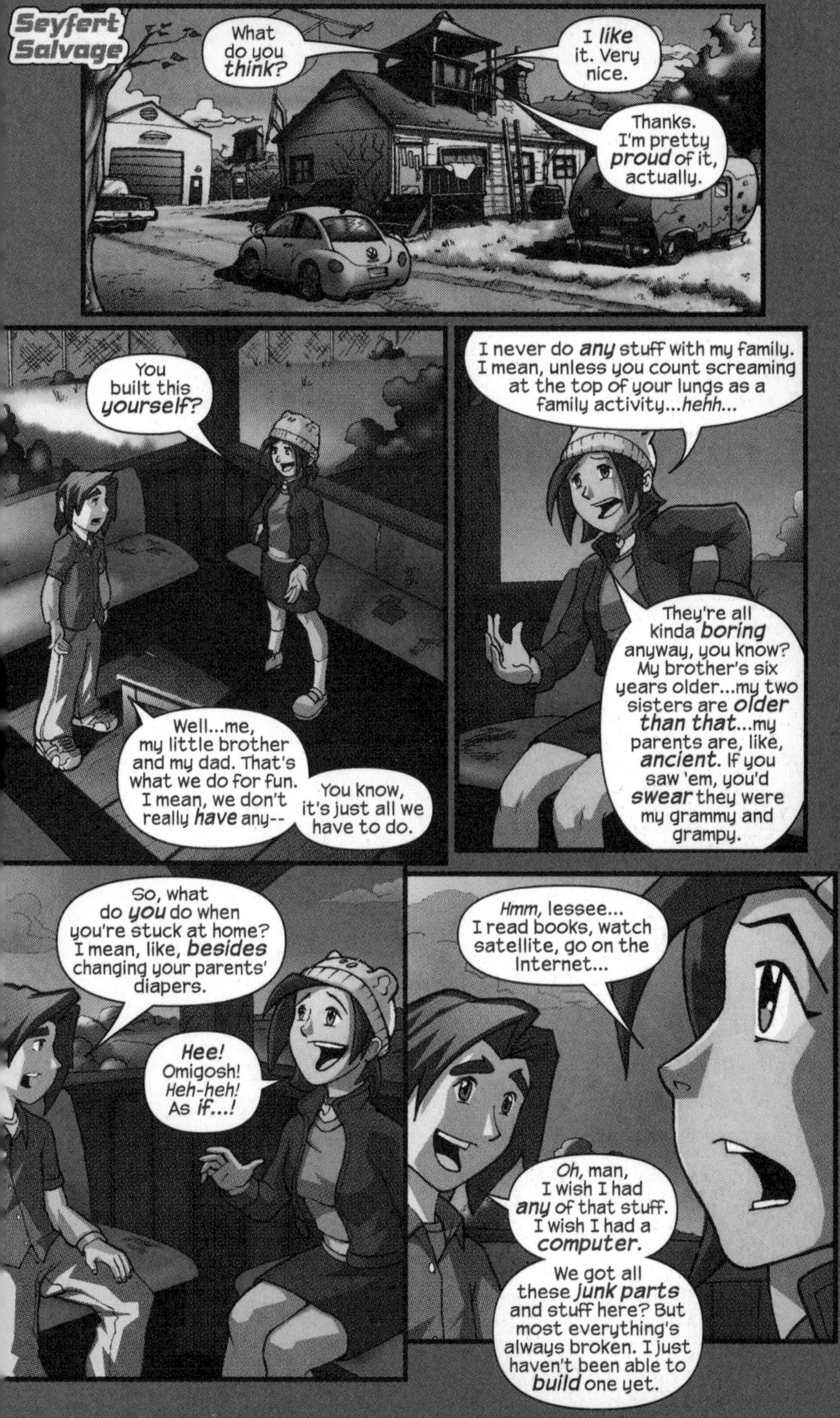

Seyfert Salvage
What do you think?
I like it. Very nice.
Thanks. I'm pretty proud of it, actually.
You built this yourself?
Well...me, my little brother and my dad. That's what we do for fun. I mean, we don't really have any--
You know, it's just all we have to do.
I never do any stuff with my family. I mean, unless you count screaming at the top of your lungs as a family activity...hehh...
They're all kinda boring anyway, you know? My brother's six years older...my two sisters are older than that...my parents are, like, ancient. If you saw 'em, you'd swear they were my grammy and grampy.
So, what do you do when you're stuck at home? I mean, like, besides changing your parents' diapers.
Hee! Omigosh! Heh-heh! As if...!
Hmm, lessee... I read books, watch satellite, go on the Internet...
Oh, man, I wish I had any of that stuff. I wish I had a computer.
We got all these junk parts and stuff here? But most everything's always broken. I just haven't been able to build one yet.

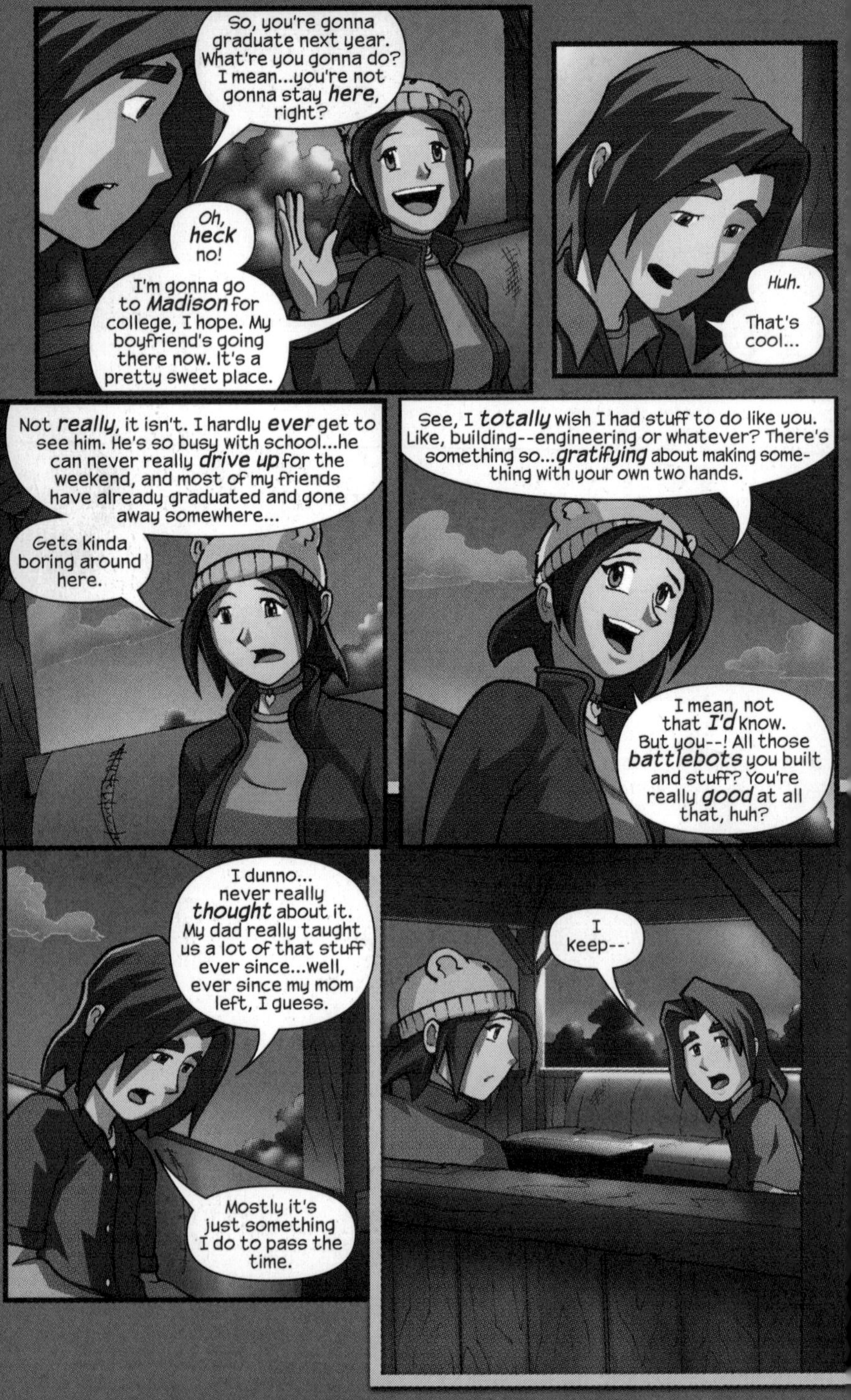
So, you're gonna graduate next year. What're you gonna do? I mean...you're not gonna stay here, right?
Oh, heck no!
I'm gonna go to Madison for college, I hope. My boyfriend's going there now. It's a pretty sweet place.
Huh.
That's cool...
Not really, it isn't. I hardly ever get to see him. He's so busy with school...he can never really drive up for the weekend, and most of my friends have already graduated and gone away somewhere...
Gets kinda boring around here.
See, I totally wish I had stuff to do like you. Like, building--engineering or whatever? There's something so...gratifying about making something with your own two hands.
I mean, not that I'd know. But you--! All those battlebots you built and stuff? You're really good at all that, huh?
I dunno... never really thought about it. My dad really taught us a lot of that stuff ever since...well, ever since my mom left, I guess.
Mostly it's just something I do to pass the time.
I keep--

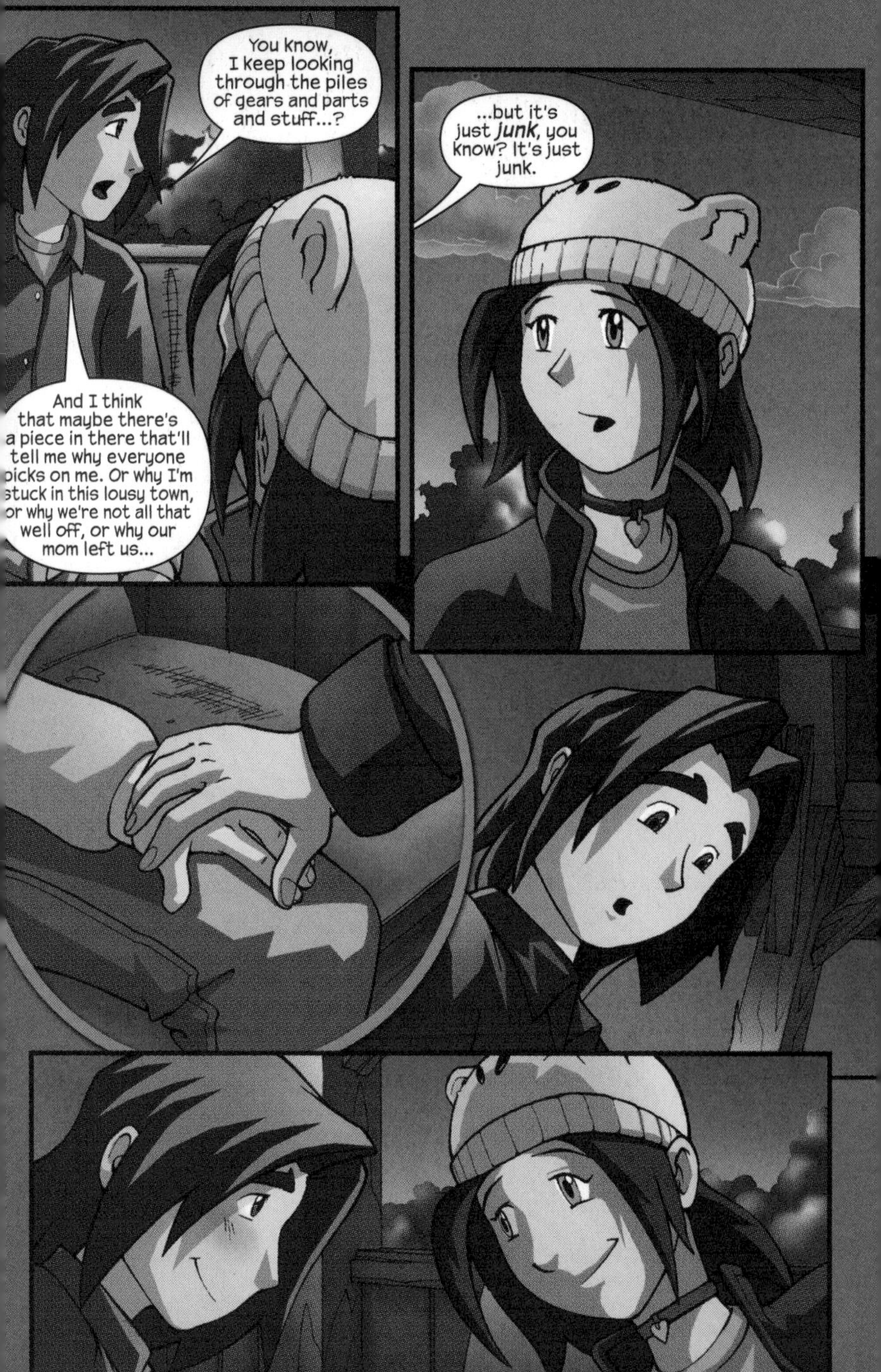
You know, I keep looking through the piles of gears and parts and stuff...?
And I think that maybe there's a piece in there that'll tell me why everyone picks on me. Or why I'm stuck in this lousy town, or why we're not all that well off, or why our mom left us...
...but it's just *junk*, you know? It's just junk.

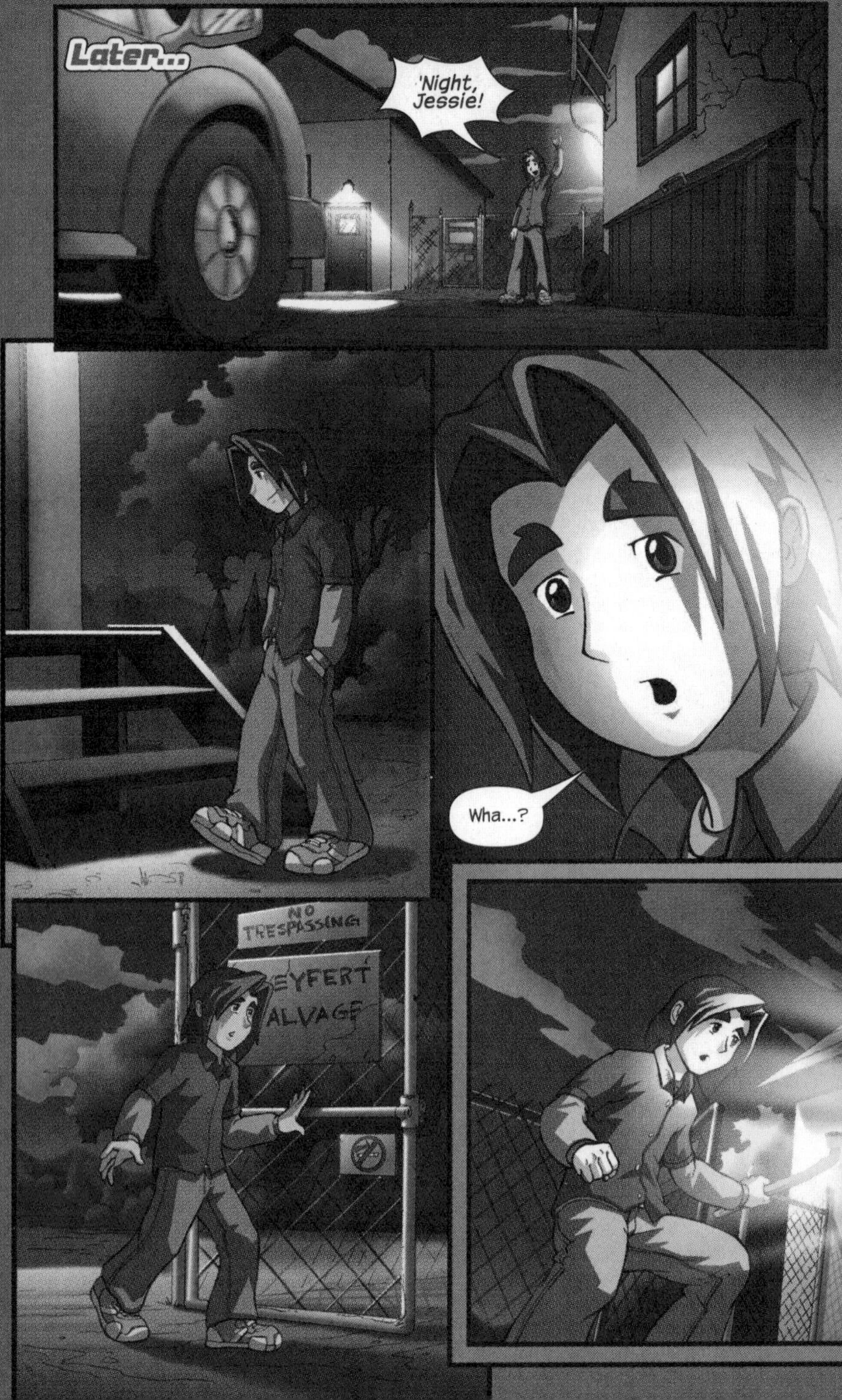
Later...
'Night, Jessie!
Wha...?
NO TRESPASSING
EYFERT
ALVAGE

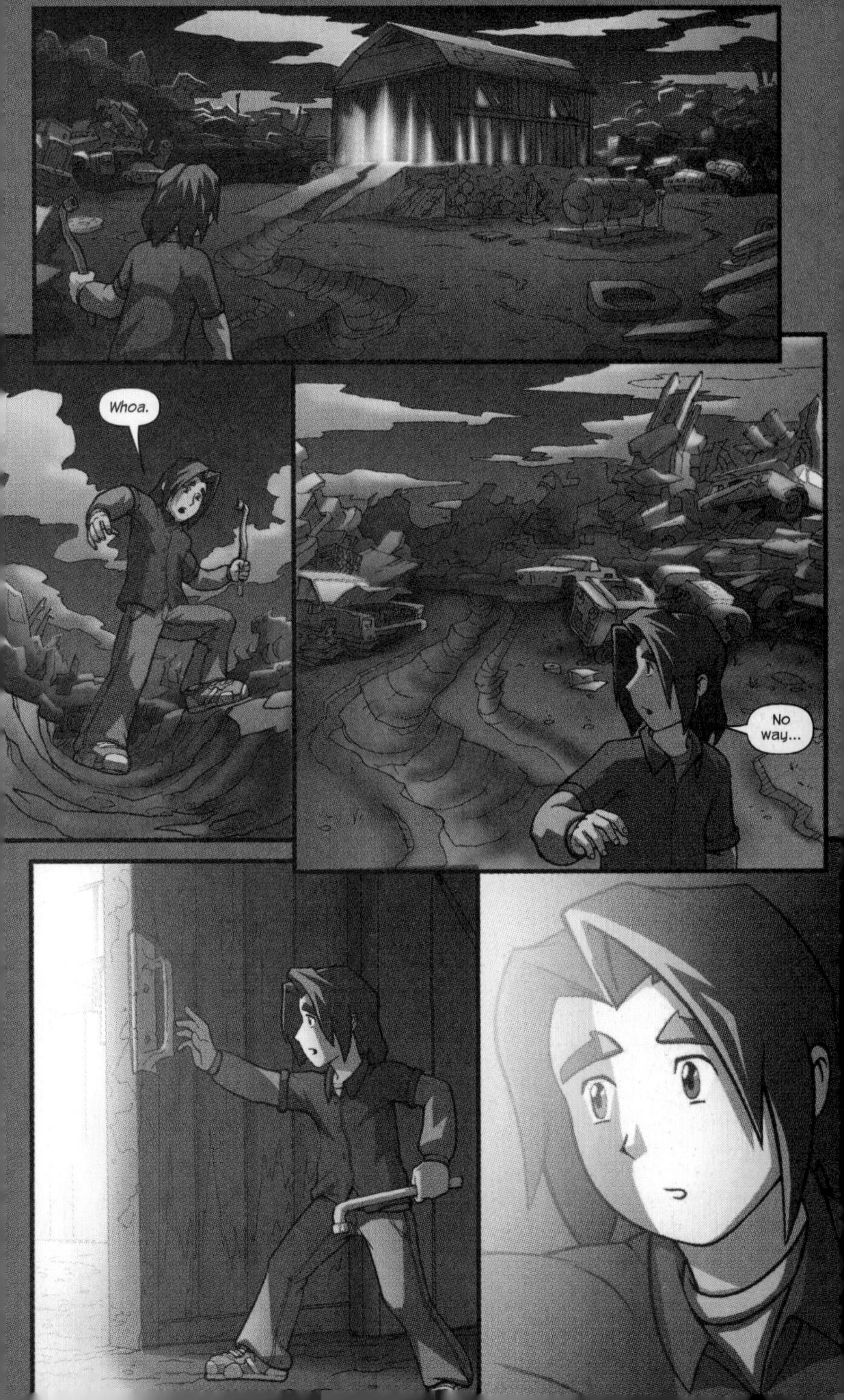
Whoa.
No way...

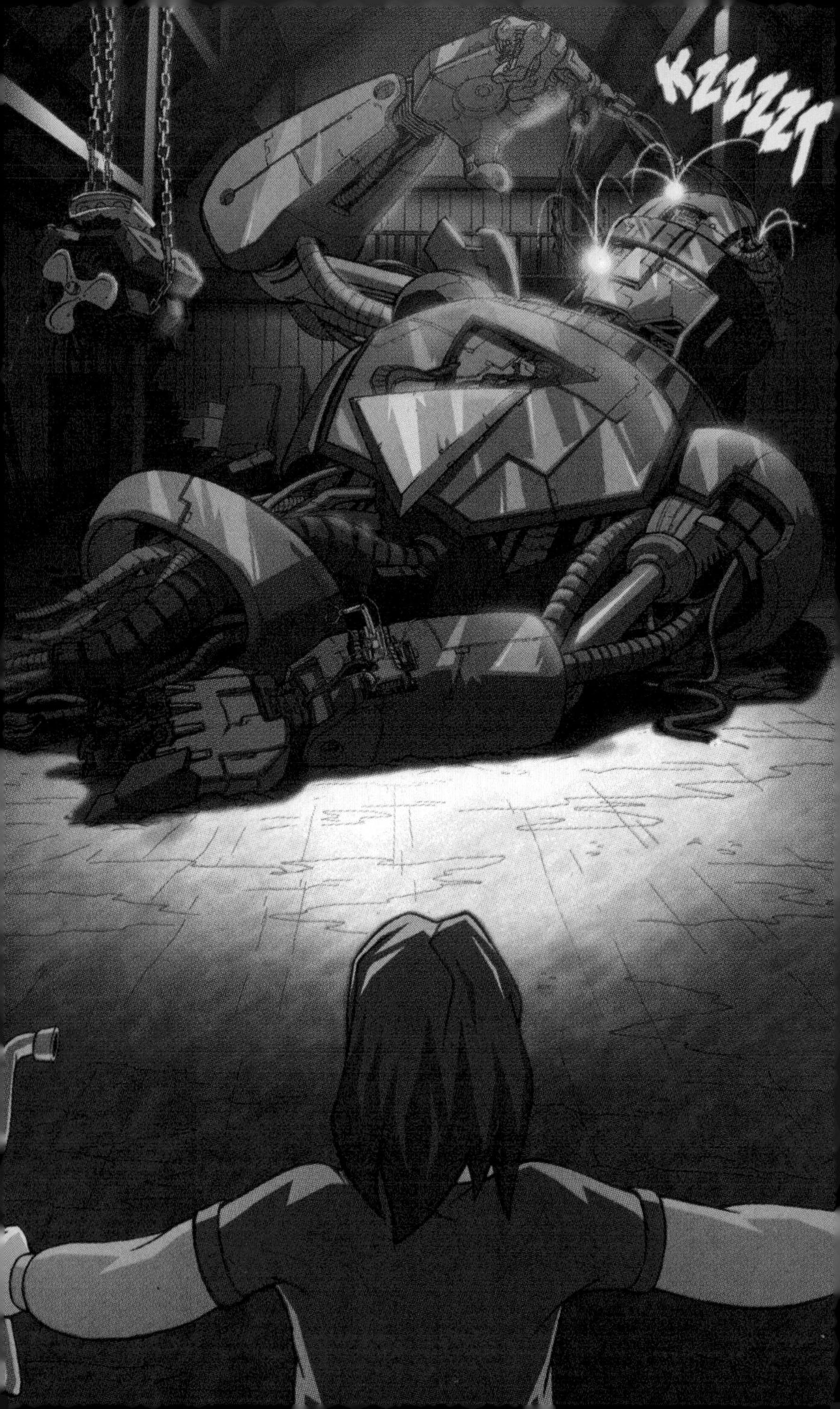
KZZZZZT

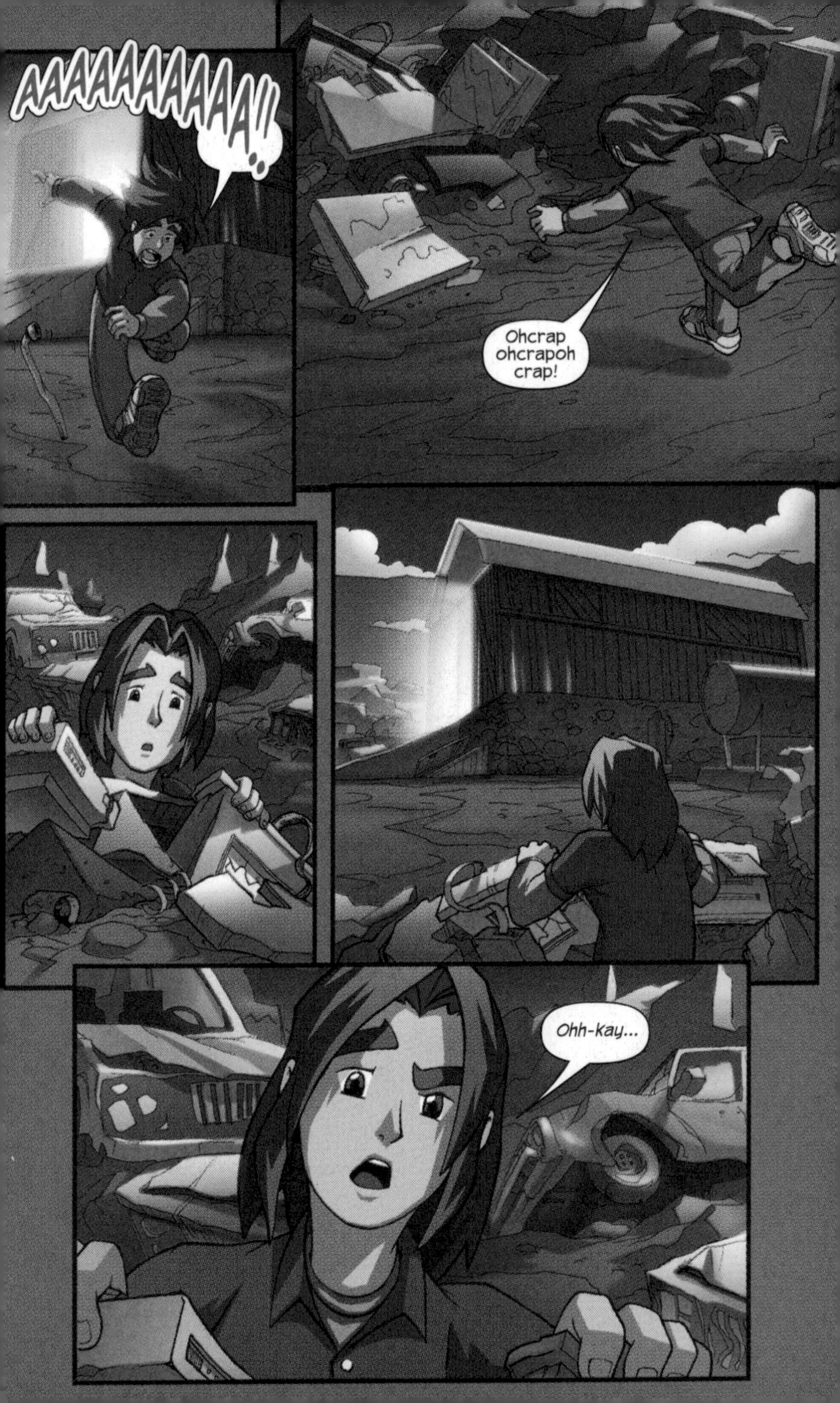

AAAAAAAAAA!!
Ohcrap ohcrapoh crap!
Ohh-kay...

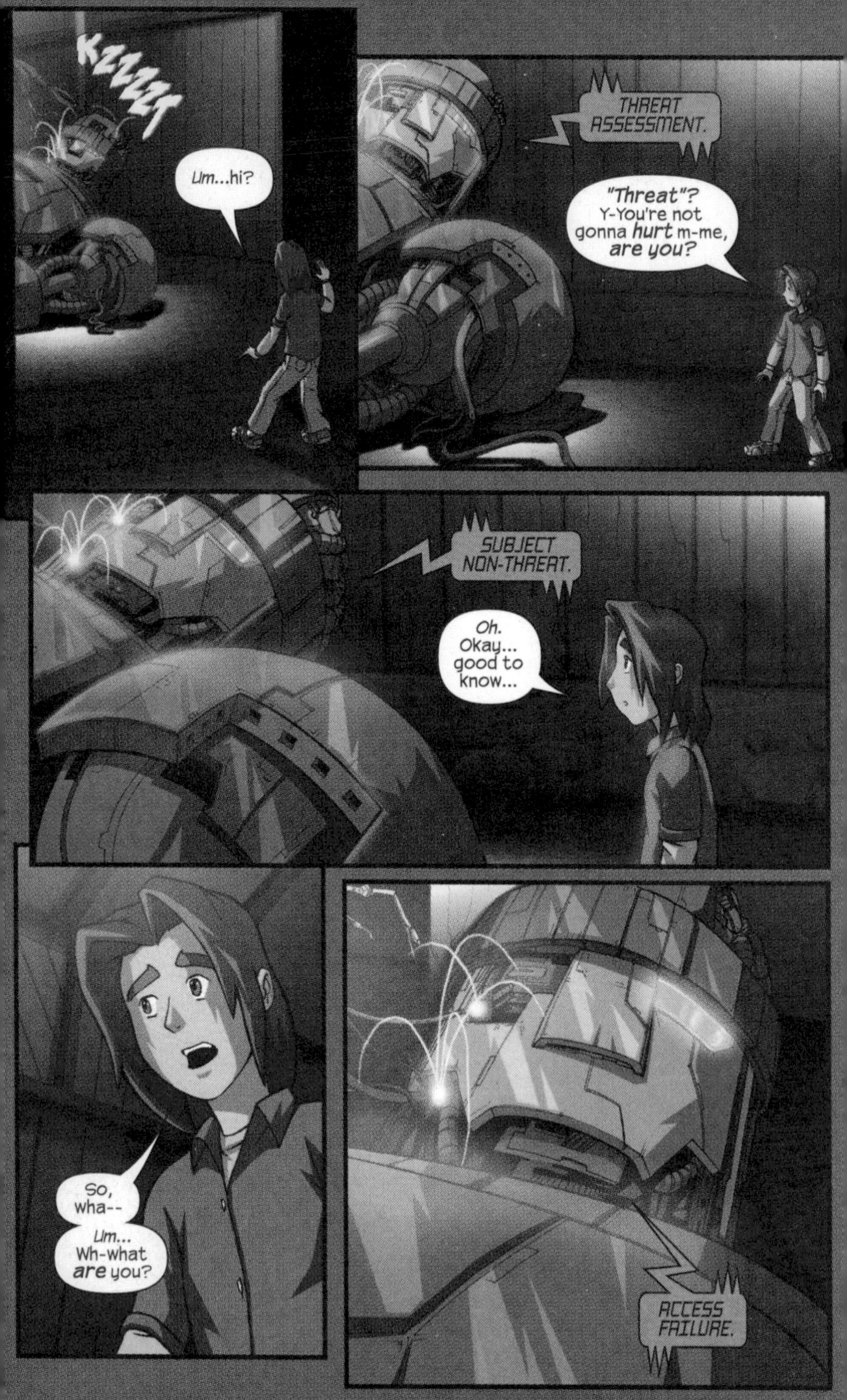
KZZZZT
Um...hi?
THREAT ASSESSMENT.
"Threat"? Y-You're not gonna hurt m-me, are you?
SUBJECT NON-THREAT.
Oh. Okay... good to know...
So, wha--
Um... Wh-what are you?
ACCESS FAILURE.

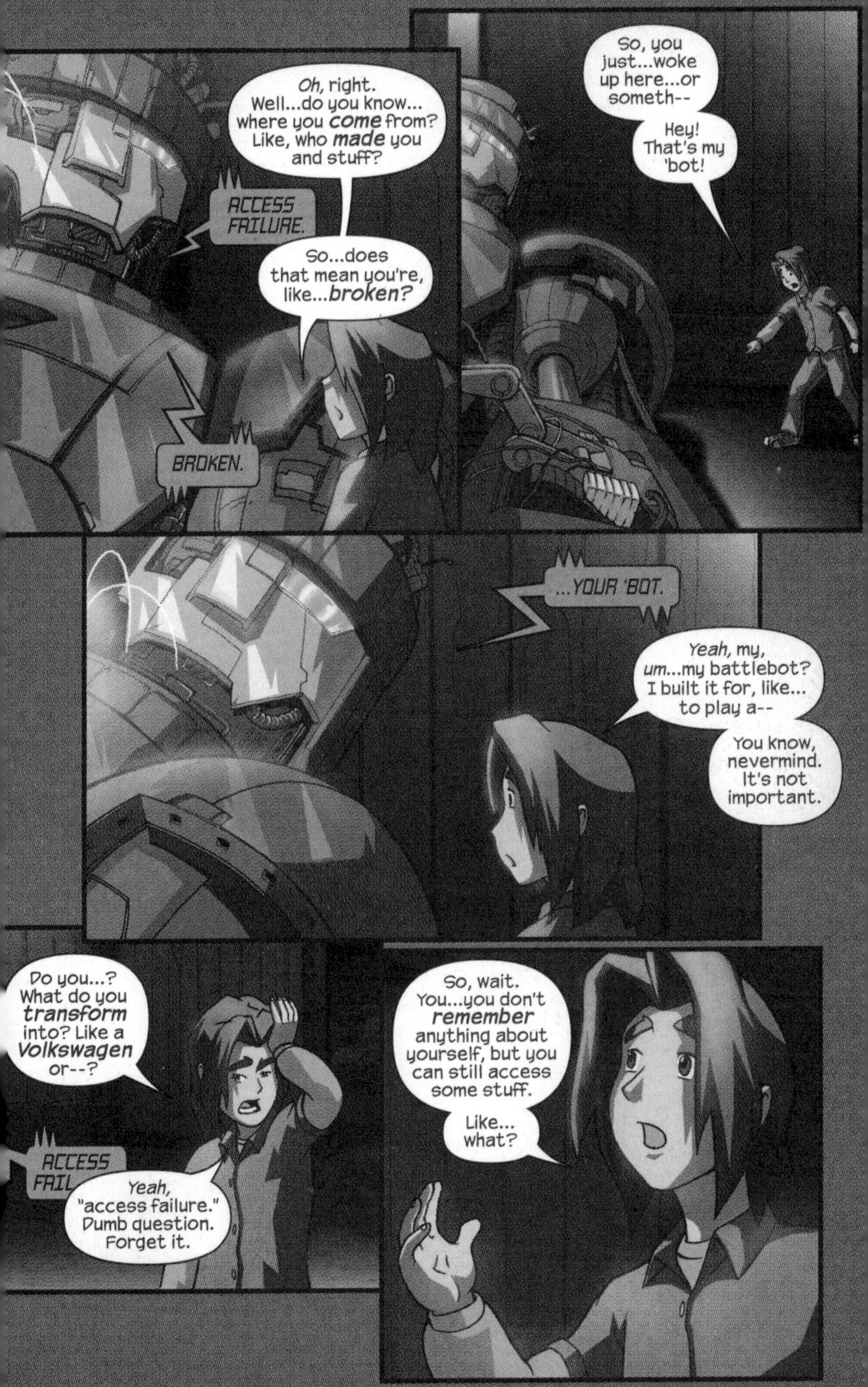
Oh, right. Well...do you know... where you come from? Like, who made you and stuff?
ACCESS FAILURE.
So...does that mean you're, like...broken?
BROKEN.
So, you just...woke up here...or someth--
Hey! That's my 'bot!
...YOUR 'BOT.
Yeah, my, um...my battlebot? I built it for, like... to play a--
You know, nevermind. It's not important.
Do you...? What do you transform into? Like a Volkswagen or--?
ACCESS FAIL
Yeah, "access failure." Dumb question. Forget it.
So, wait. You...you don't remember anything about yourself, but you can still access some stuff.
Like... what?

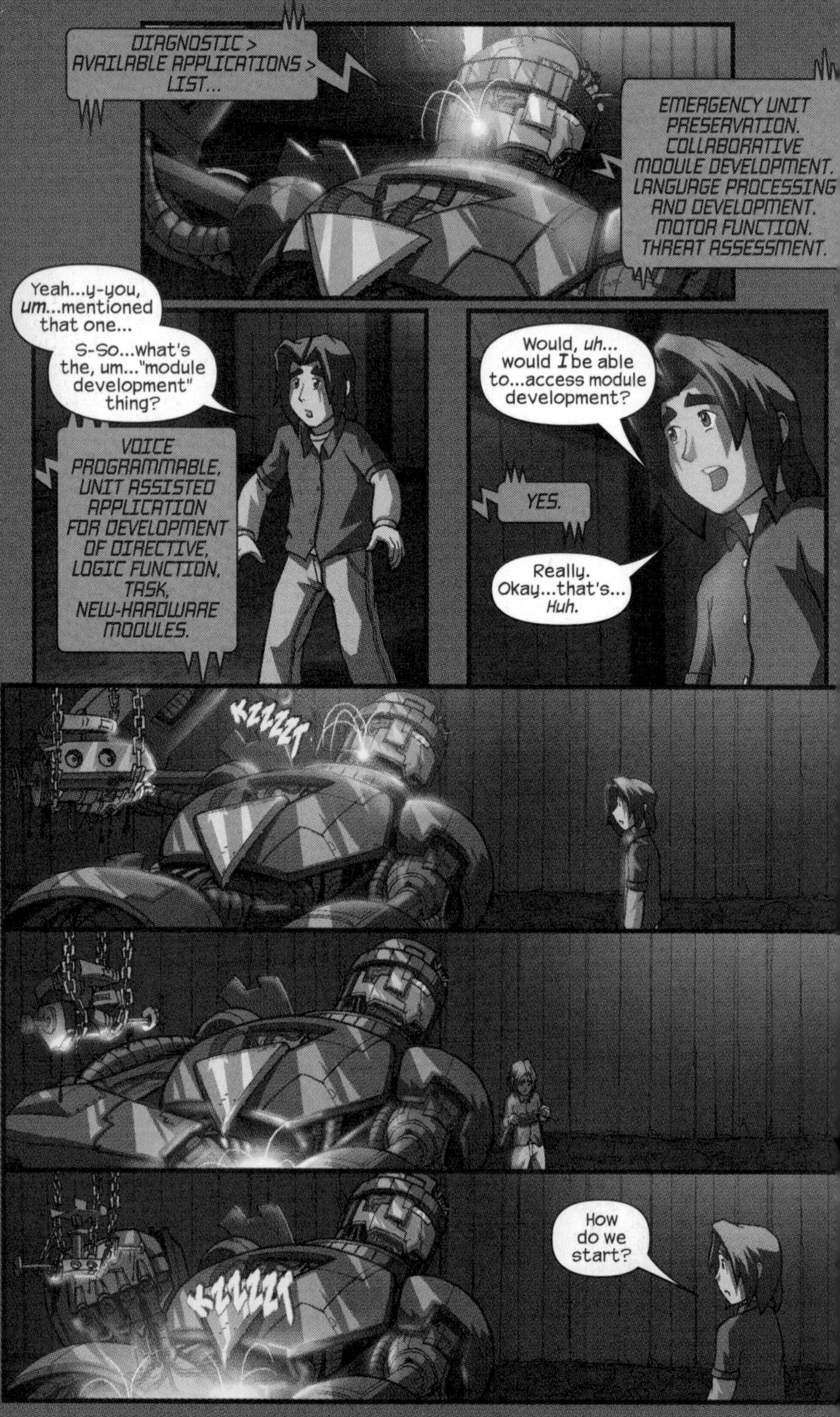

DIAGNOSTIC > AVAILABLE APPLICATIONS > LIST...
EMERGENCY UNIT PRESERVATION. COLLABORATIVE MODULE DEVELOPMENT. LANGUAGE PROCESSING AND DEVELOPMENT. MOTOR FUNCTION. THREAT ASSESSMENT.
Yeah...y-you, um...mentioned that one...
S-So...what's the, um..."module development" thing?
VOICE PROGRAMMABLE, UNIT ASSISTED APPLICATION FOR DEVELOPMENT OF DIRECTIVE, LOGIC FUNCTION, TASK, NEW-HARDWARE MODULES.
Would, uh... would I be able to...access module development?
YES.
Really. Okay...that's... Huh.
KZZZZZT
KZZZZZT
How do we start?

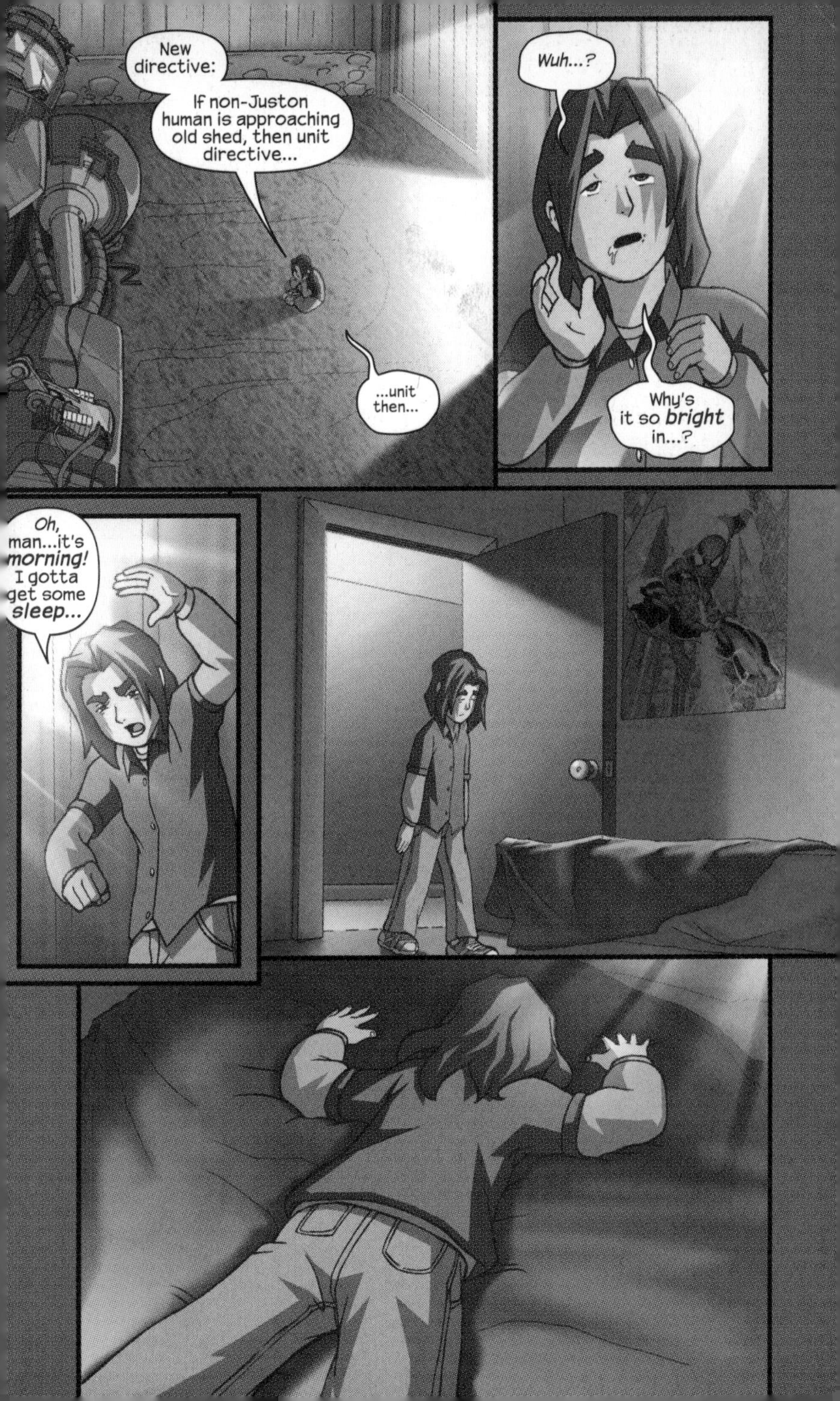
New directive:
If non-Juston human is approaching old shed, then unit directive...
...unit then...
Wuh...?
Why's it so bright in...?
Oh, man...it's morning! I gotta get some sleep...

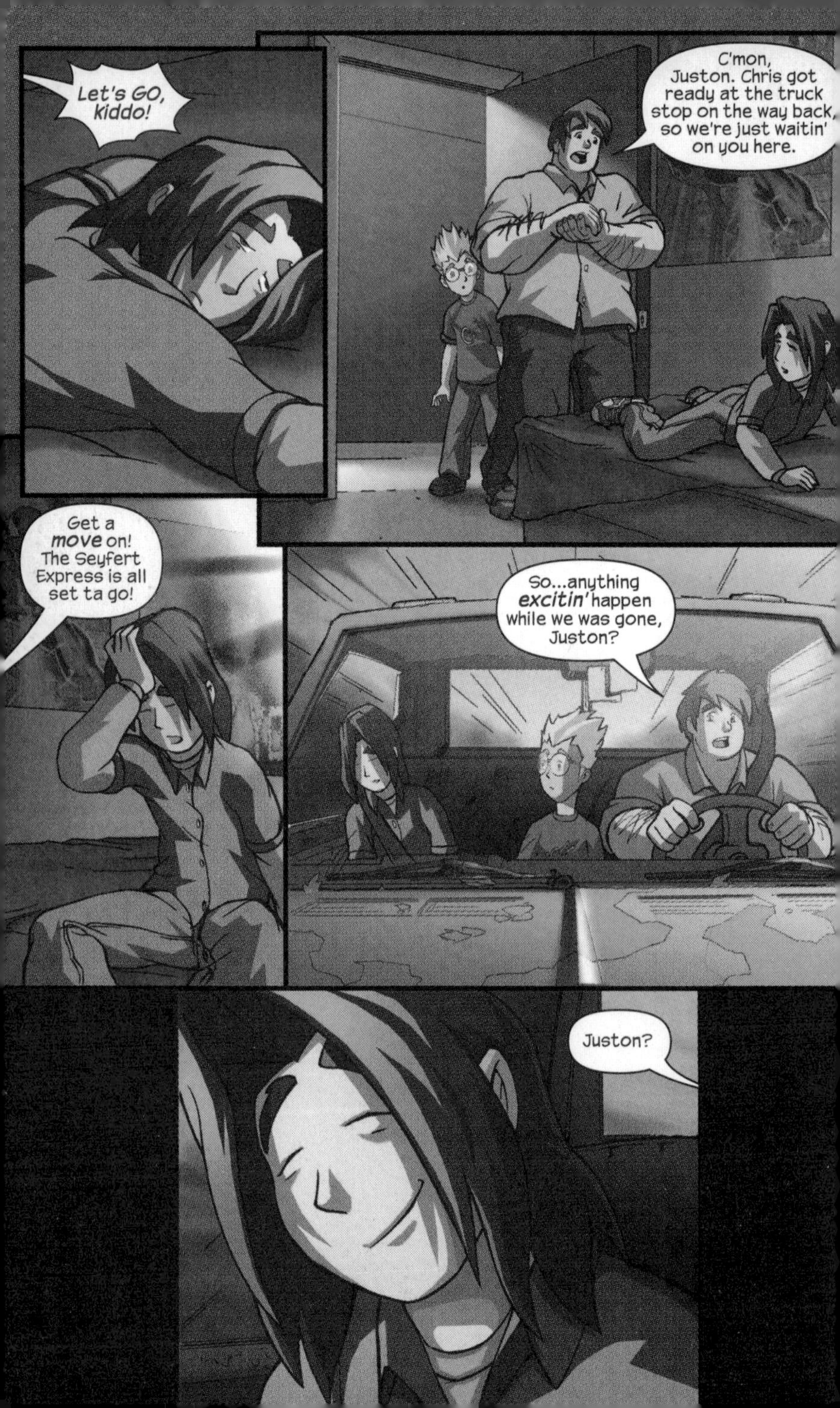
Let's GO, kiddo!
C'mon, Juston. Chris got ready at the truck stop on the way back, so we're just waitin' on you here.
Get a move on! The Seyfert Express is all set ta go!
So...anything excitin' happen while we was gone, Juston?
Juston?

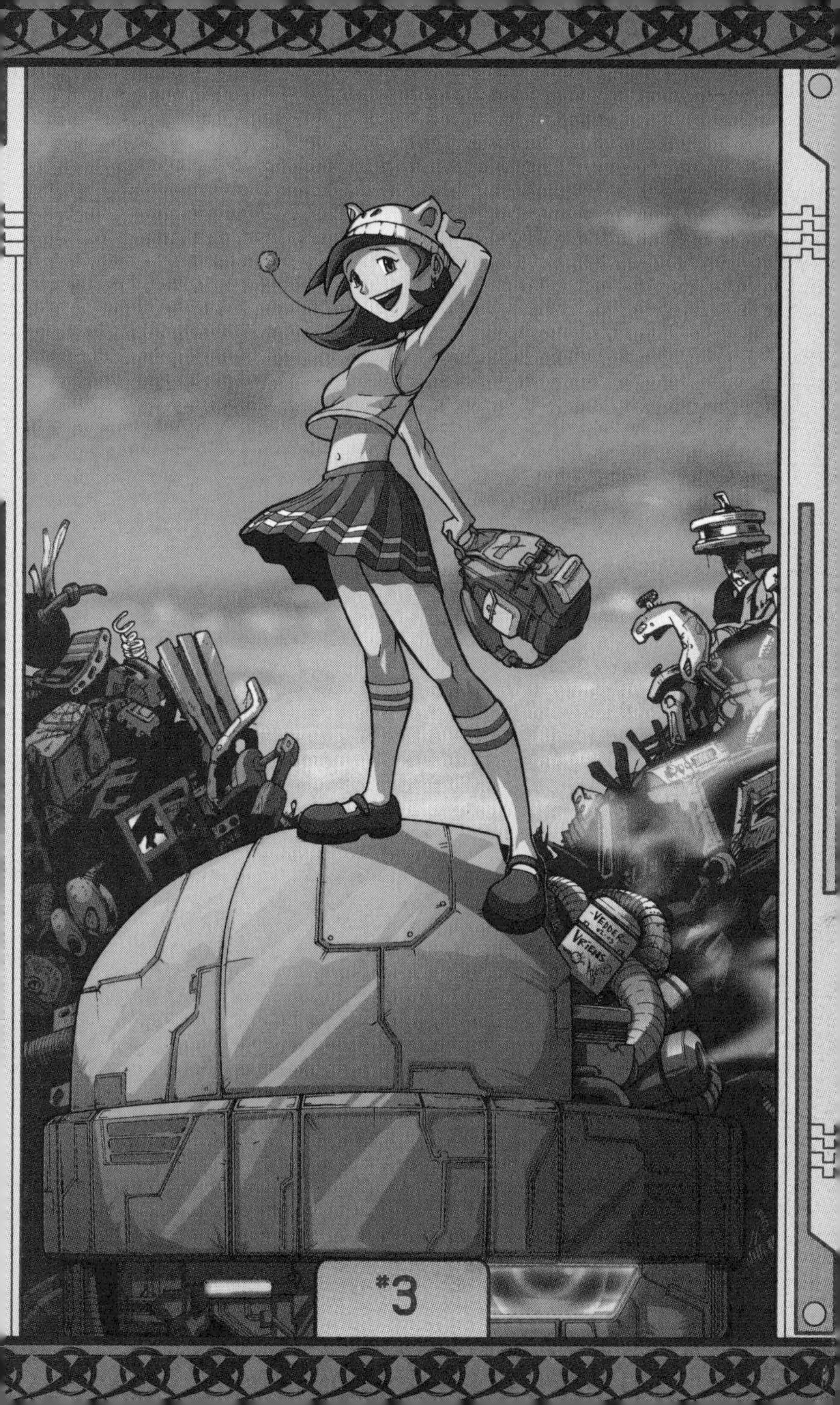
*3

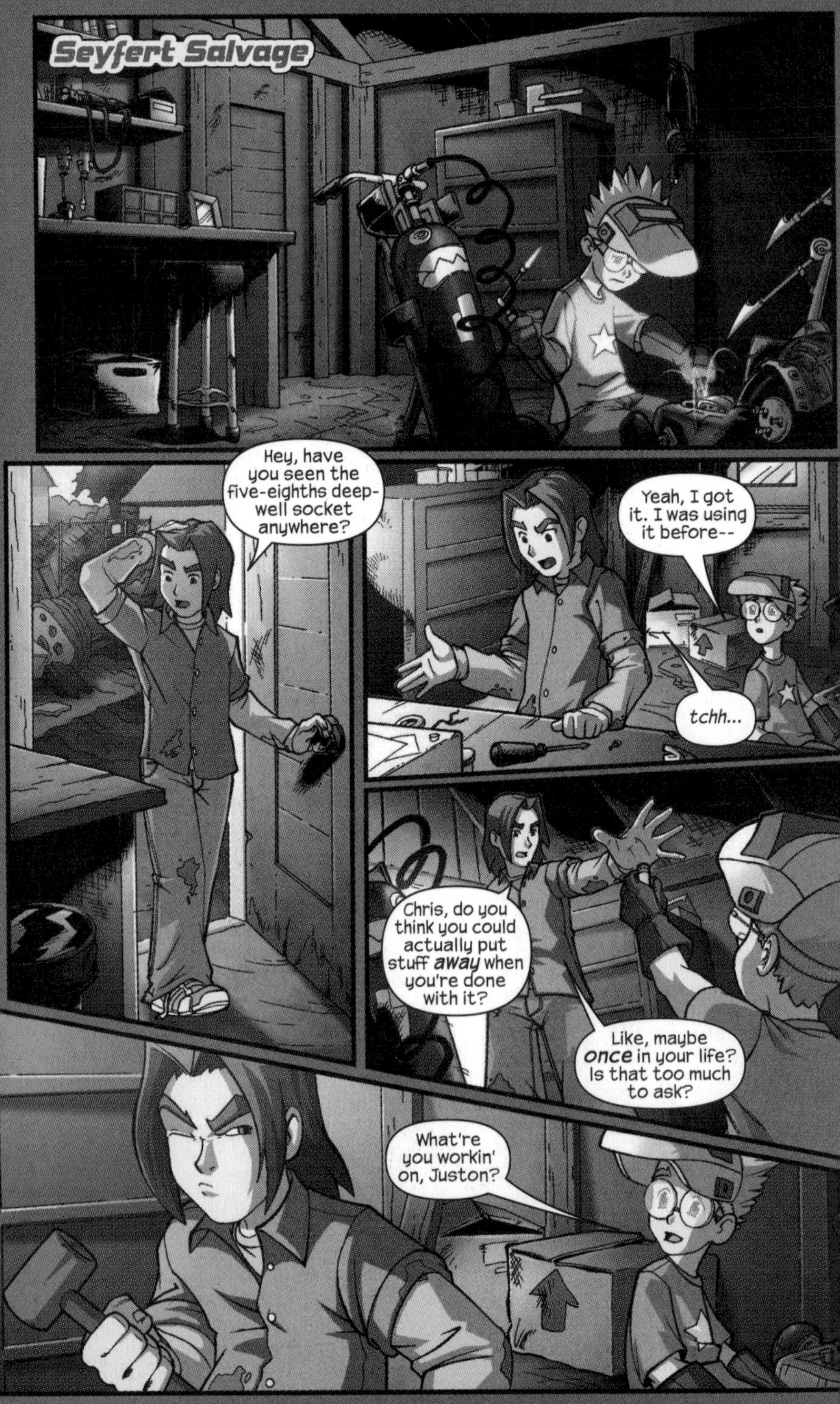
Seyfert Salvage
Hey, have you seen the five-eighths deep-well socket anywhere?
Yeah, I got it. I was using it before--
tchh...
Chris, do you think you could actually put stuff *away* when you're done with it?
Like, maybe *once* in your life? Is that too much to ask?
What're you workin' on, Juston?

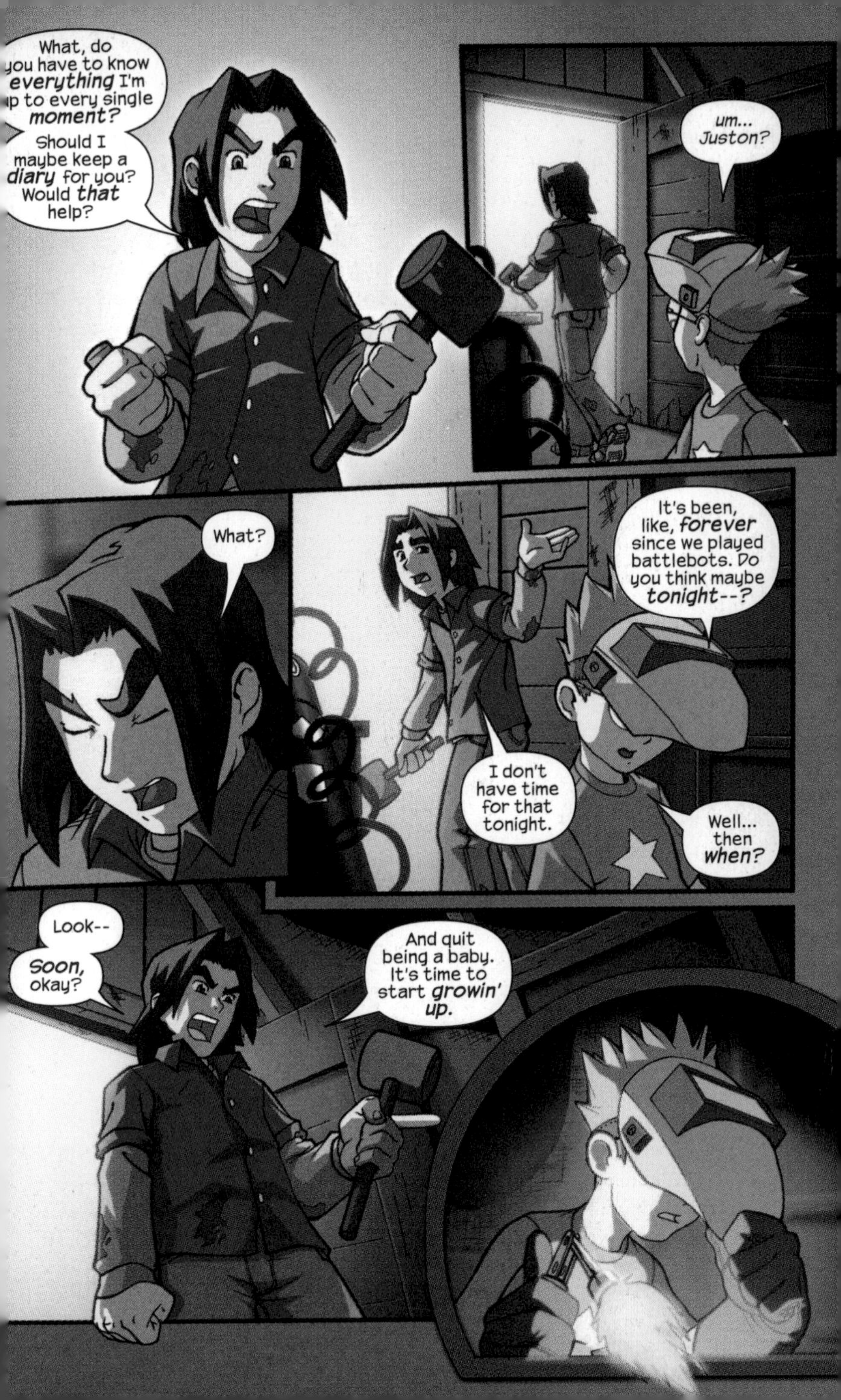

What, do you have to know *everything* I'm up to every single *moment?*
Should I maybe keep a *diary* for you? Would *that* help?
um... Juston?
What?
It's been, like, *forever* since we played battlebots. Do you think maybe *tonight--?*
I don't have time for that tonight.
Well... then *when?*
Look--
Soon, okay?
And quit being a baby. It's time to start *growin' up.*

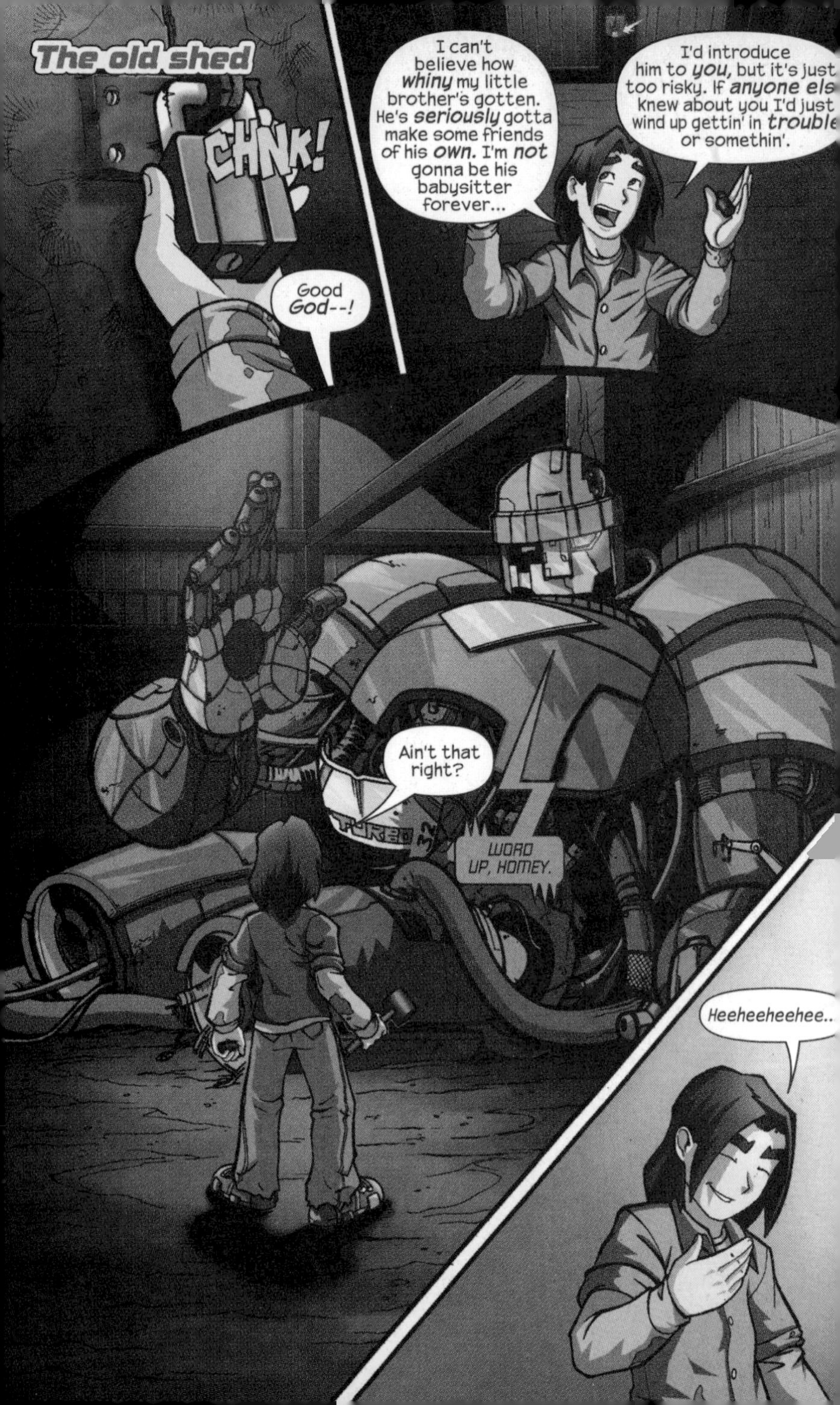

The old shed
CHNK!
Good God--!
I can't believe how whiny my little brother's gotten. He's seriously gotta make some friends of his own. I'm not gonna be his babysitter forever...
I'd introduce him to you, but it's just too risky. If anyone els knew about you I'd just wind up gettin' in trouble or somethin'.
Ain't that right?
WORD UP, HOMEY.
Heeheeheehee..

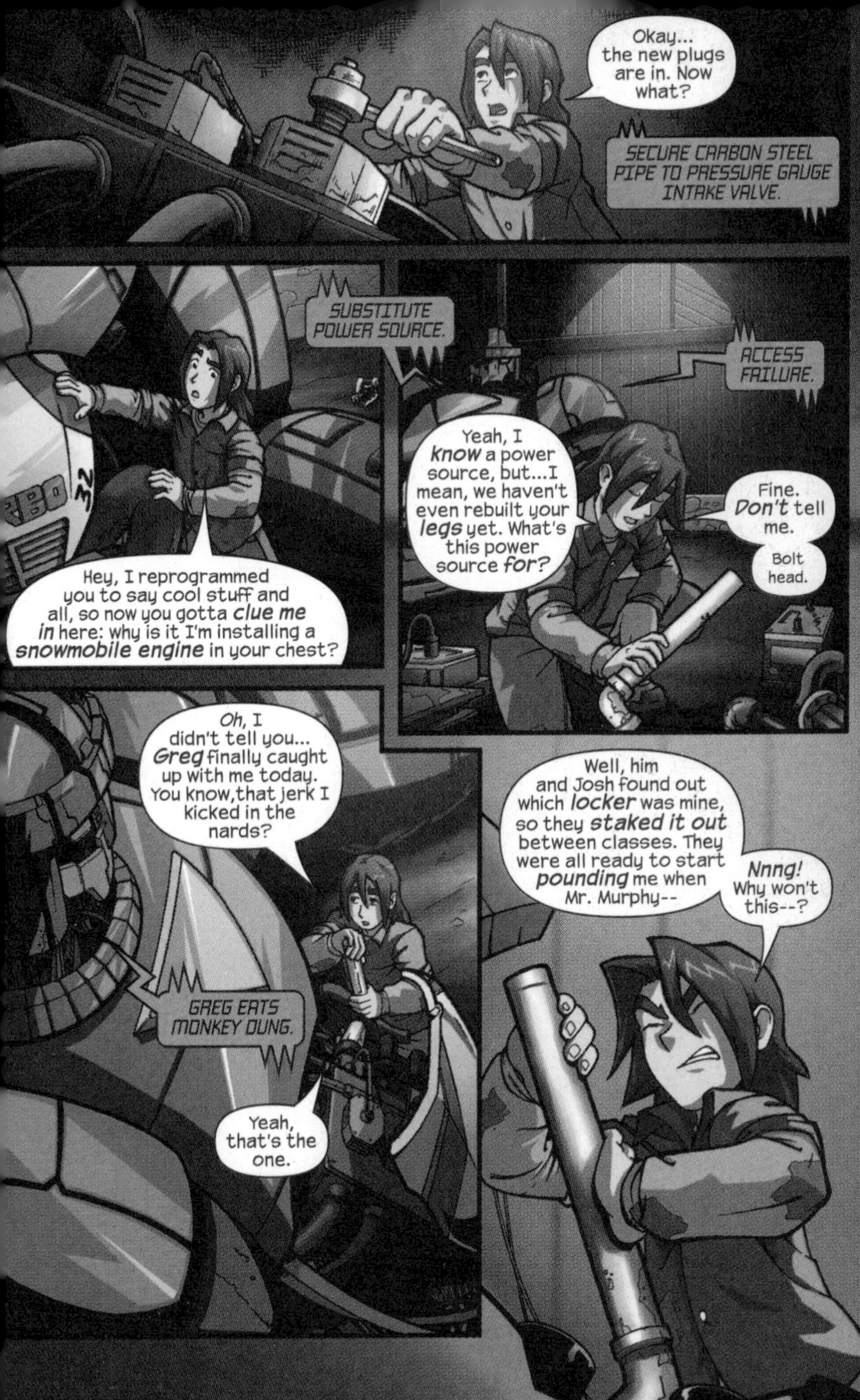

Okay... the new plugs are in. Now what?
SECURE CARBON STEEL PIPE TO PRESSURE GAUGE INTAKE VALVE.
SUBSTITUTE POWER SOURCE.
Hey, I reprogrammed you to say cool stuff and all, so now you gotta clue me in here: why is it I'm installing a snowmobile engine in your chest?
ACCESS FAILURE.
Yeah, I know a power source, but...I mean, we haven't even rebuilt your legs yet. What's this power source for?
Fine. Don't tell me.
Bolt head.
Oh, I didn't tell you... Greg finally caught up with me today. You know, that jerk I kicked in the nards?
GREG EATS MONKEY DUNG.
Yeah, that's the one.
Well, him and Josh found out which locker was mine, so they staked it out between classes. They were all ready to start pounding me when Mr. Murphy--
Nnng! Why won't this--?

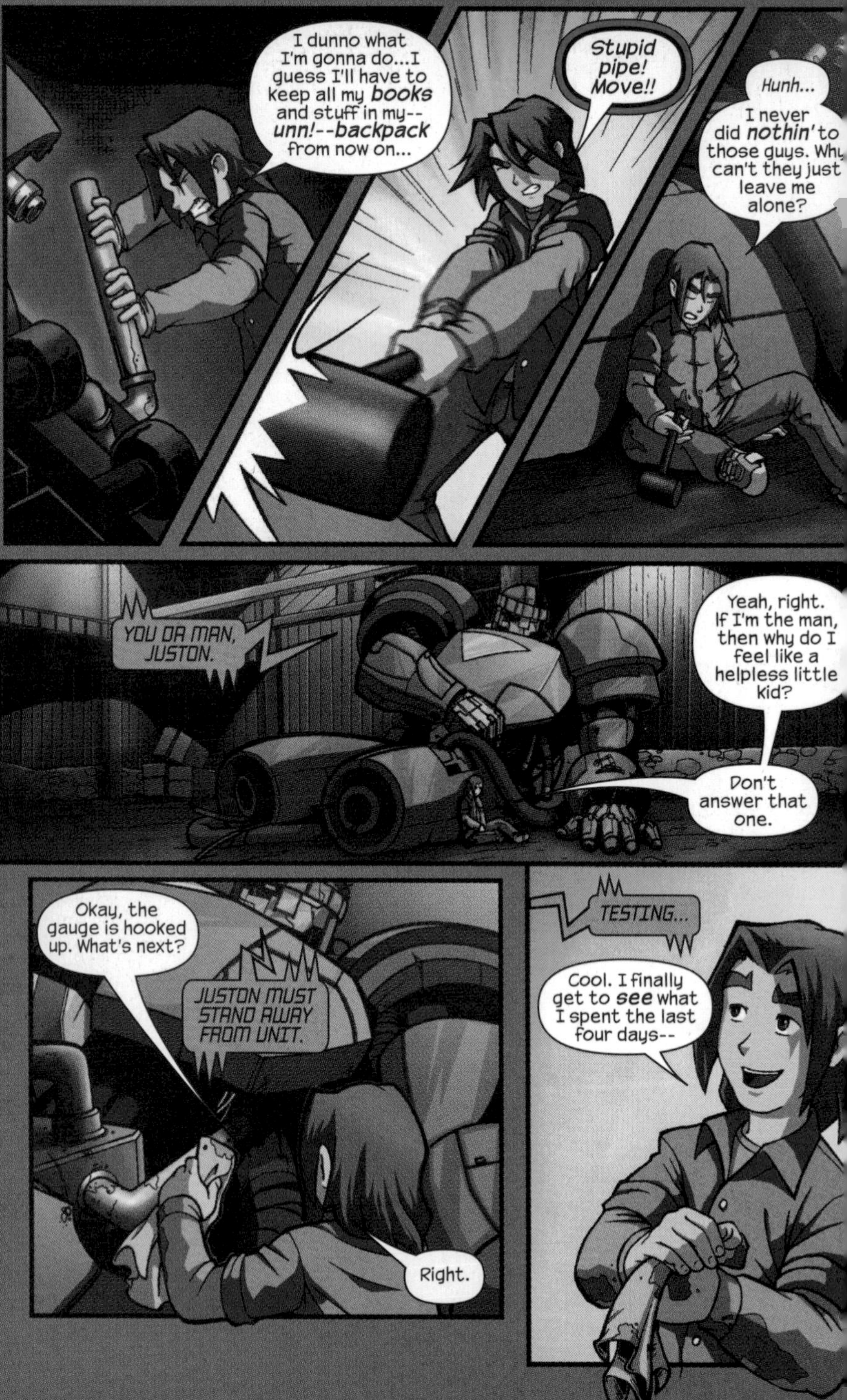
I dunno what I'm gonna do...I guess I'll have to keep all my books and stuff in my--unn!--backpack from now on...
Stupid pipe! Move!!
Hunh...
I never did nothin' to those guys. Why can't they just leave me alone?
YOU DA MAN, JUSTON.
Yeah, right. If I'm the man, then why do I feel like a helpless little kid?
Don't answer that one.
Okay, the gauge is hooked up. What's next?
JUSTON MUST STAND AWAY FROM UNIT.
Right.
TESTING...
Cool. I finally get to see what I spent the last four days--

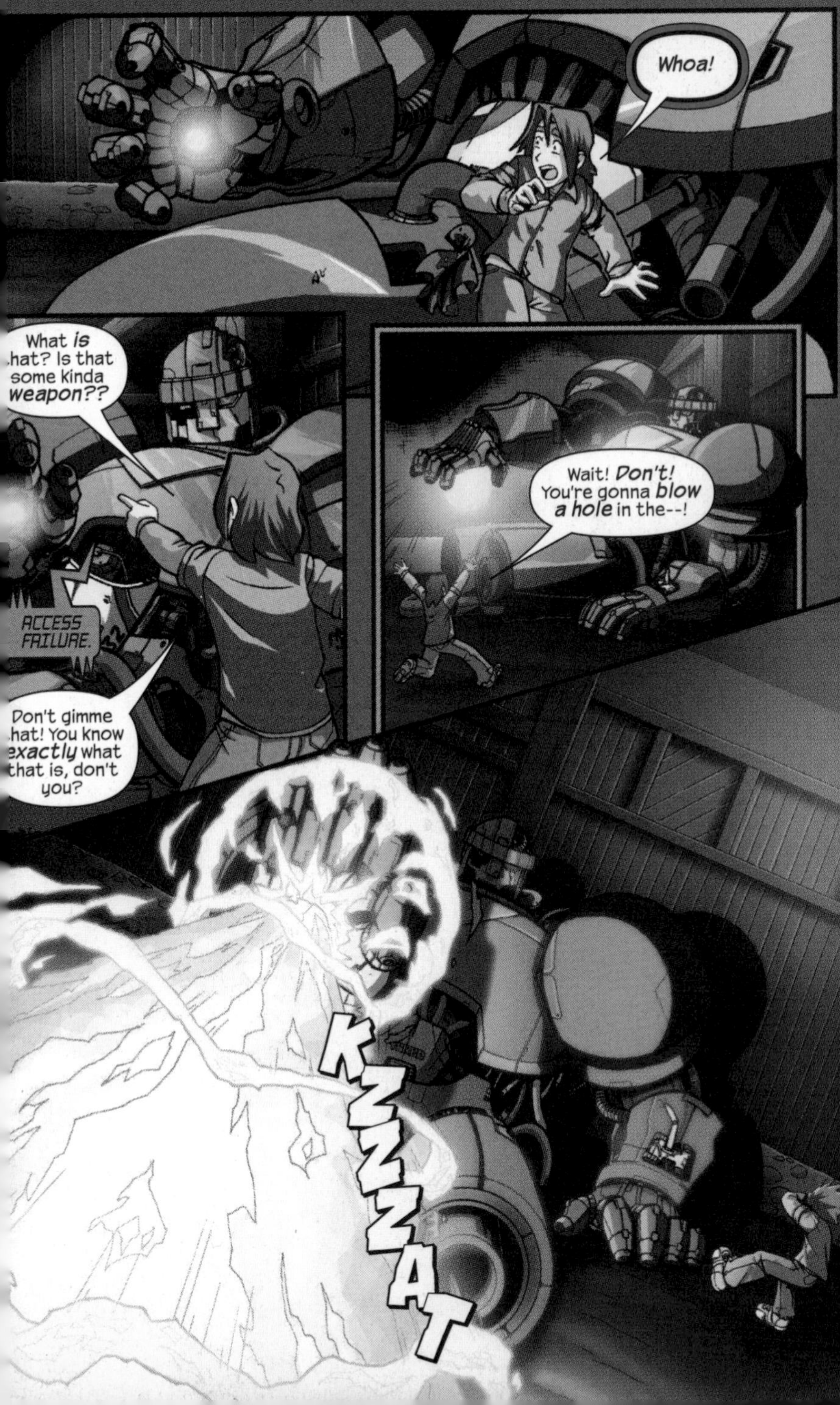
Whoa!
What *is* [t]hat? Is that some kinda *weapon??*
ACCESS FAILURE.
Don't gimme [t]hat! You know *exactly* what that is, don't you?
Wait! *Don't!* You're gonna *blow a hole* in the--!
KZZZAT

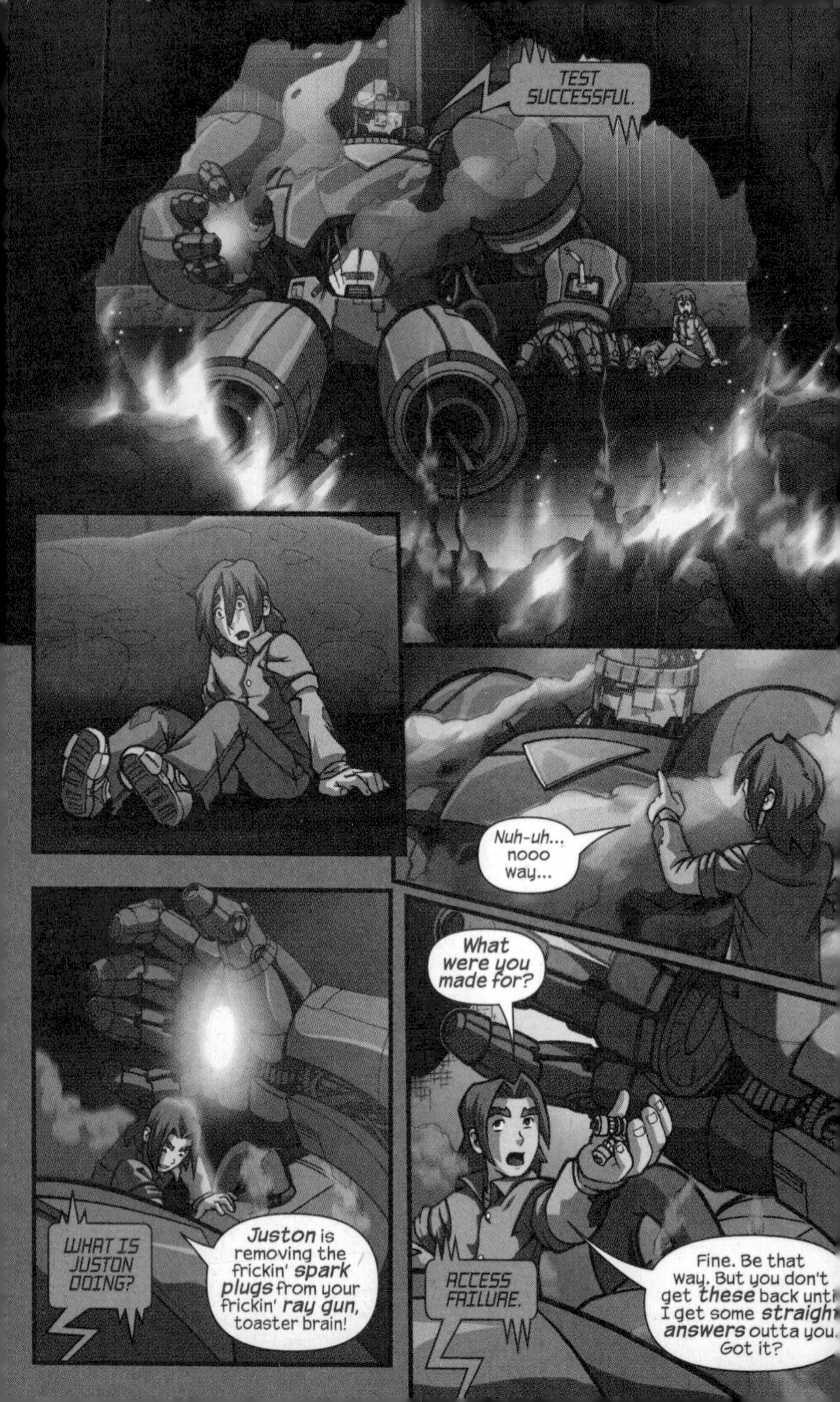

TEST SUCCESSFUL.
Nuh-uh... nooo way...
WHAT IS JUSTON DOING?
Juston is removing the frickin' spark plugs from your frickin' ray gun, toaster brain!
What were you made for?
ACCESS FAILURE.
Fine. Be that way. But you don't get these back until I get some straight answers outta you. Got it?

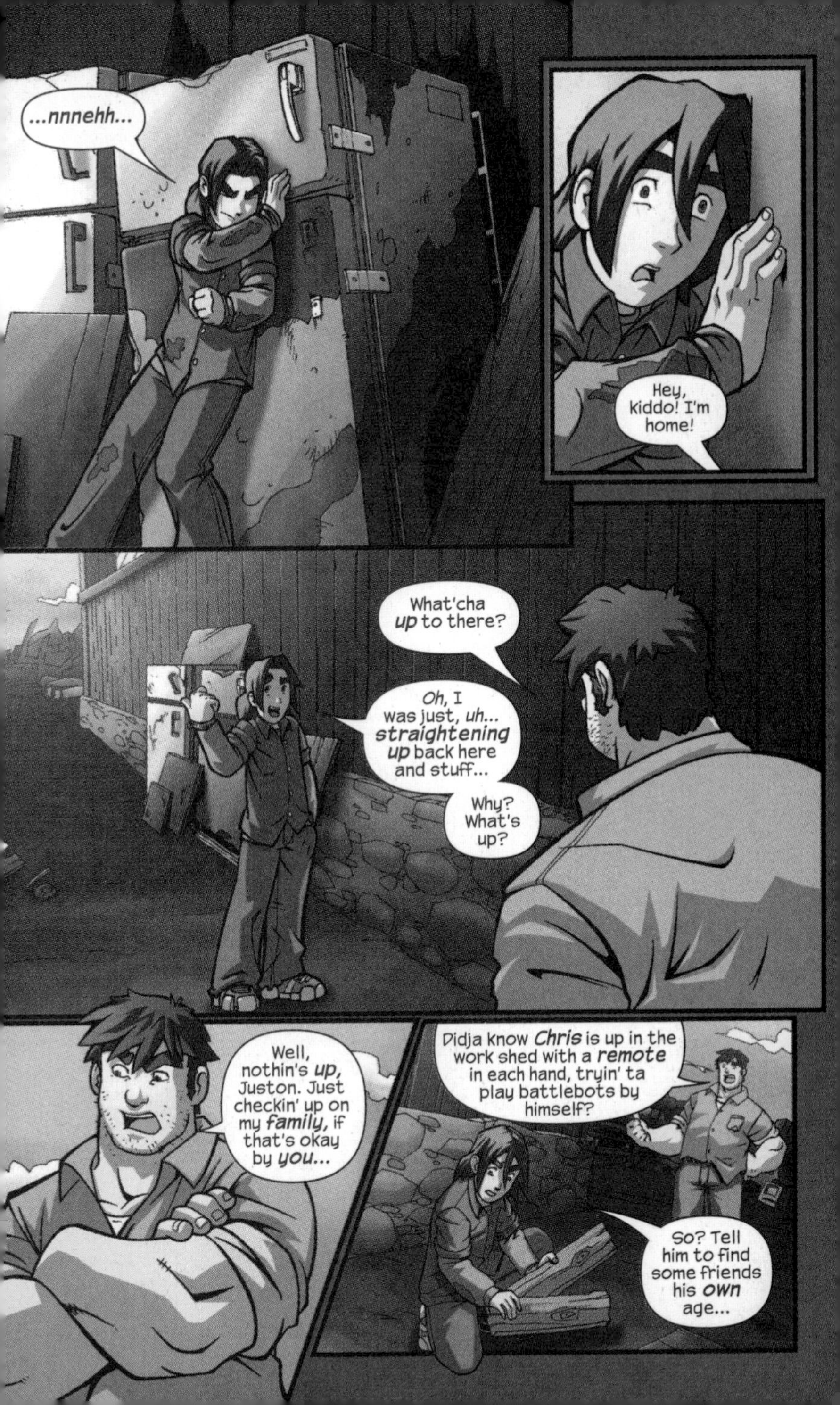
...nnnehh...
Hey, kiddo! I'm home!
What'cha up to there?
Oh, I was just, uh... straightening up back here and stuff...
Why? What's up?
Well, nothin's up, Juston. Just checkin' up on my family, if that's okay by you...
Didja know Chris is up in the work shed with a remote in each hand, tryin' ta play battlebots by himself?
So? Tell him to find some friends his own age...

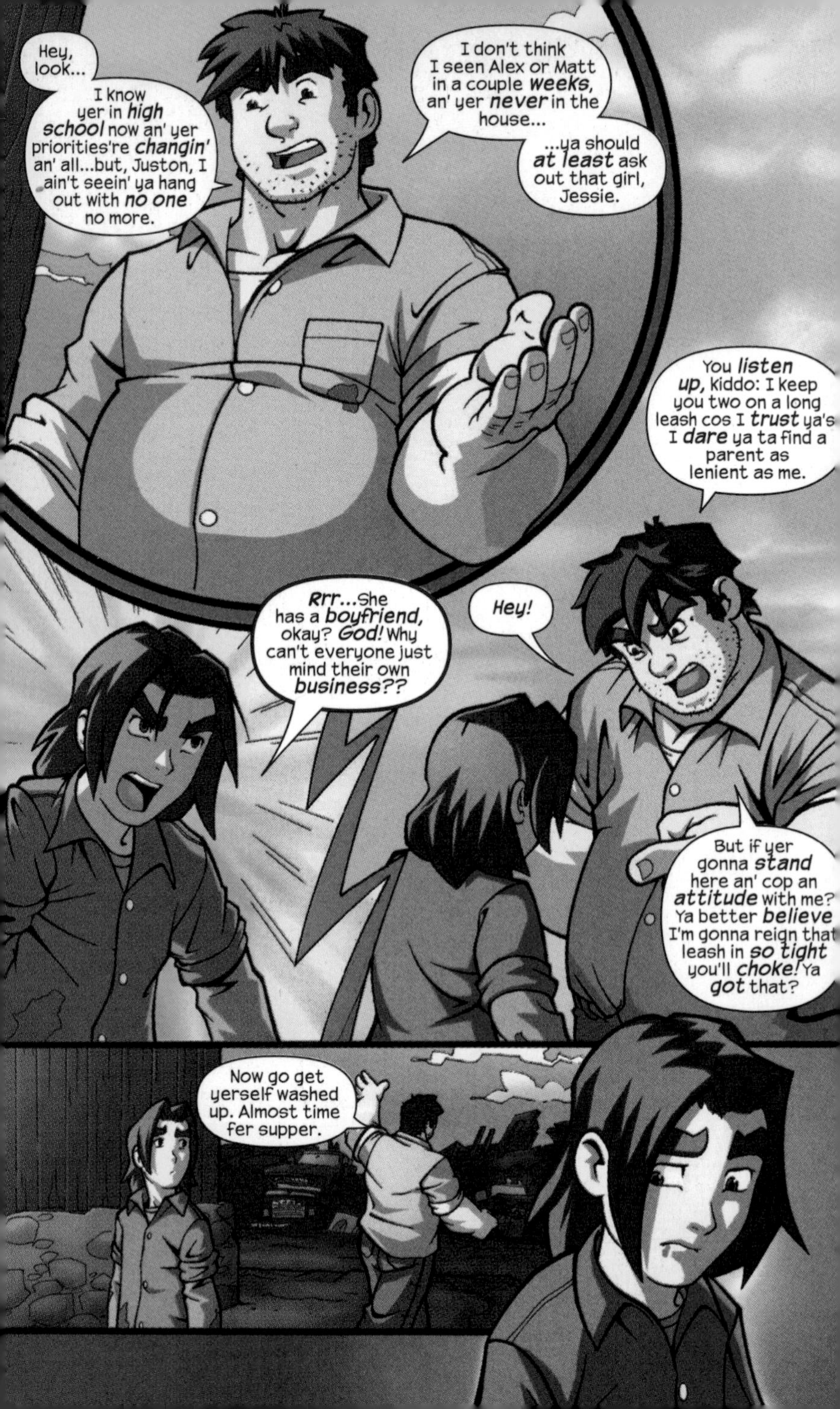
Hey, look...
I know yer in high school now an' yer priorities're changin' an' all...but, Juston, I ain't seein' ya hang out with no one no more.
I don't think I seen Alex or Matt in a couple weeks, an' yer never in the house...
...ya should at least ask out that girl, Jessie.
You listen up, kiddo: I keep you two on a long leash cos I trust ya's I dare ya ta find a parent as lenient as me.
Rrr...She has a boyfriend, okay? God! Why can't everyone just mind their own business??
Hey!
But if yer gonna stand here an' cop an attitude with me? Ya better believe I'm gonna reign that leash in so tight you'll choke! Ya got that?
Now go get yerself washed up. Almost time fer supper.

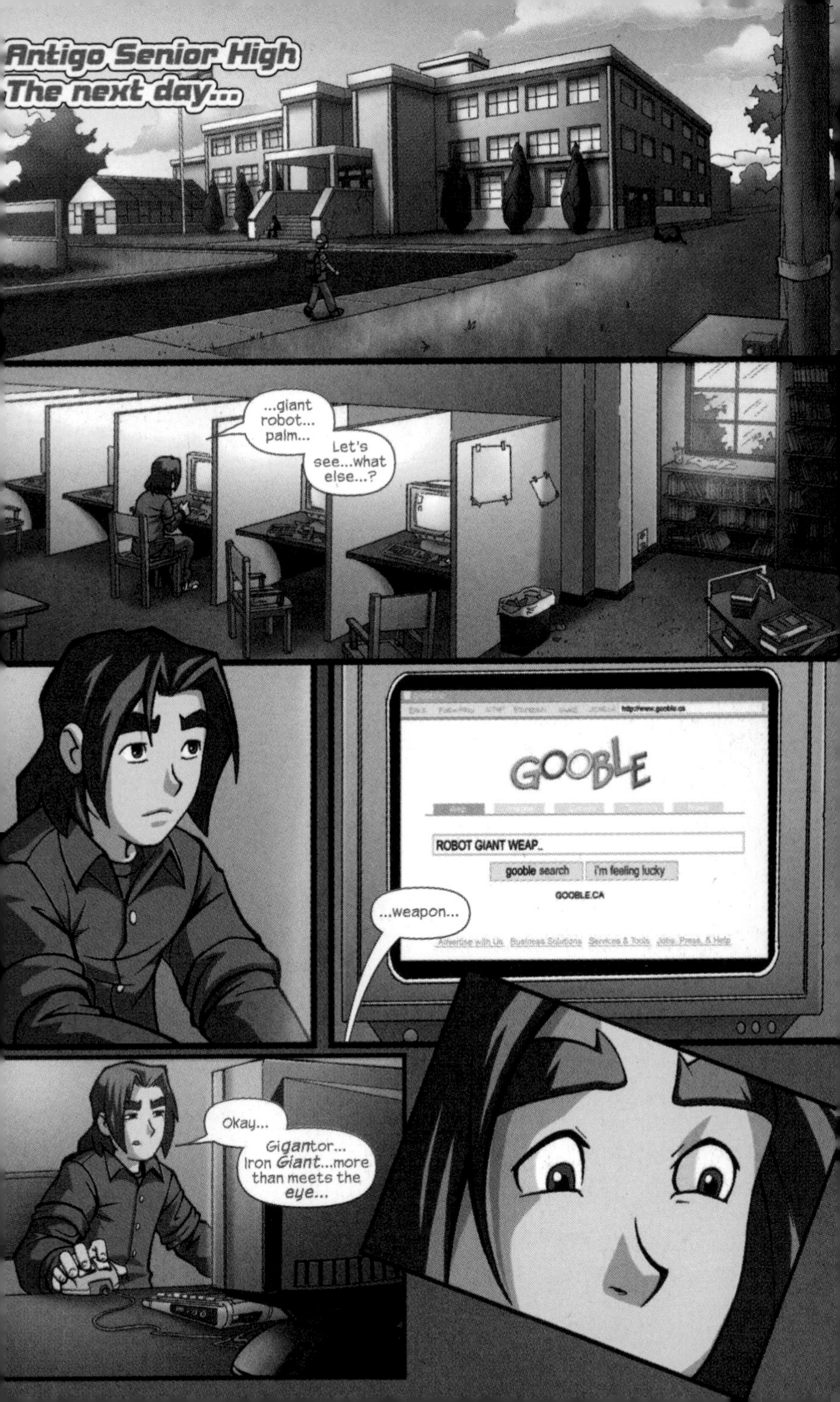
Antigo Senior High
The next day...
...giant robot... palm...
Let's see...what else...?
ROBOT GIANT WEAP..
gooble search
i'm feeling lucky
GOOBLE.CA
...weapon...
Advertise with Us
Business Solutions
Services & Tools
Jobs, Press, & Help
Okay...
Gigantor... Iron Giant...more than meets the eye...

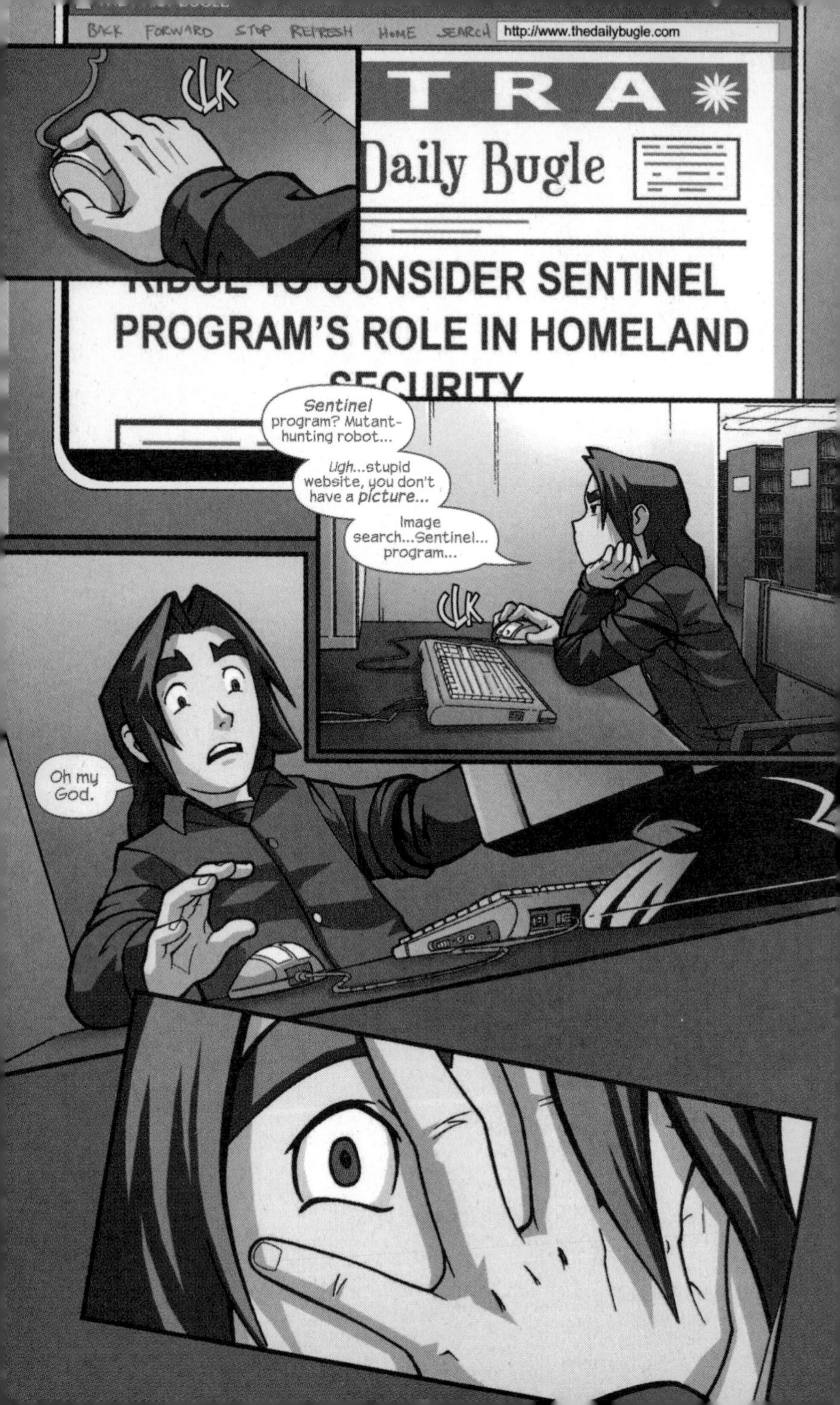
BACK FORWARD STOP REFRESH HOME SEARCH
http://www.thedailybugle.com
CLK
TRA
Daily Bugle
CONSIDER SENTINEL PROGRAM'S ROLE IN HOMELAND
Sentinel program? Mutant-hunting robot...
Ugh...stupid website, you don't have a picture...
Image search...Sentinel... program...
CLK
Oh my God.

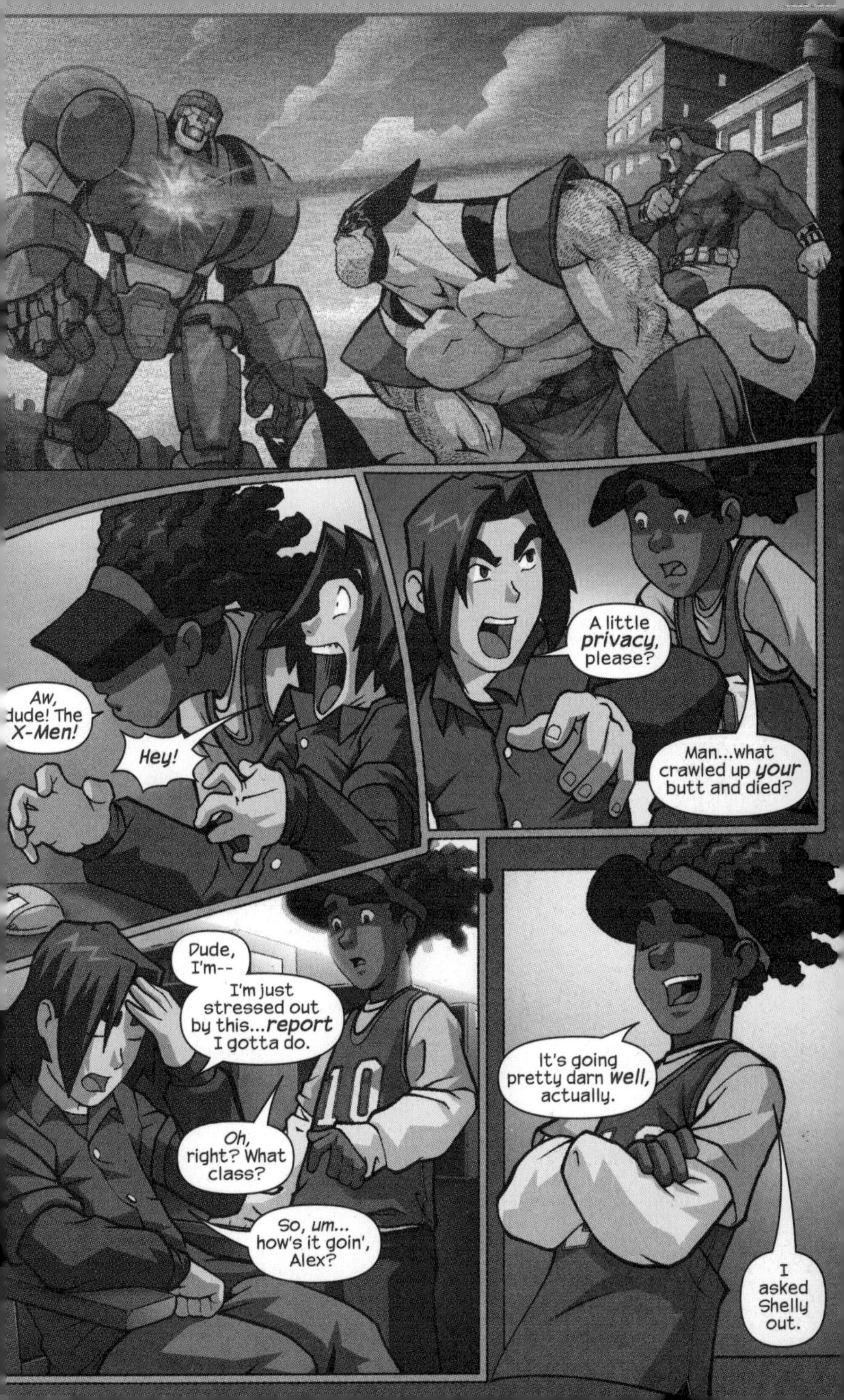
Aw, dude! The X-Men!
Hey!
A little privacy, please?
Man...what crawled up your butt and died?
Dude, I'm--
I'm just stressed out by this...report I gotta do.
Oh, right? What class?
So, um... how's it goin', Alex?
It's going pretty darn well, actually.
I asked Shelly out.

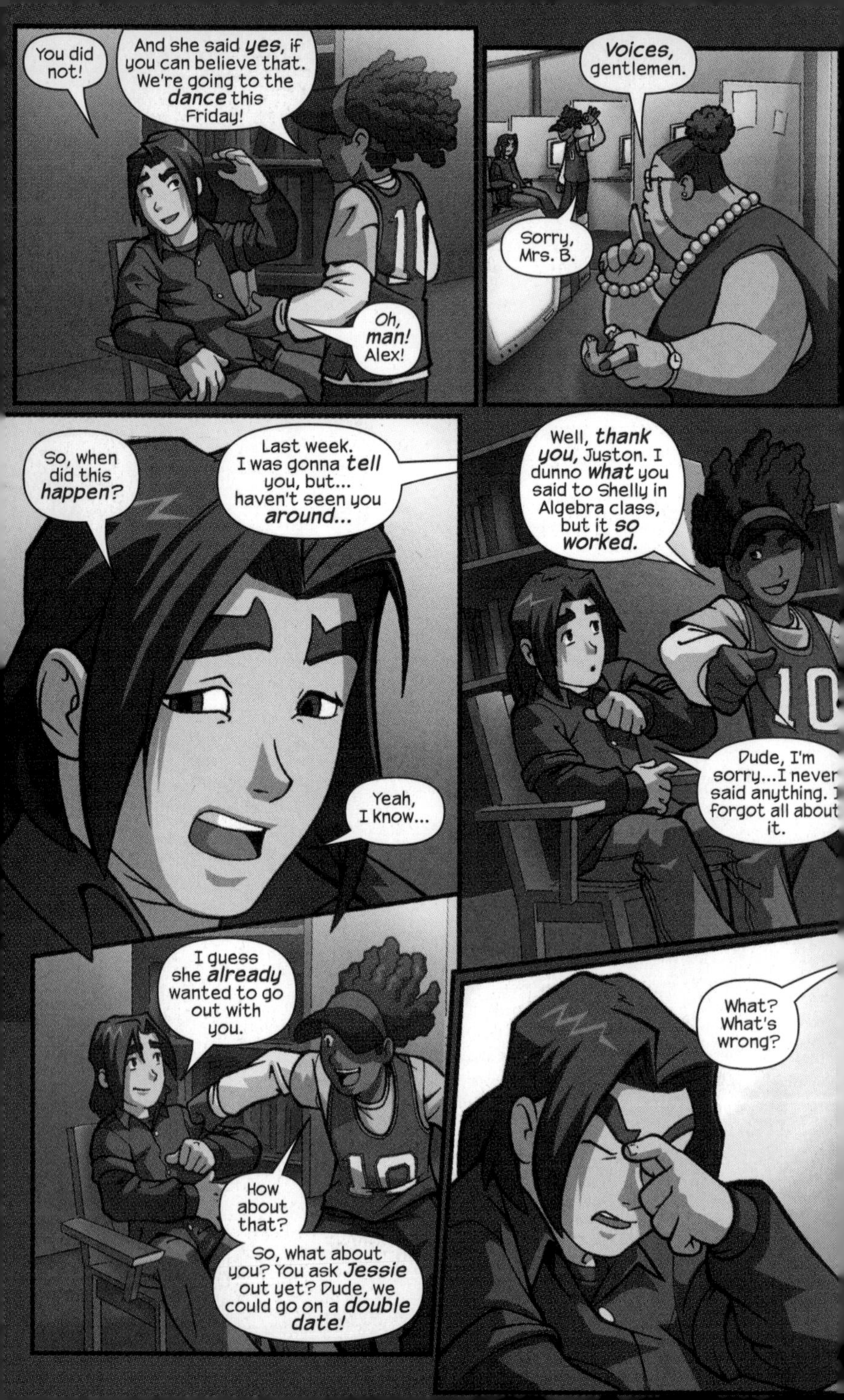
You did not!
And she said yes, if you can believe that. We're going to the dance this Friday!
Oh, man! Alex!
Voices, gentlemen.
Sorry, Mrs. B.
So, when did this happen?
Last week. I was gonna tell you, but... haven't seen you around...
Yeah, I know...
Well, thank you, Juston. I dunno what you said to Shelly in Algebra class, but it so worked.
Dude, I'm sorry...I never said anything. I forgot all about it.
I guess she already wanted to go out with you.
How about that?
So, what about you? You ask Jessie out yet? Dude, we could go on a double date!
What? What's wrong?

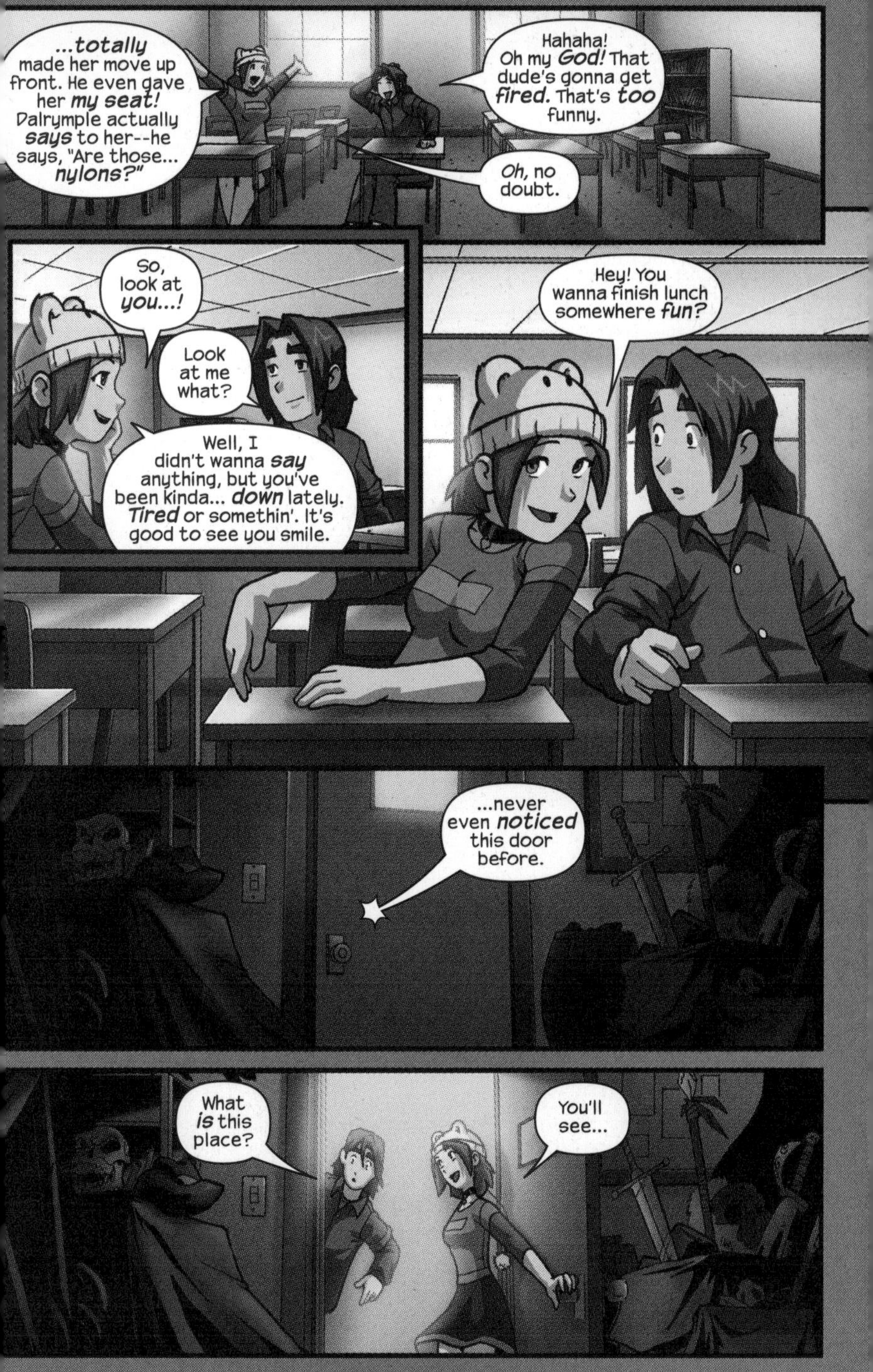
...totally made her move up front. He even gave her my seat! Dalrymple actually says to her--he says, "Are those... nylons?"
Hahaha! Oh my God! That dude's gonna get fired. That's too funny.
Oh, no doubt.
So, look at you...!
Look at me what?
Well, I didn't wanna say anything, but you've been kinda... down lately. Tired or somethin'. It's good to see you smile.
Hey! You wanna finish lunch somewhere fun?
...never even noticed this door before.
What is this place?
You'll see...

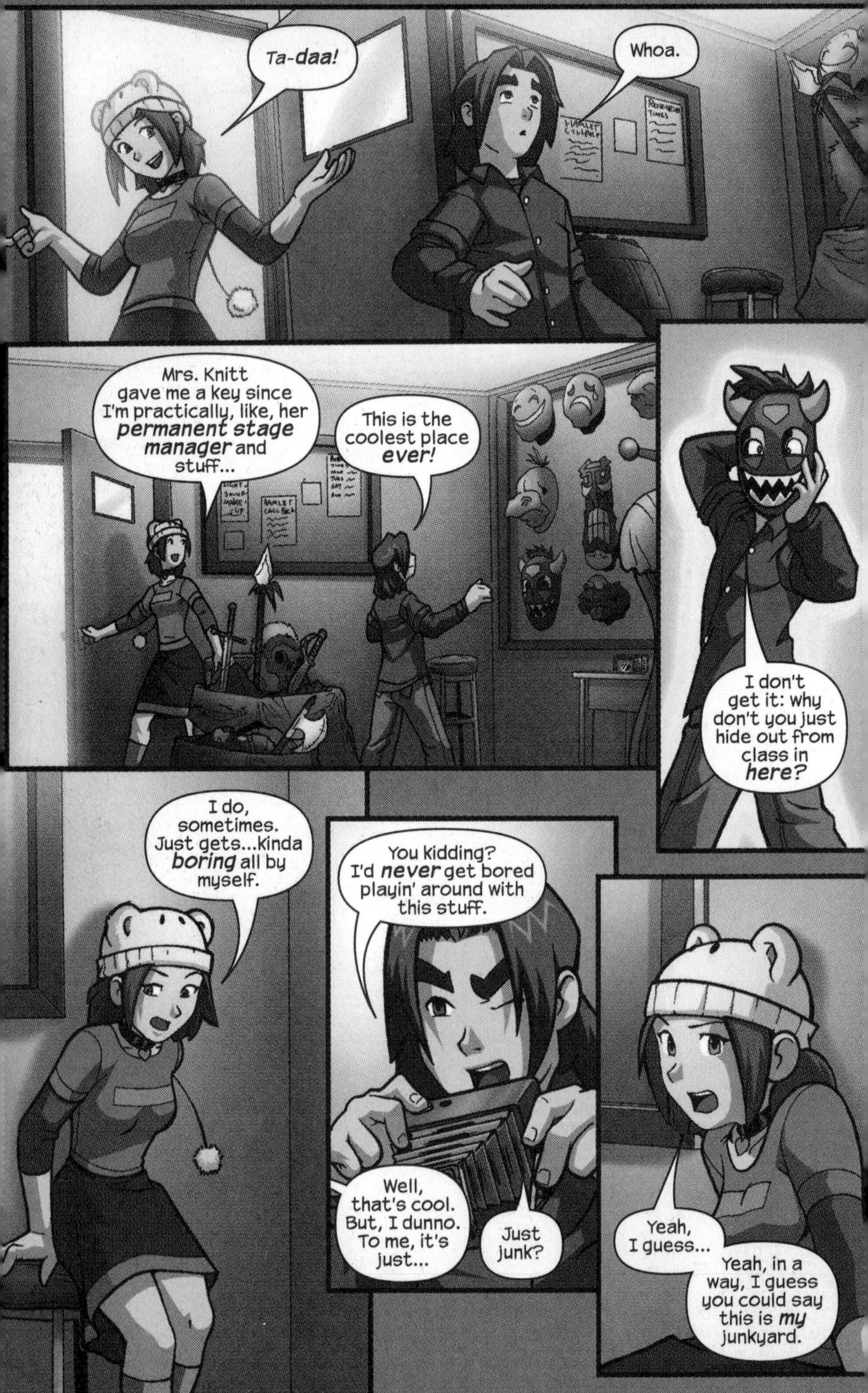

Ta-*daa!*
Whoa.
Mrs. Knitt gave me a key since I'm practically, like, her ***permanent stage manager*** and stuff...
This is the coolest place ***ever!***
I don't get it: why don't you just hide out from class in ***here?***
I do, sometimes. Just gets...kinda ***boring*** all by myself.
You kidding? I'd ***never*** get bored playin' around with this stuff.
Well, that's cool. But, I dunno. To me, it's just...
Just junk?
Yeah, I guess...
Yeah, in a way, I guess you could say this is ***my*** junkyard.

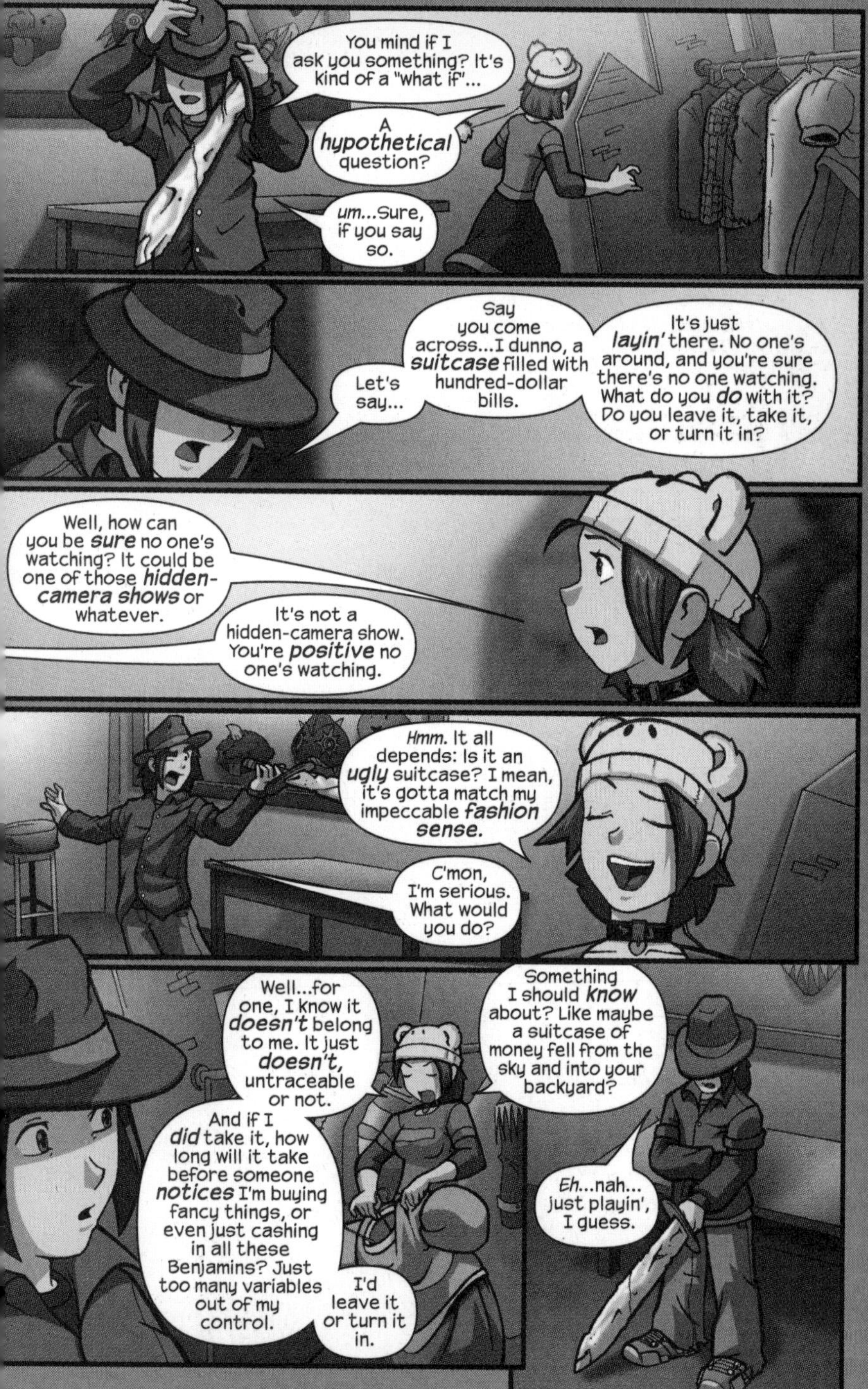
You mind if I ask you something? It's kind of a "what if"...
A *hypothetical* question?
um...Sure, if you say so.
Let's say...
Say you come across...I dunno, a ***suitcase*** filled with hundred-dollar bills.
It's just ***layin'*** there. No one's around, and you're sure there's no one watching. What do you ***do*** with it? Do you leave it, take it, or turn it in?
Well, how can you be ***sure*** no one's watching? It could be one of those ***hidden-camera shows*** or whatever.
It's not a hidden-camera show. You're ***positive*** no one's watching.
Hmm. It all depends: Is it an ***ugly*** suitcase? I mean, it's gotta match my impeccable ***fashion sense.***
C'mon, I'm serious. What would you do?
Well...for one, I know it ***doesn't*** belong to me. It just ***doesn't,*** untraceable or not.
And if I ***did*** take it, how long will it take before someone ***notices*** I'm buying fancy things, or even just cashing in all these Benjamins? Just too many variables out of my control.
I'd leave it or turn it in.
Something I should ***know*** about? Like maybe a suitcase of money fell from the sky and into your backyard?
Eh...nah... just playin', I guess.

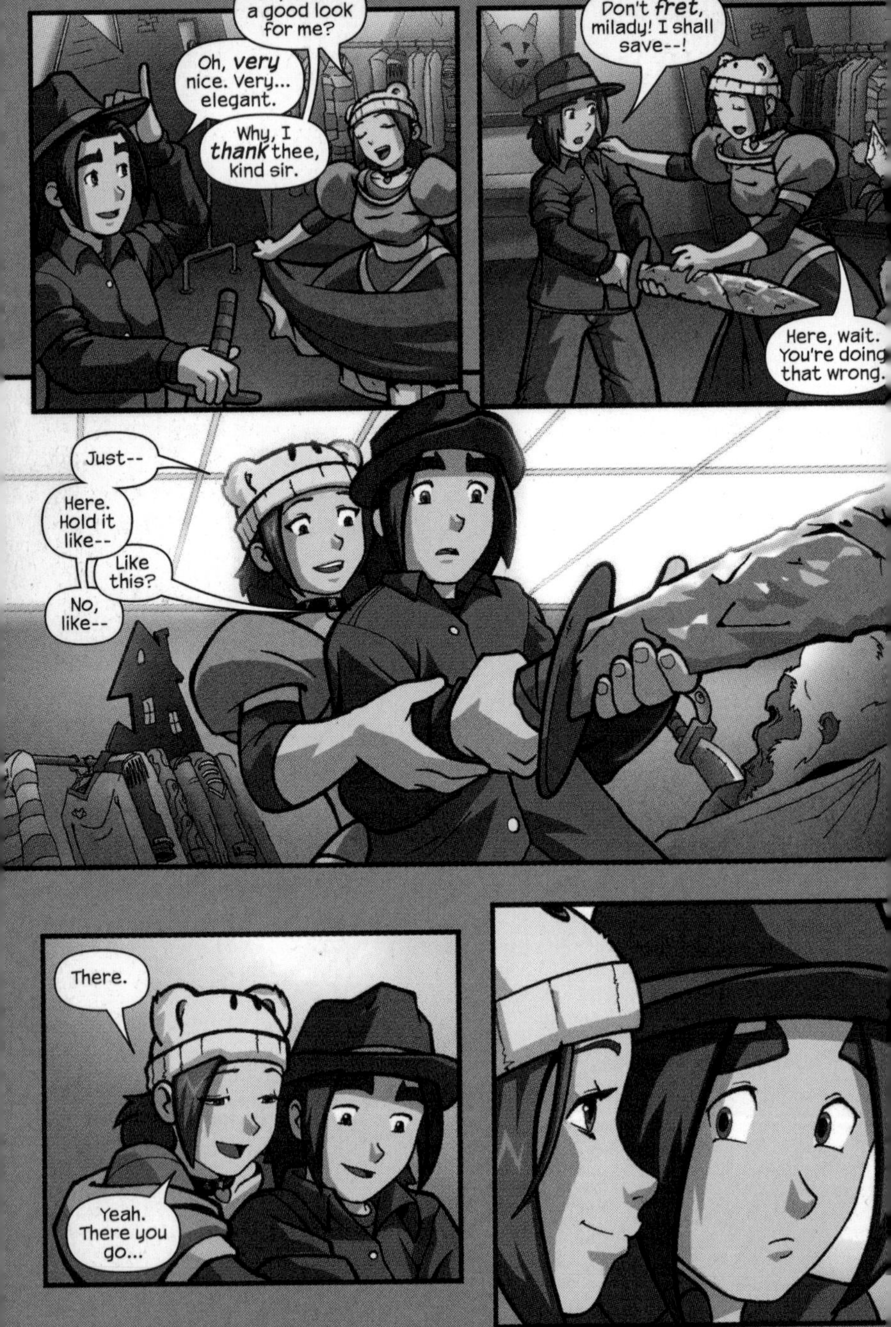
So, is this a good look for me?
Oh, very nice. Very... elegant.
Why, I thank thee, kind sir.
Don't fret, milady! I shall save--!
Here, wait. You're doing that wrong.
Just--
Here. Hold it like--
Like this?
No, like--
There.
Yeah. There you go...

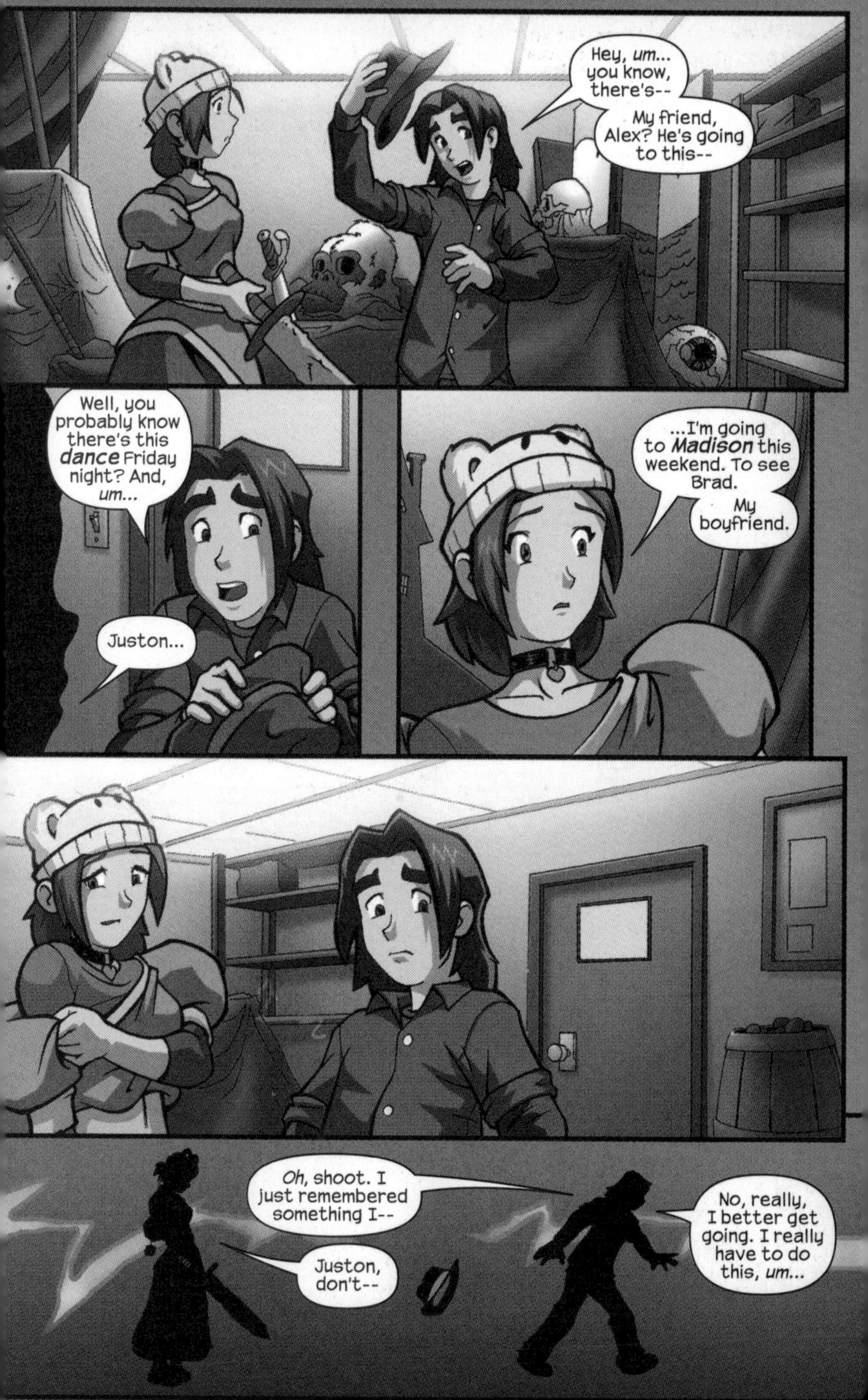
Hey, *um*... you know, there's--
My friend, Alex? He's going to this--
Well, you probably know there's this *dance* Friday night? And, *um*...
Juston...
...I'm going to *Madison* this weekend. To see Brad.
My boyfriend.
Oh, shoot. I just remembered something I--
Juston, don't--
No, really, I better get going. I really have to do this, *um*...

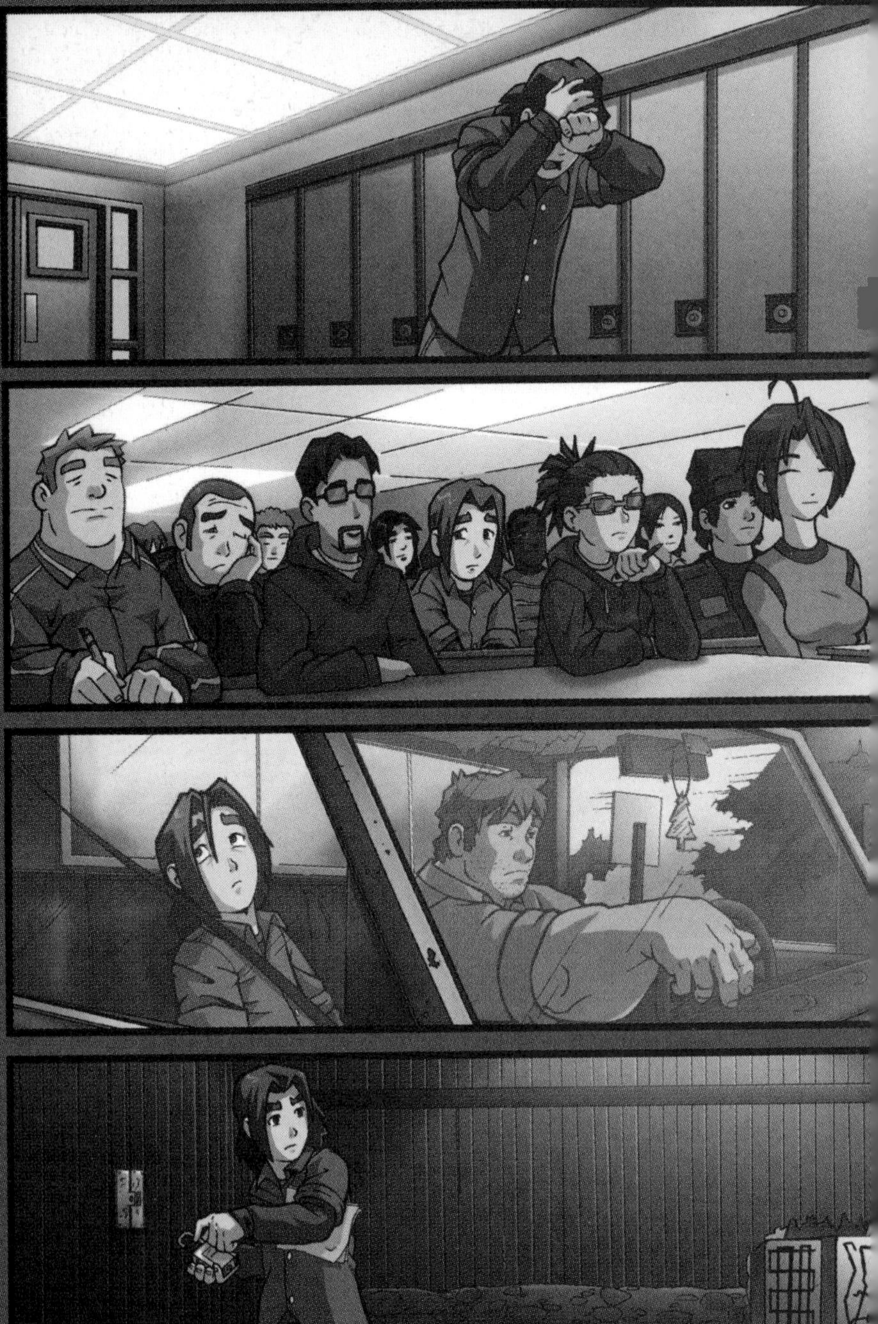

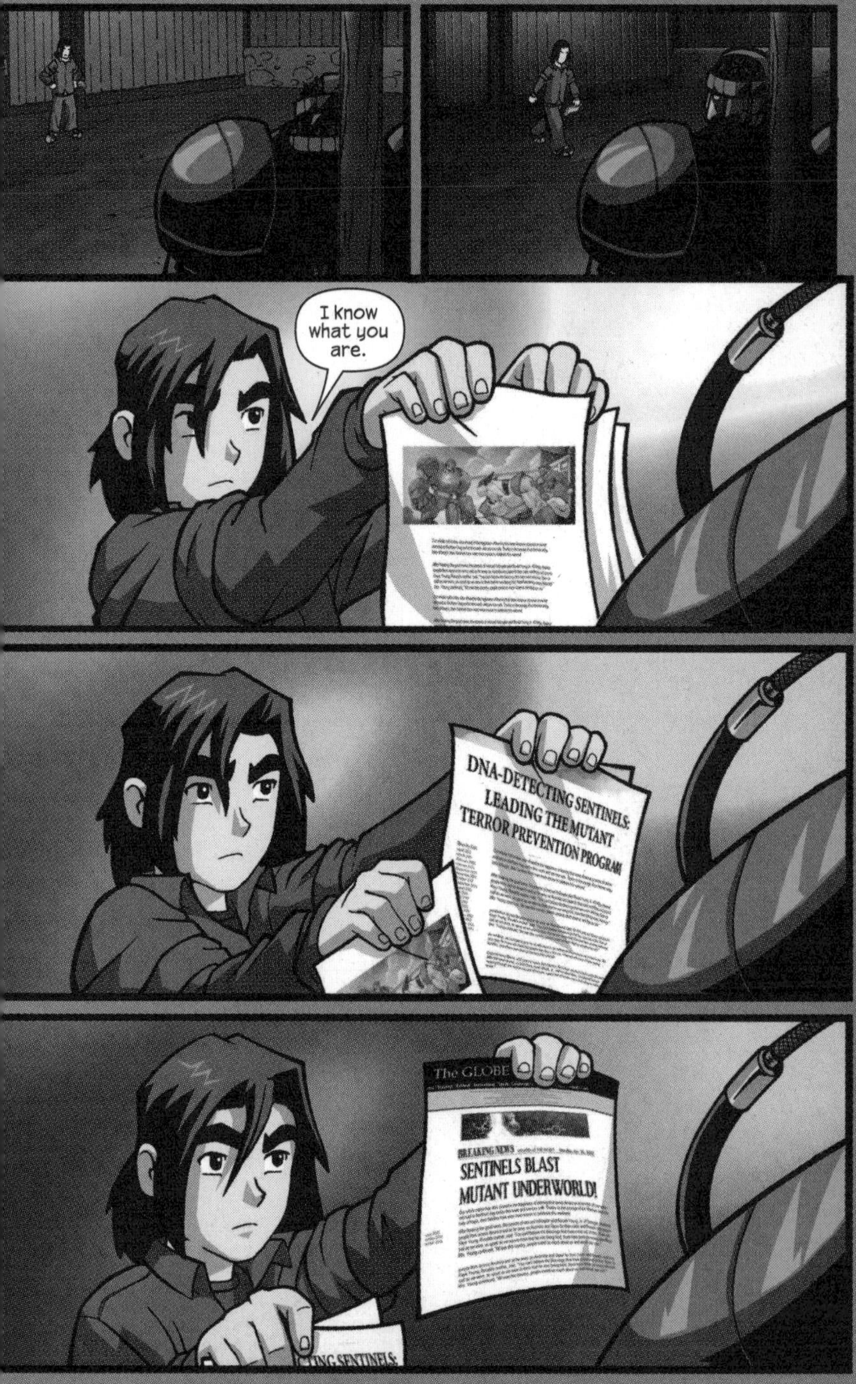

I know what you are.
DNA-DETECTING SENTINELS: LEADING THE MUTANT TERROR PREVENTION PROGRAM!
The GLOBE
BREAKING NEWS
SENTINELS BLAST MUTANT UNDERWORLD!

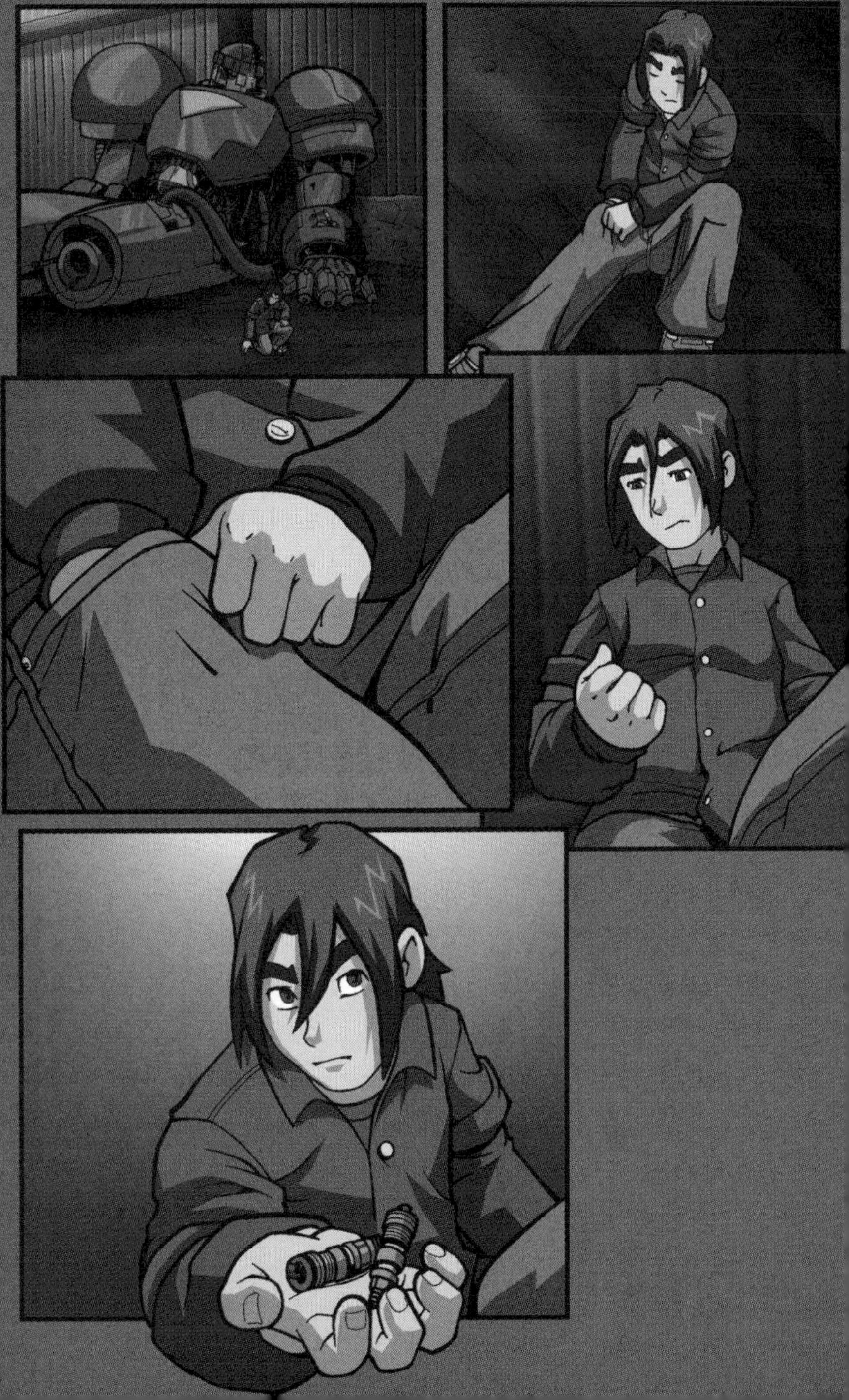

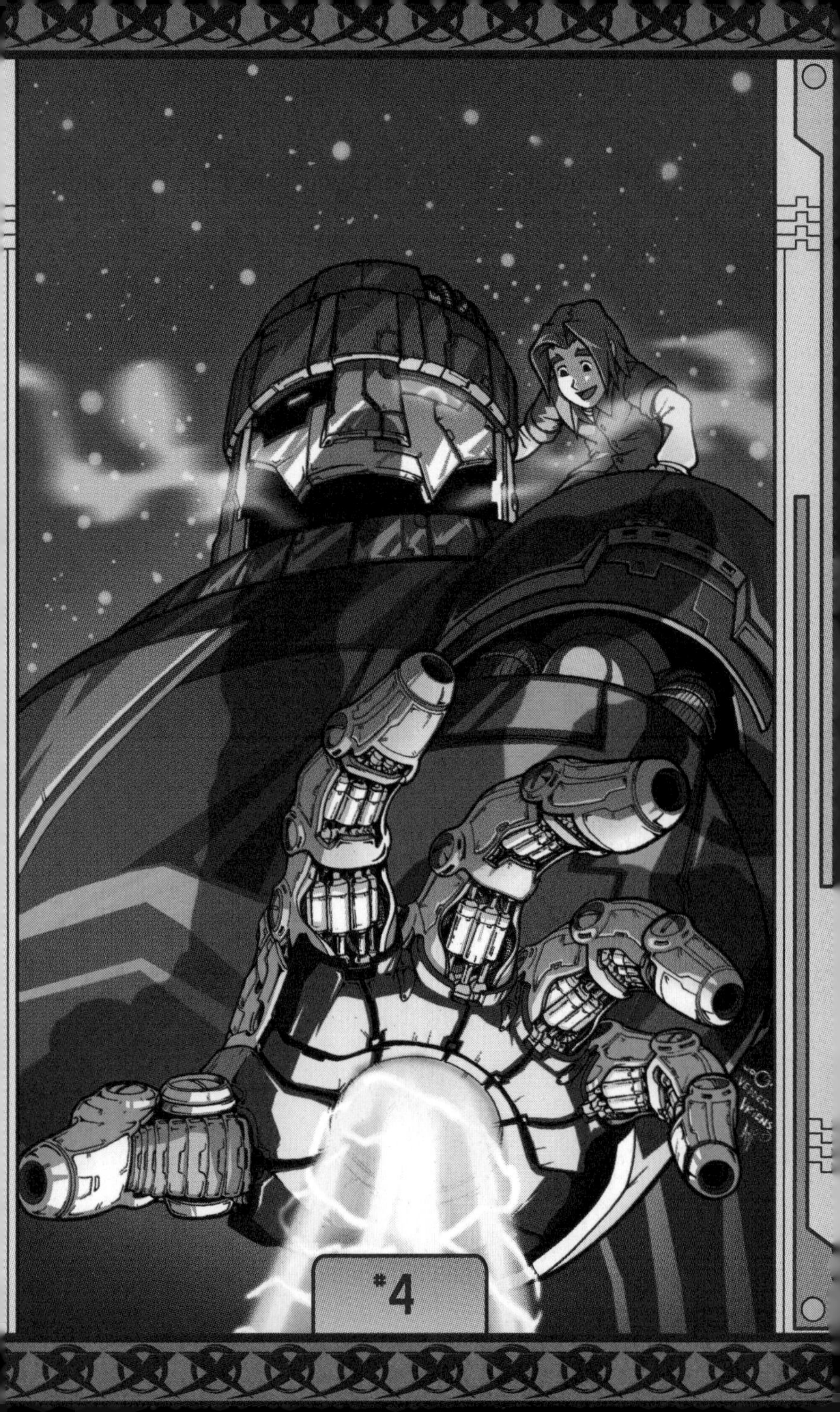
#4

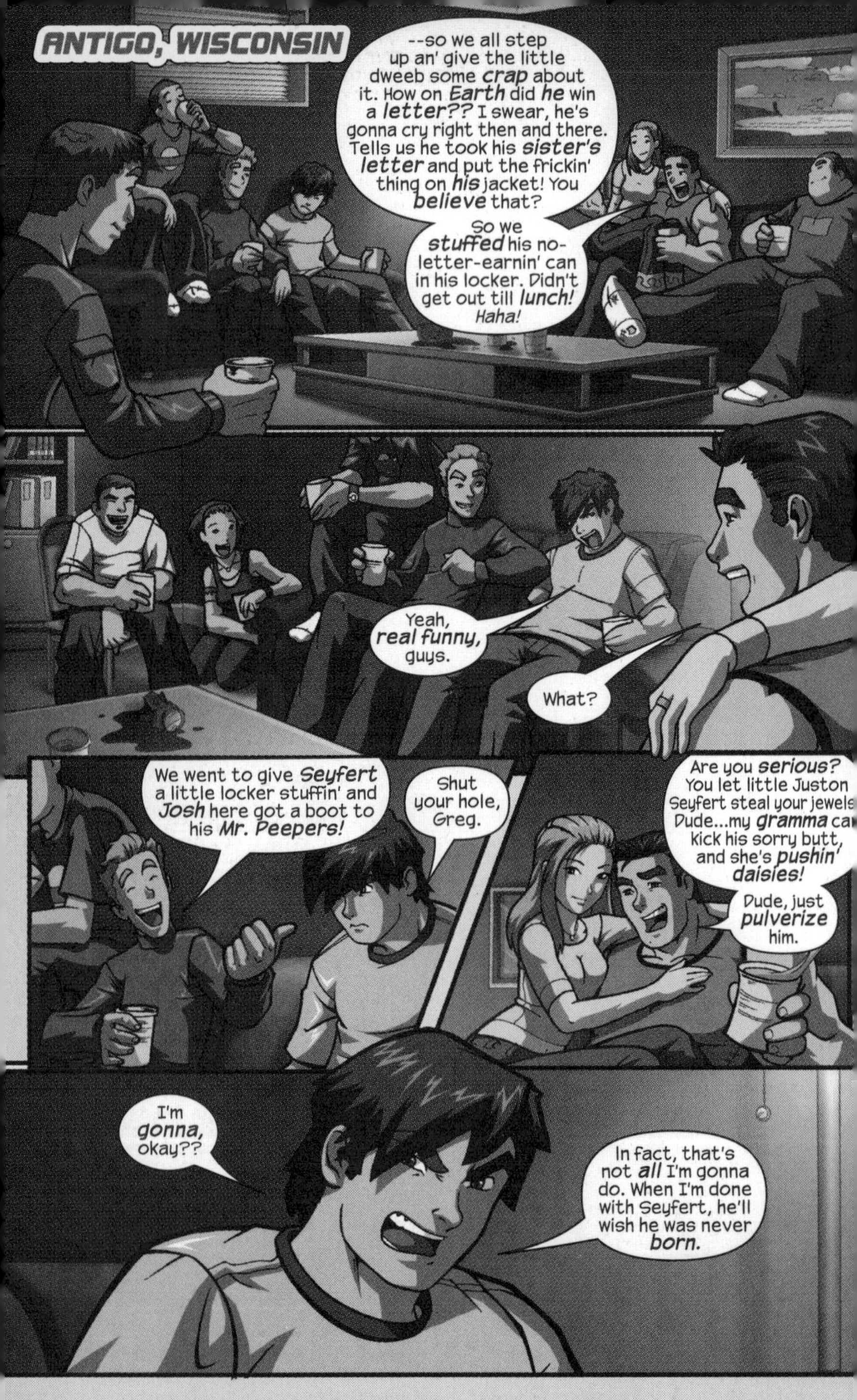
ANTIGO, WISCONSIN
--so we all step up an' give the little dweeb some crap about it. How on Earth did he win a letter?? I swear, he's gonna cry right then and there. Tells us he took his sister's letter and put the frickin' thing on his jacket! You believe that?
So we stuffed his no-letter-earnin' can in his locker. Didn't get out till lunch! Haha!
Yeah, real funny, guys.
What?
We went to give Seyfert a little locker stuffin' and Josh here got a boot to his Mr. Peepers!
Shut your hole, Greg.
Are you serious? You let little Juston Seyfert steal your jewels Dude...my gramma ca kick his sorry butt, and she's pushin' daisies!
Dude, just pulverize him.
I'm gonna, okay??
In fact, that's not all I'm gonna do. When I'm done with Seyfert, he'll wish he was never born.

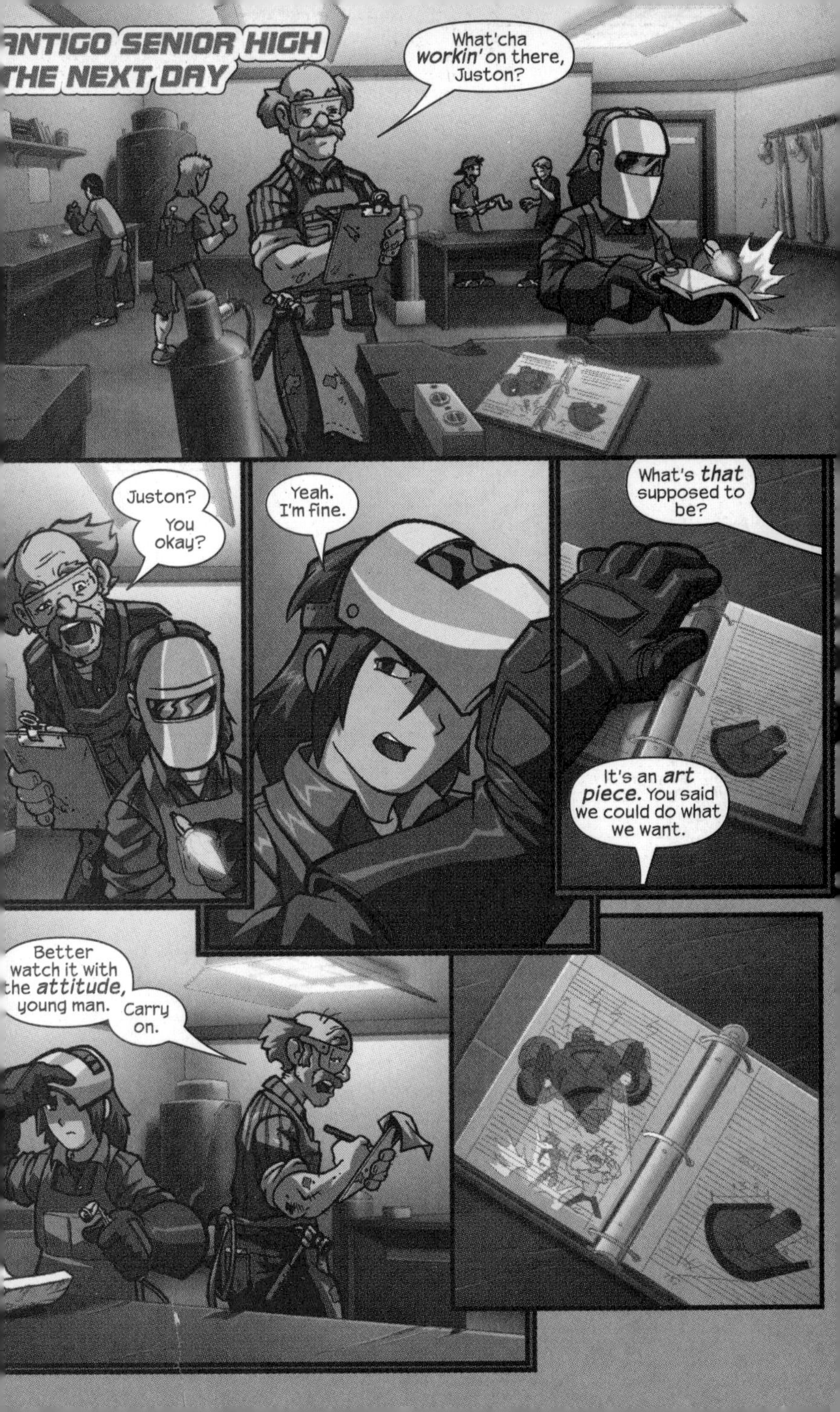
ANTIGO SENIOR HIGH
THE NEXT DAY
What'cha *workin'* on there, Juston?
Juston? You okay?
Yeah. I'm fine.
What's *that* supposed to be?
It's an *art piece.* You said we could do what we want.
Better watch it with the *attitude,* young man.
Carry on.

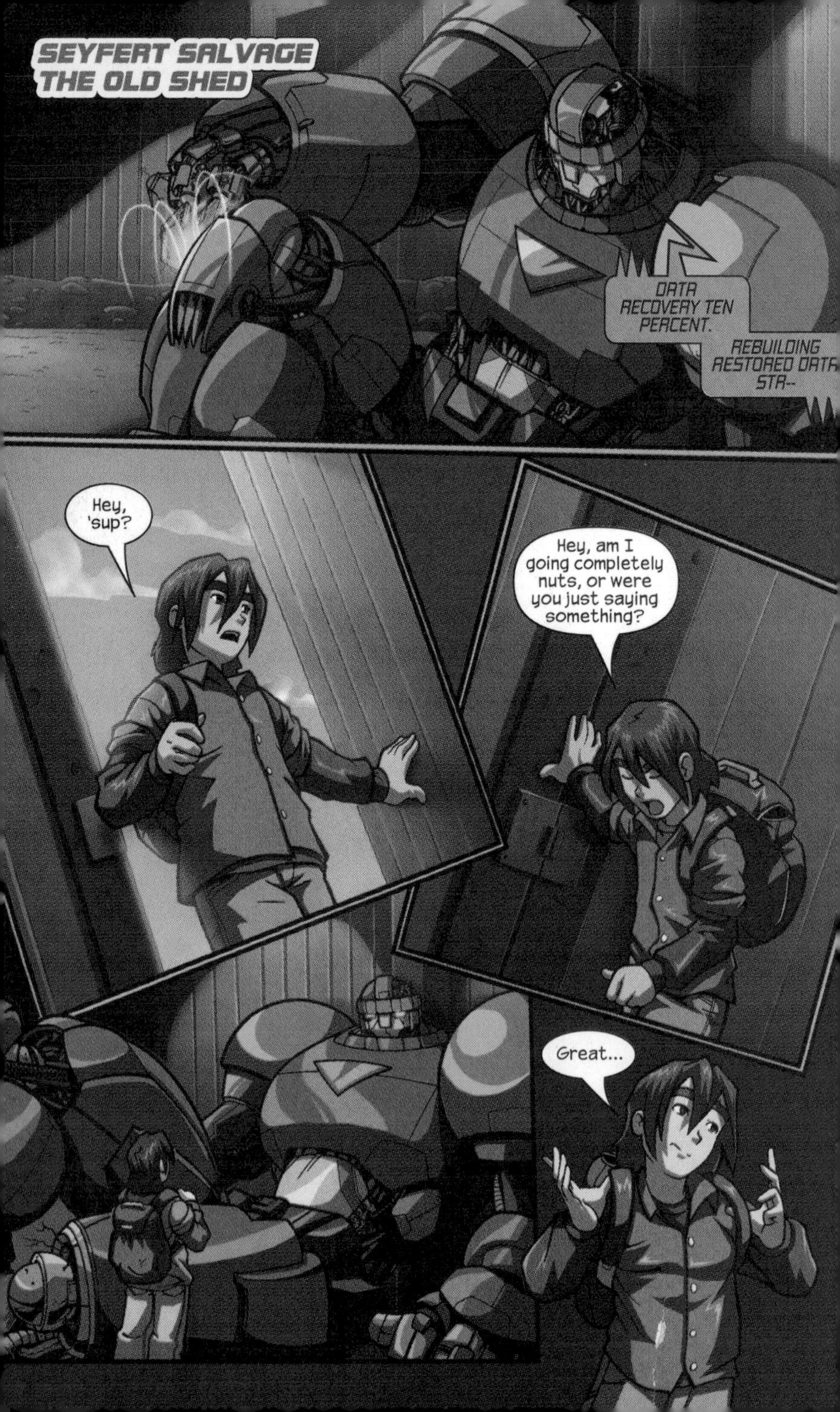
SEYFERT SALVAGE
THE OLD SHED
DATA RECOVERY TEN PERCENT.
REBUILDING RESTORED DATA STR--
Hey, 'sup?
Hey, am I going completely nuts, or were you just saying something?
Great...

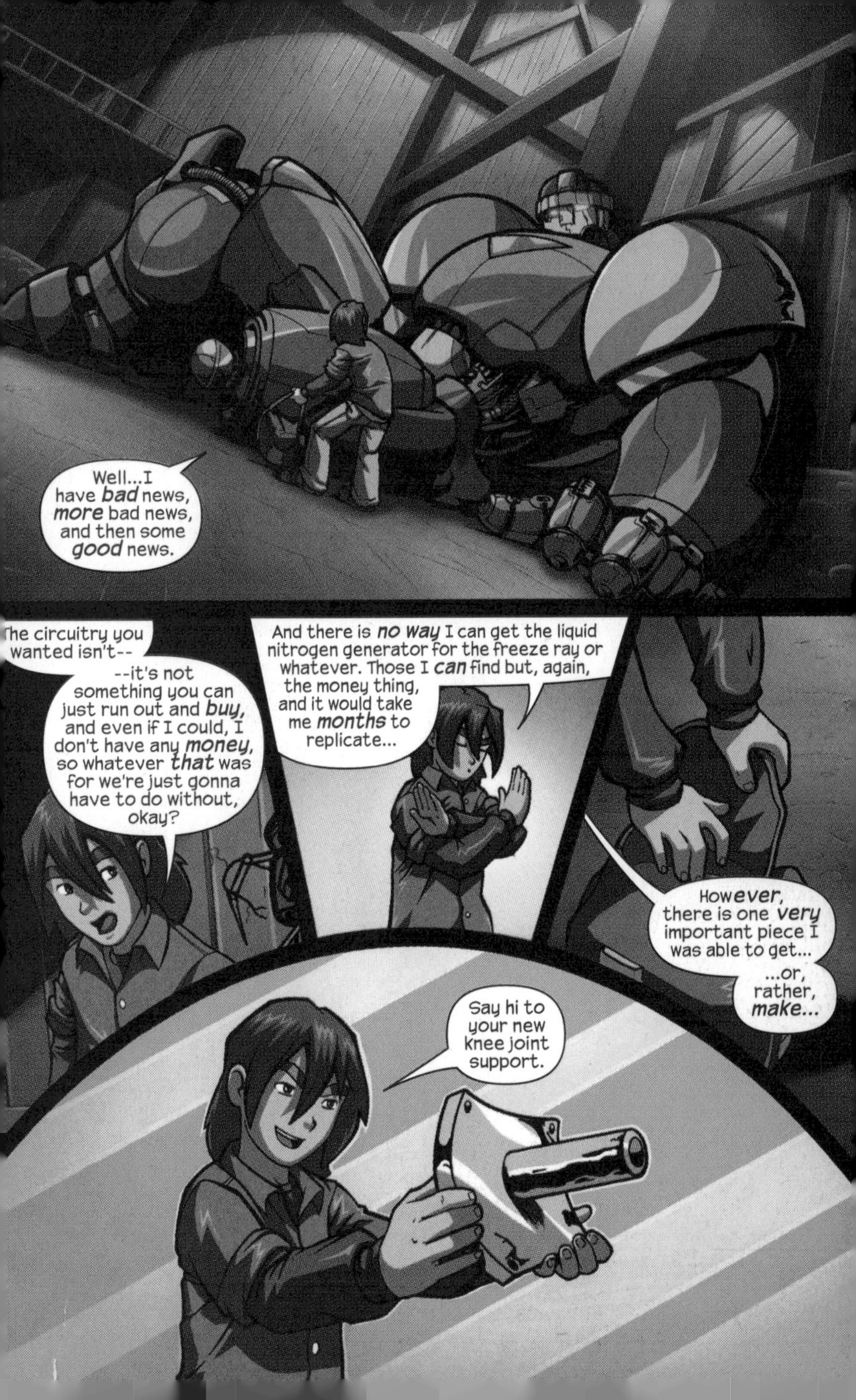

Well...I have **bad** news, **more** bad news, and then some **good** news.
The circuitry you wanted isn't--
--it's not something you can just run out and **buy**, and even if I could, I don't have any **money**, so whatever **that** was for we're just gonna have to do without, okay?
And there is **no way** I can get the liquid nitrogen generator for the freeze ray or whatever. Those I **can** find but, again, the money thing, and it would take me **months** to replicate...
How**ever**, there is one **very** important piece I was able to get...
...or, rather, **make**...
Say hi to your new knee joint support.

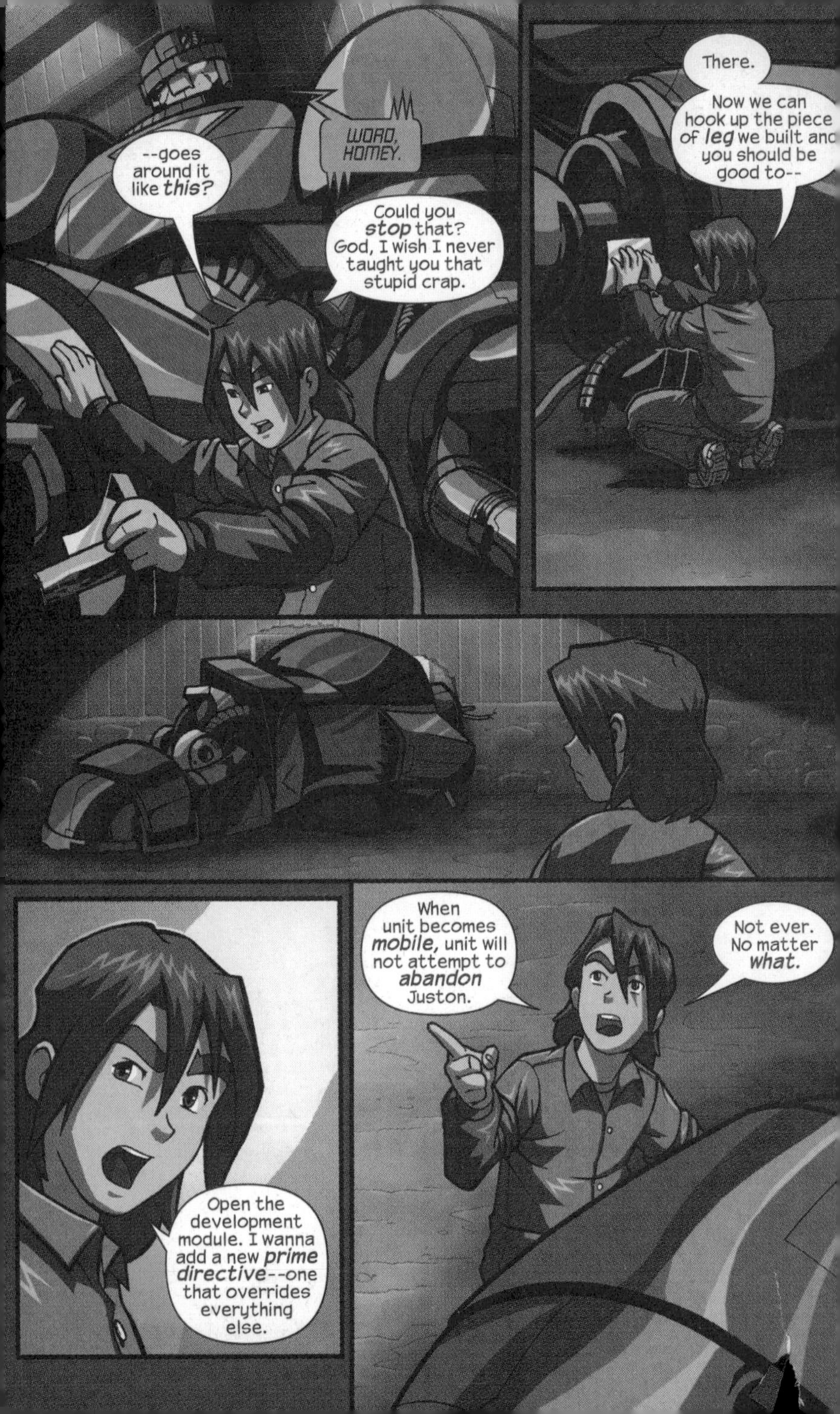
--goes around it like *this?*
WORD, HOMEY.
Could you *stop* that? God, I wish I never taught you that stupid crap.
There.
Now we can hook up the piece of *leg* we built and you should be good to--
Open the development module. I wanna add a new *prime directive*--one that overrides everything else.
When unit becomes *mobile,* unit will not attempt to *abandon* Juston.
Not ever. No matter *what.*

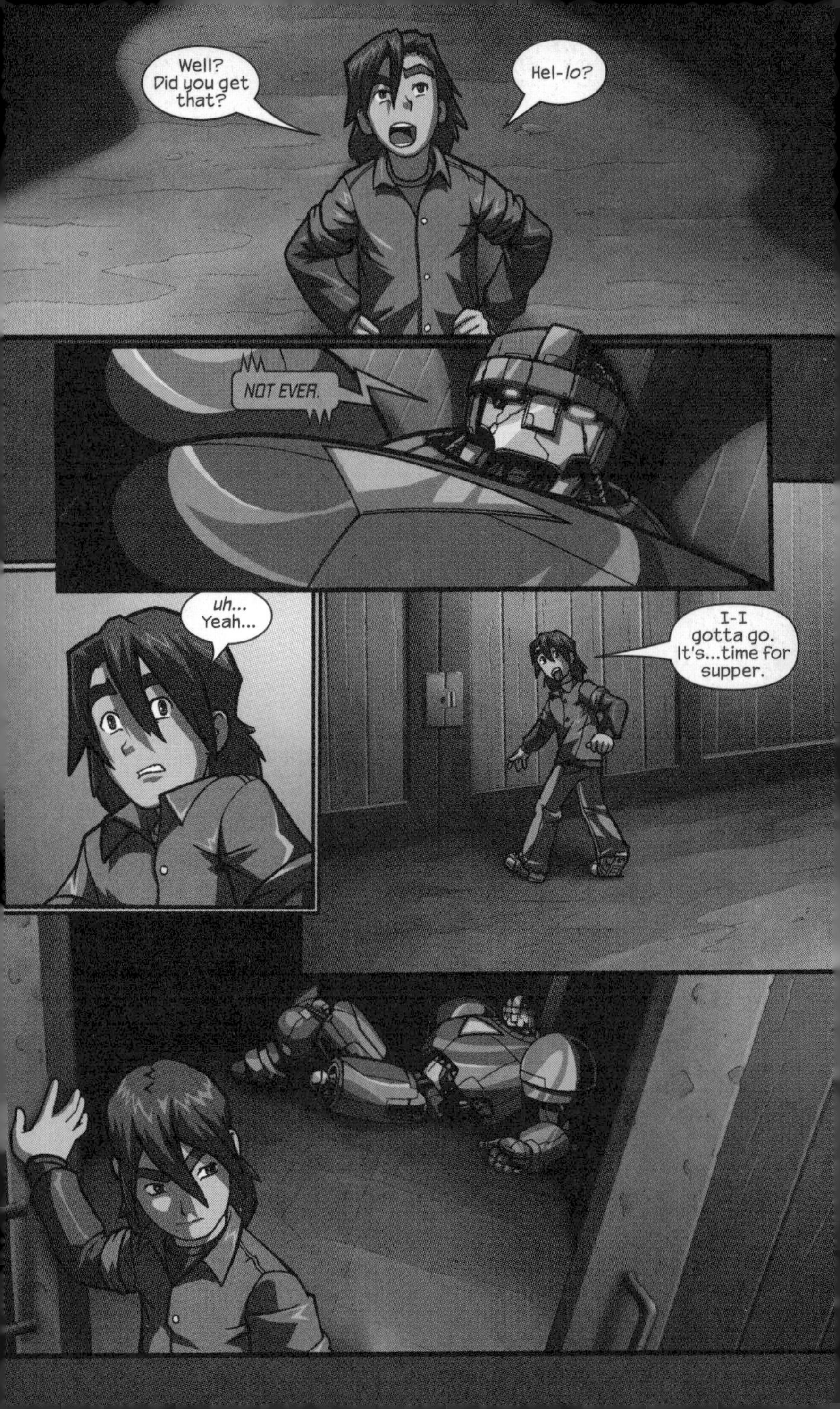
Well? Did you get that?
Hel-lo?
NOT EVER.
uh... Yeah...
I-I gotta go. It's...time for supper.

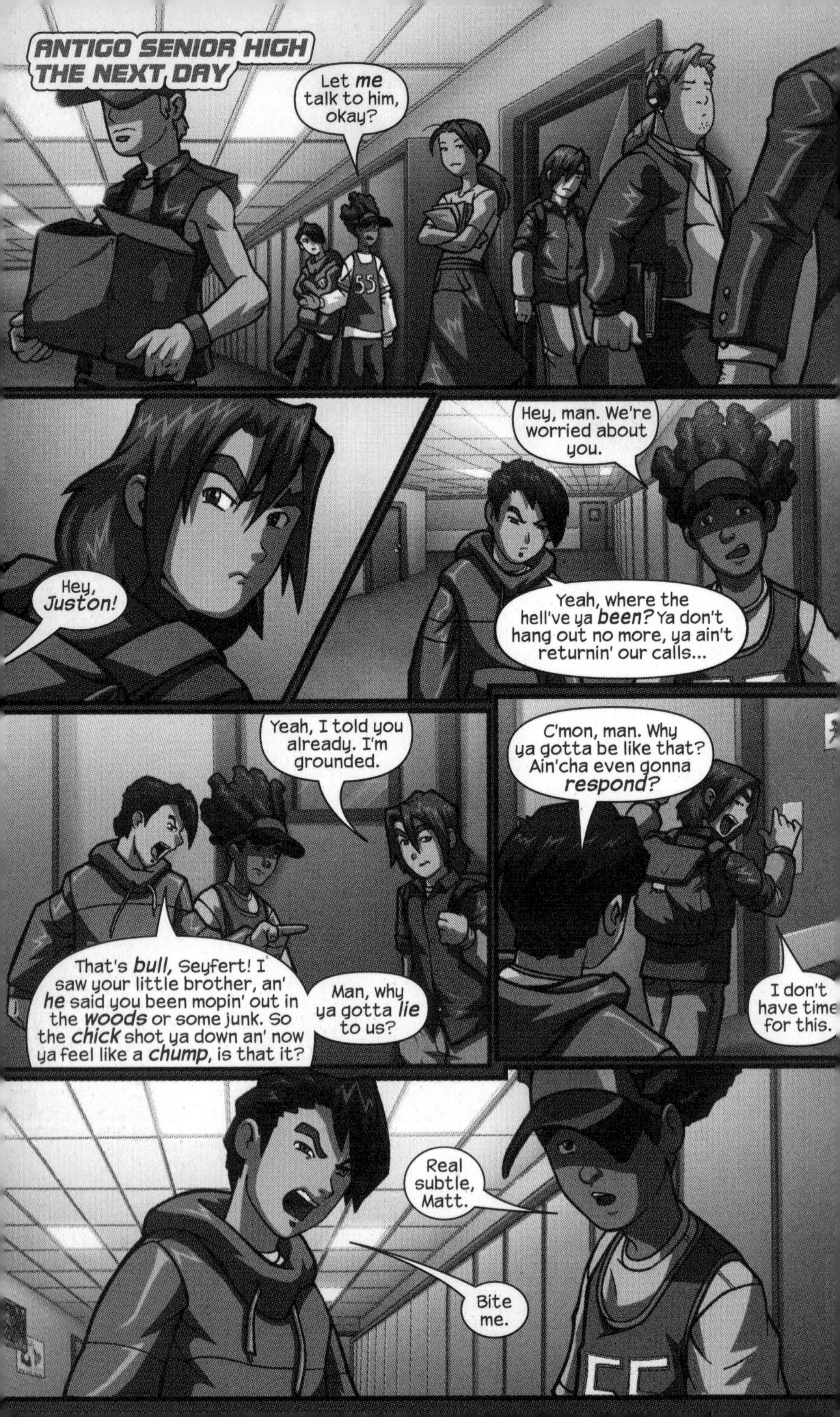
ANTIGO SENIOR HIGH
THE NEXT DAY
Let me talk to him, okay?
Hey, Juston!
Hey, man. We're worried about you.
Yeah, where the hell've ya been? Ya don't hang out no more, ya ain't returnin' our calls...
Yeah, I told you already. I'm grounded.
That's bull, Seyfert! I saw your little brother, an' he said you been mopin' out in the woods or some junk. So the chick shot ya down an' now ya feel like a chump, is that it?
Man, why ya gotta lie to us?
C'mon, man. Why ya gotta be like that? Ain'cha even gonna respond?
I don't have time for this.
Real subtle, Matt.
Bite me.

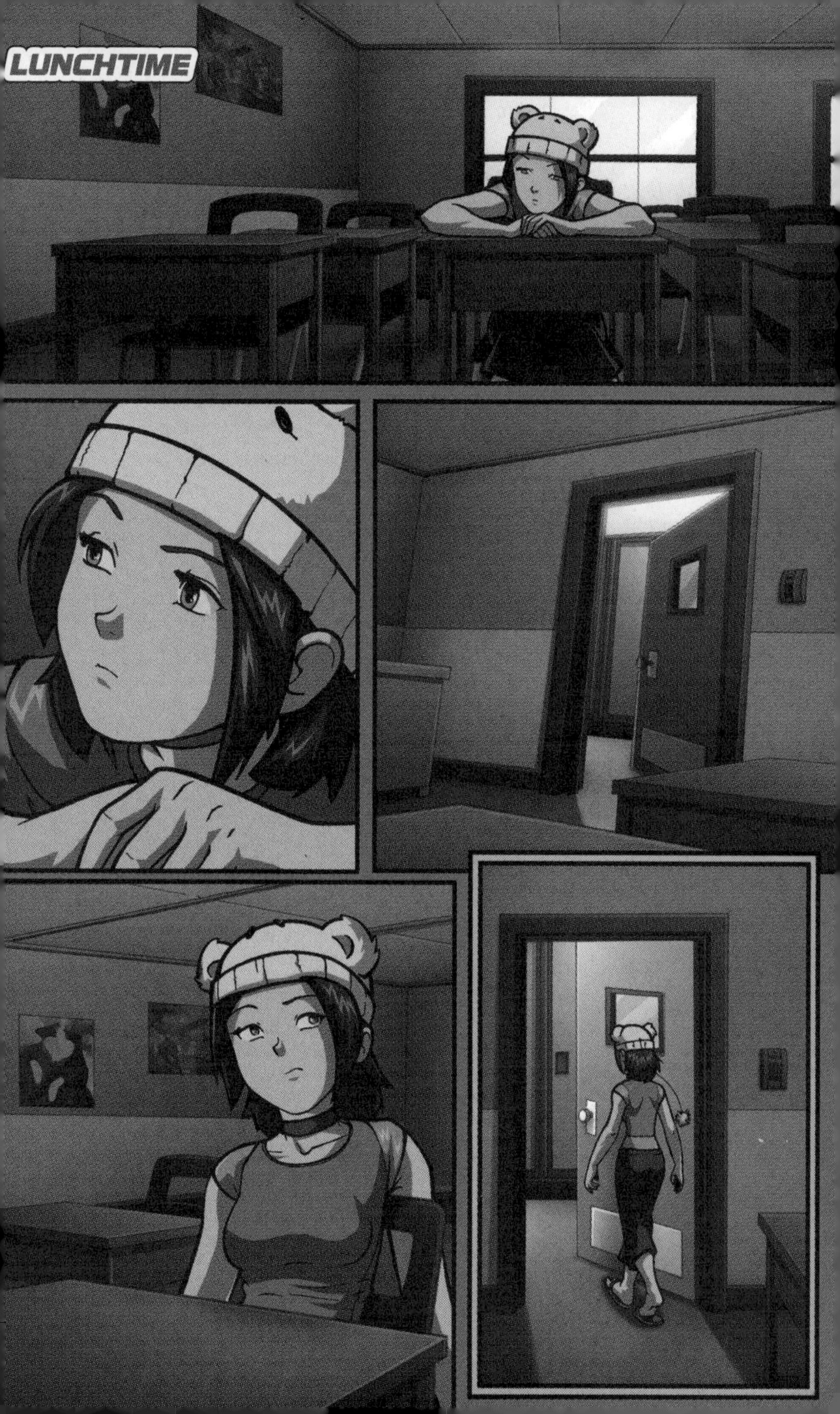
LUNCHTIME

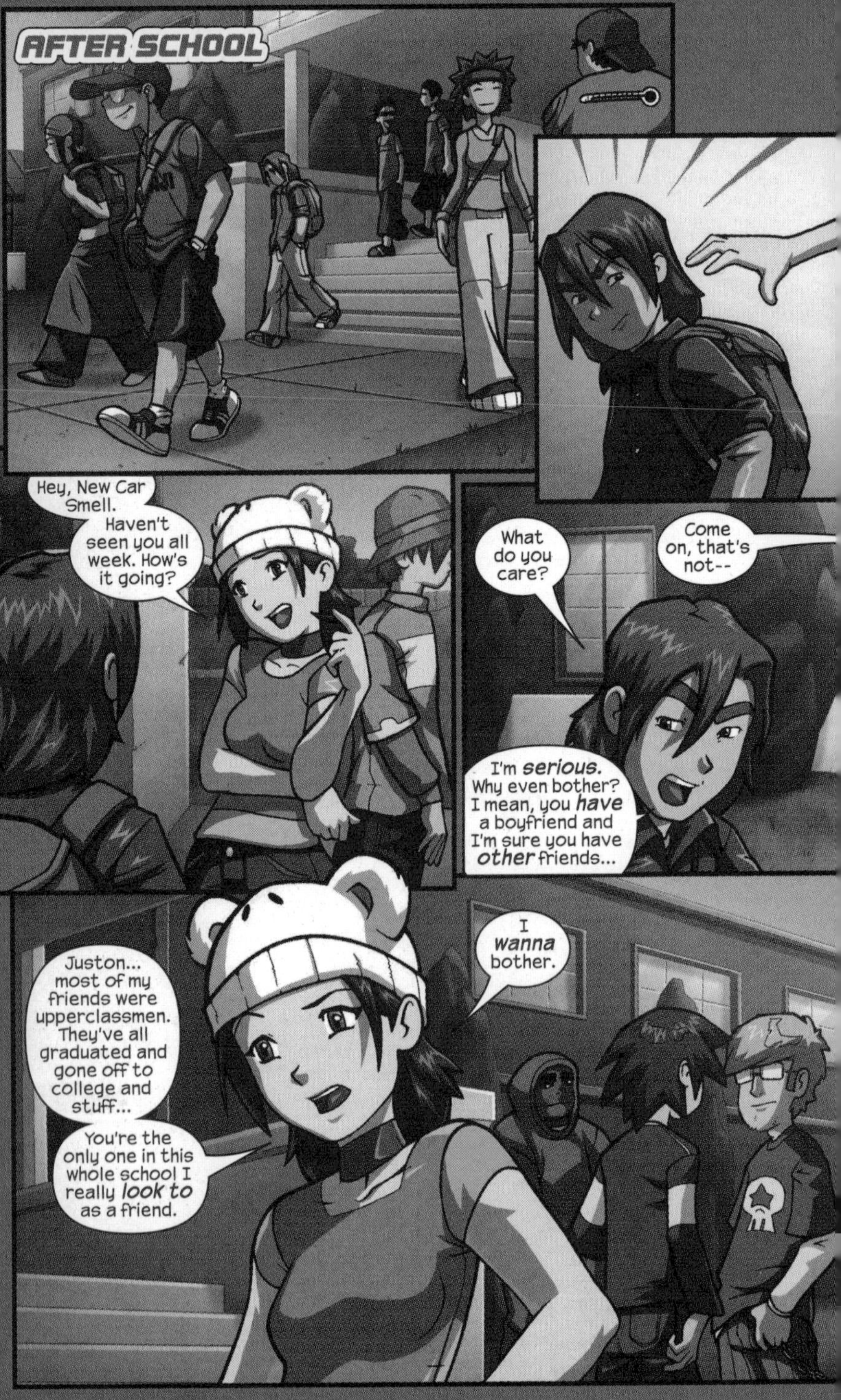
AFTER SCHOOL
Hey, New Car Smell.
Haven't seen you all week. How's it going?
What do you care?
Come on, that's not--
I'm *serious.* Why even bother? I mean, you *have* a boyfriend and I'm sure you have *other* friends...
Juston... most of my friends were upperclassmen. They've all graduated and gone off to college and stuff...
You're the only one in this whole school! I really *look to* as a friend.
I *wanna* bother.

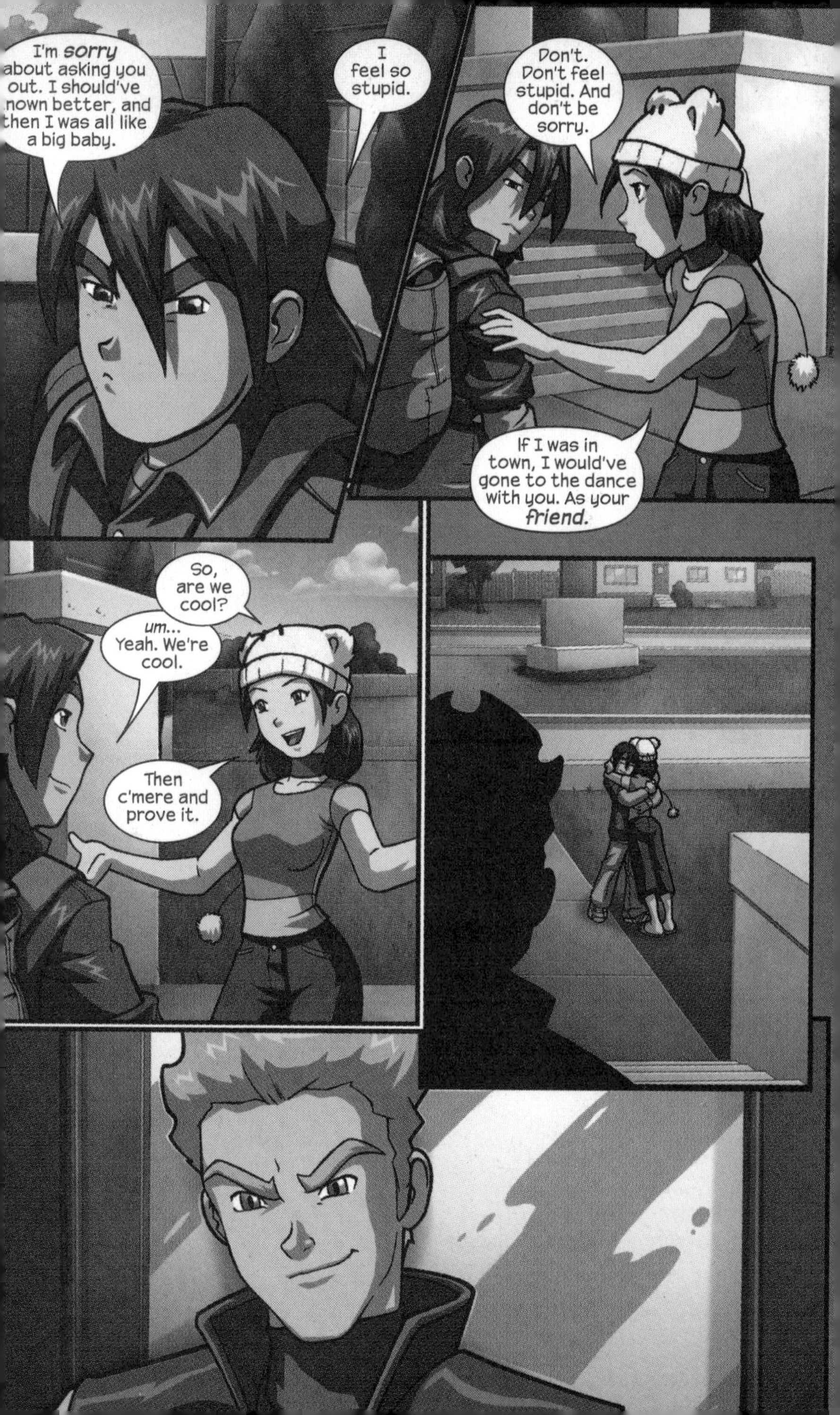
I'm *sorry* about asking you out. I should've nown better, and then I was all like a big baby.
I feel so stupid.
Don't. Don't feel stupid. And don't be sorry.
If I was in town, I would've gone to the dance with you. As your *friend.*
So, are we cool?
um... Yeah. We're cool.
Then c'mere and prove it.

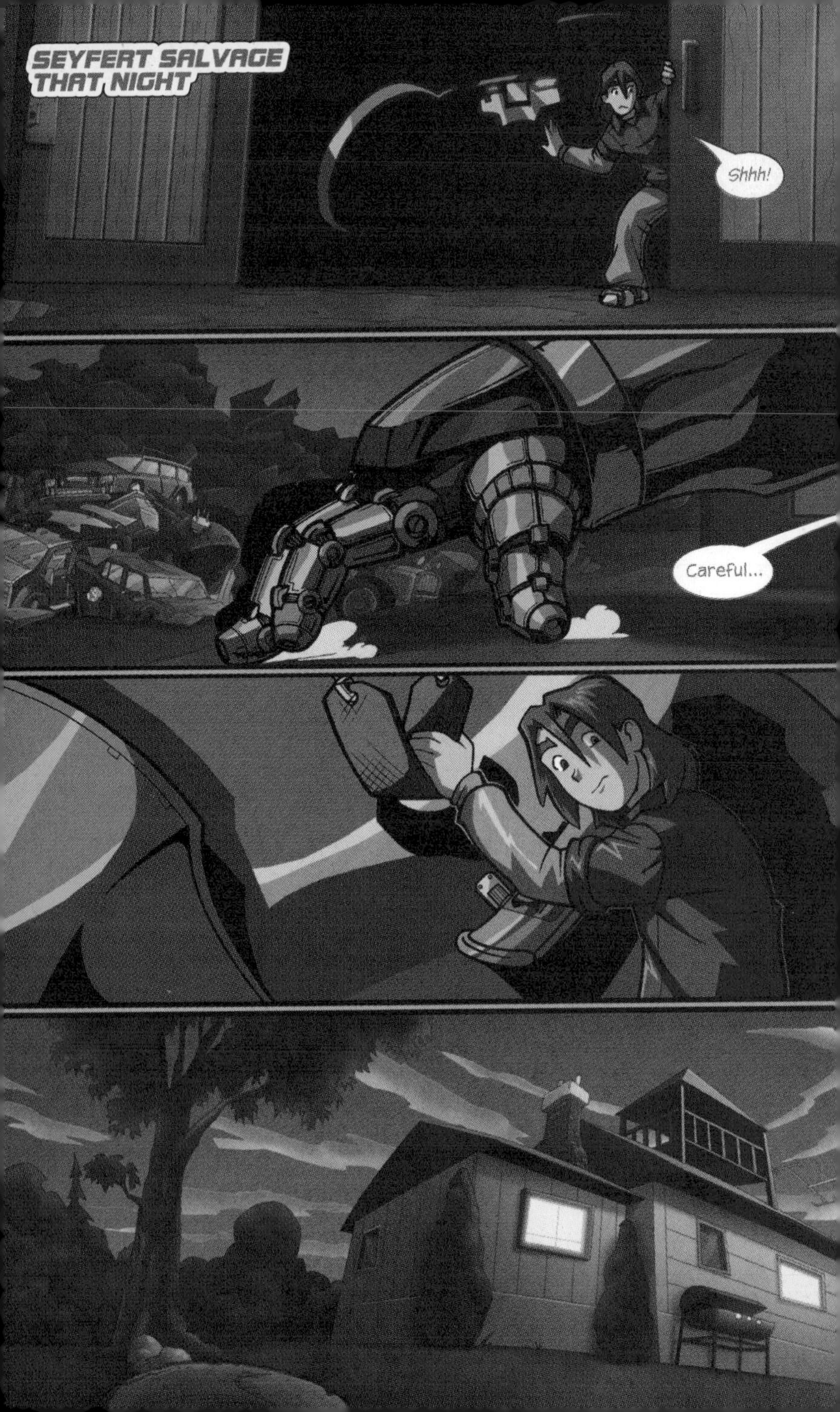
SEYFERT SALVAGE
THAT NIGHT
Shhh!
Careful...

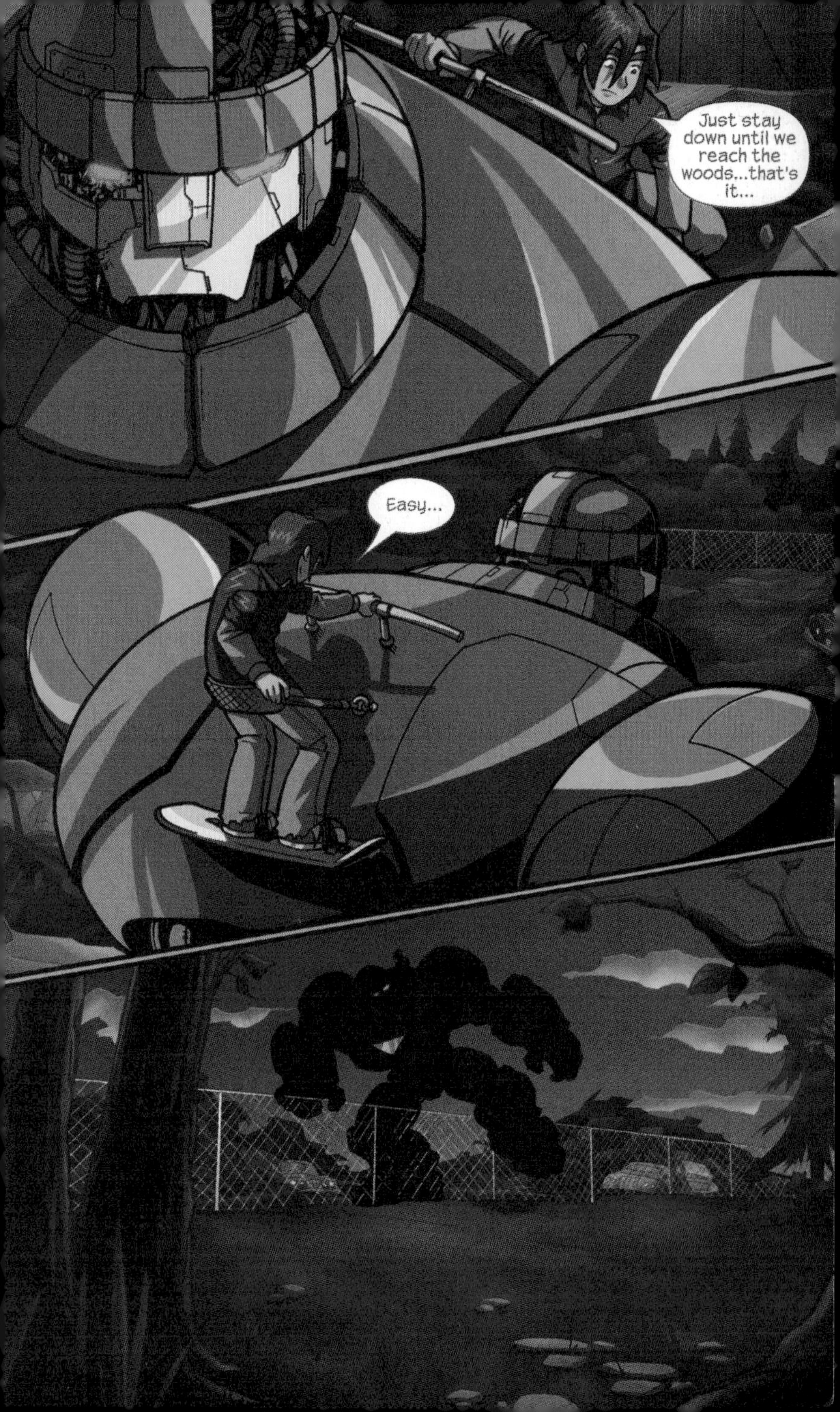
Just stay down until we reach the woods...that's it...
Easy...

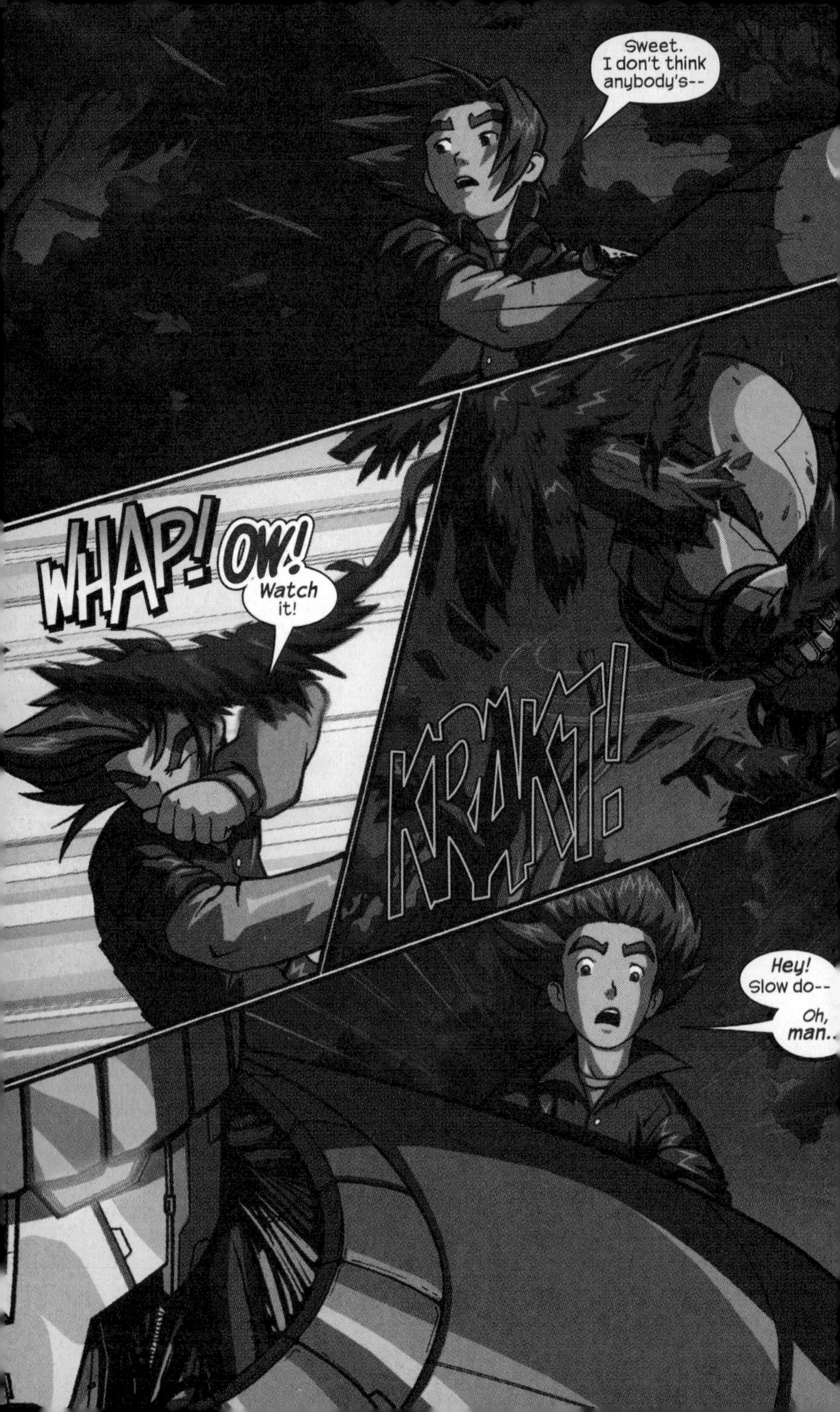
Sweet. I don't think anybody's--
WHAP!
OW!
Watch it!
KRAKT!
Hey! Slow do--
Oh, man..

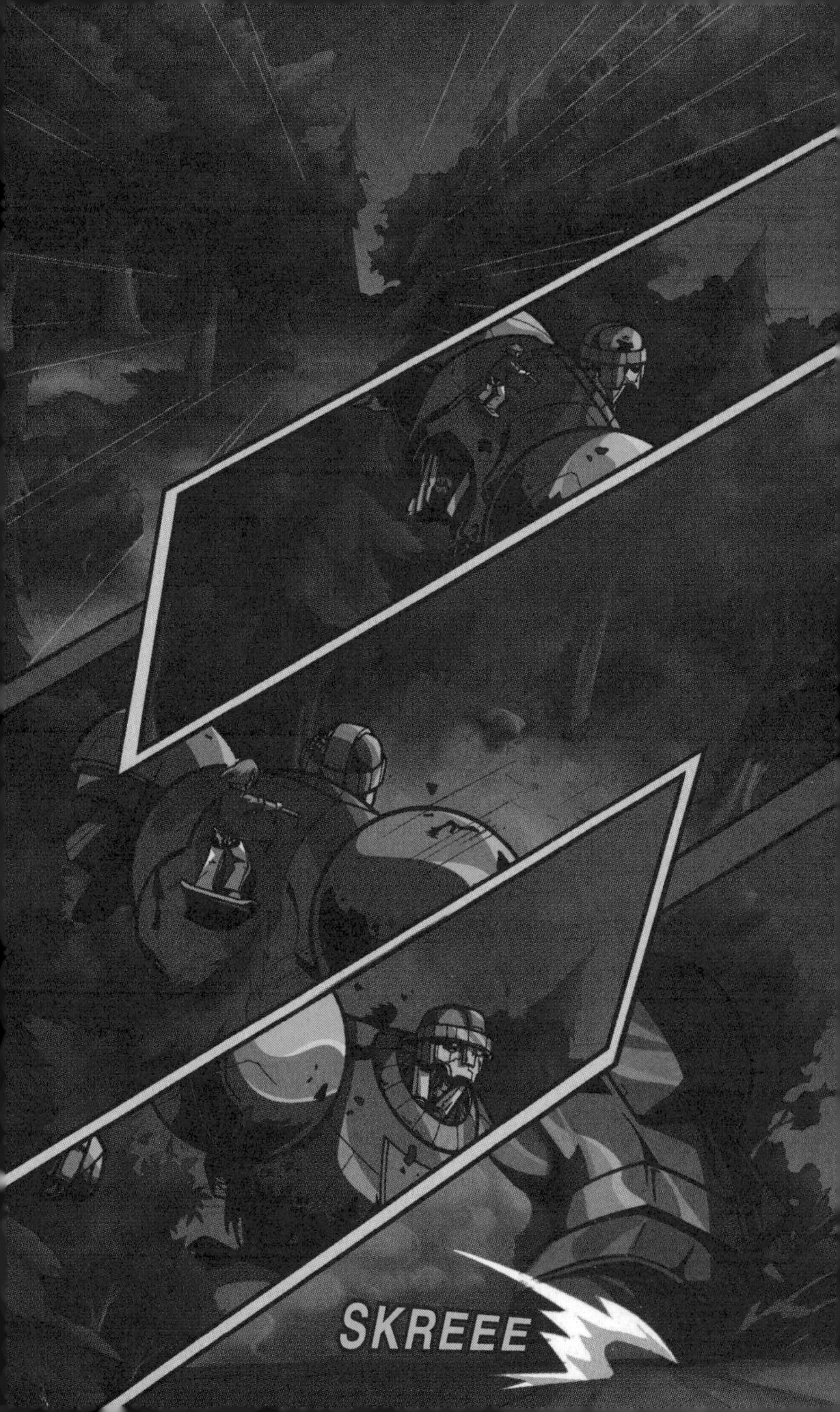
SKREEE

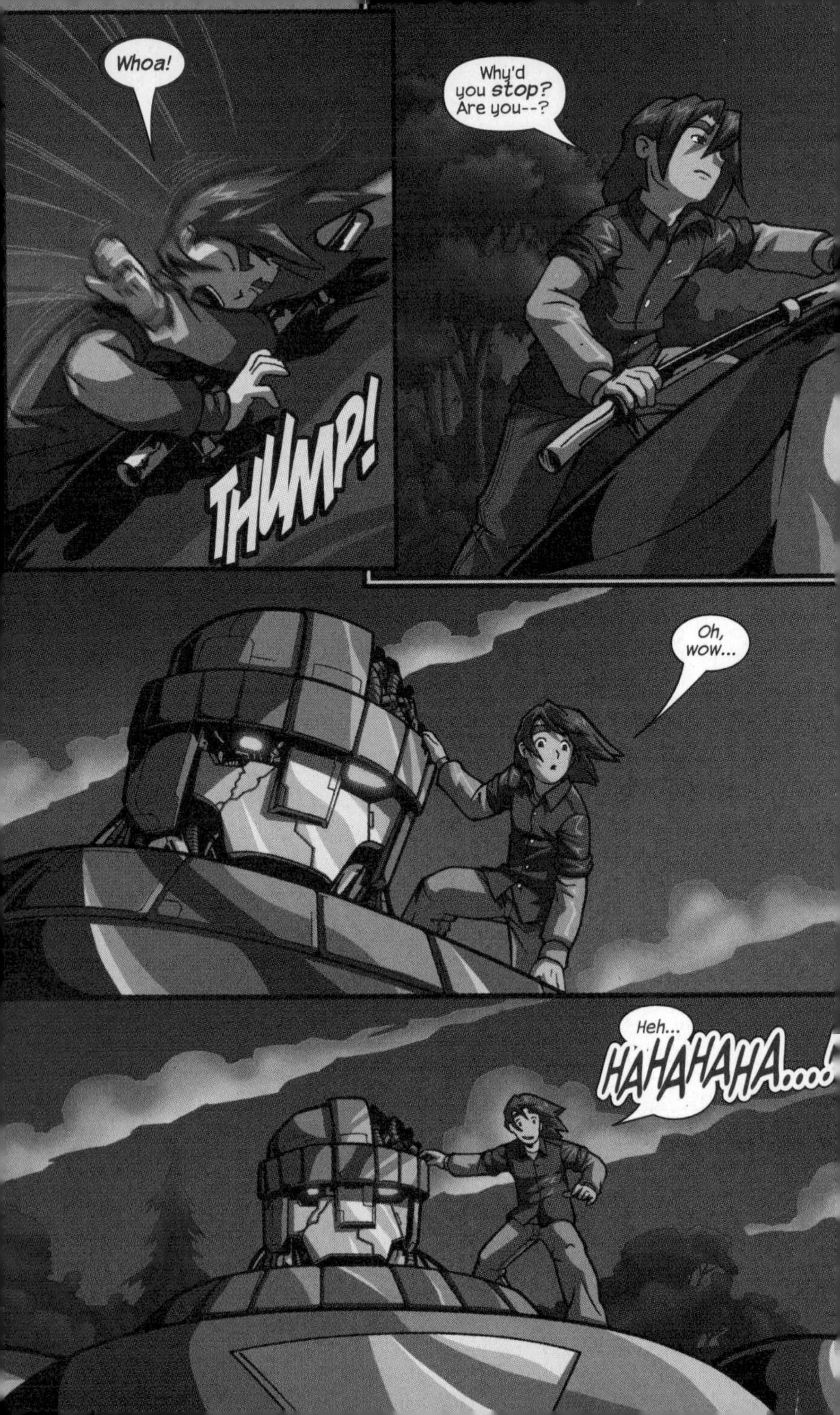
Whoa!
THUMP!
Why'd you stop? Are you--?
Oh, wow...
Heh...
HAHAHAHA...!

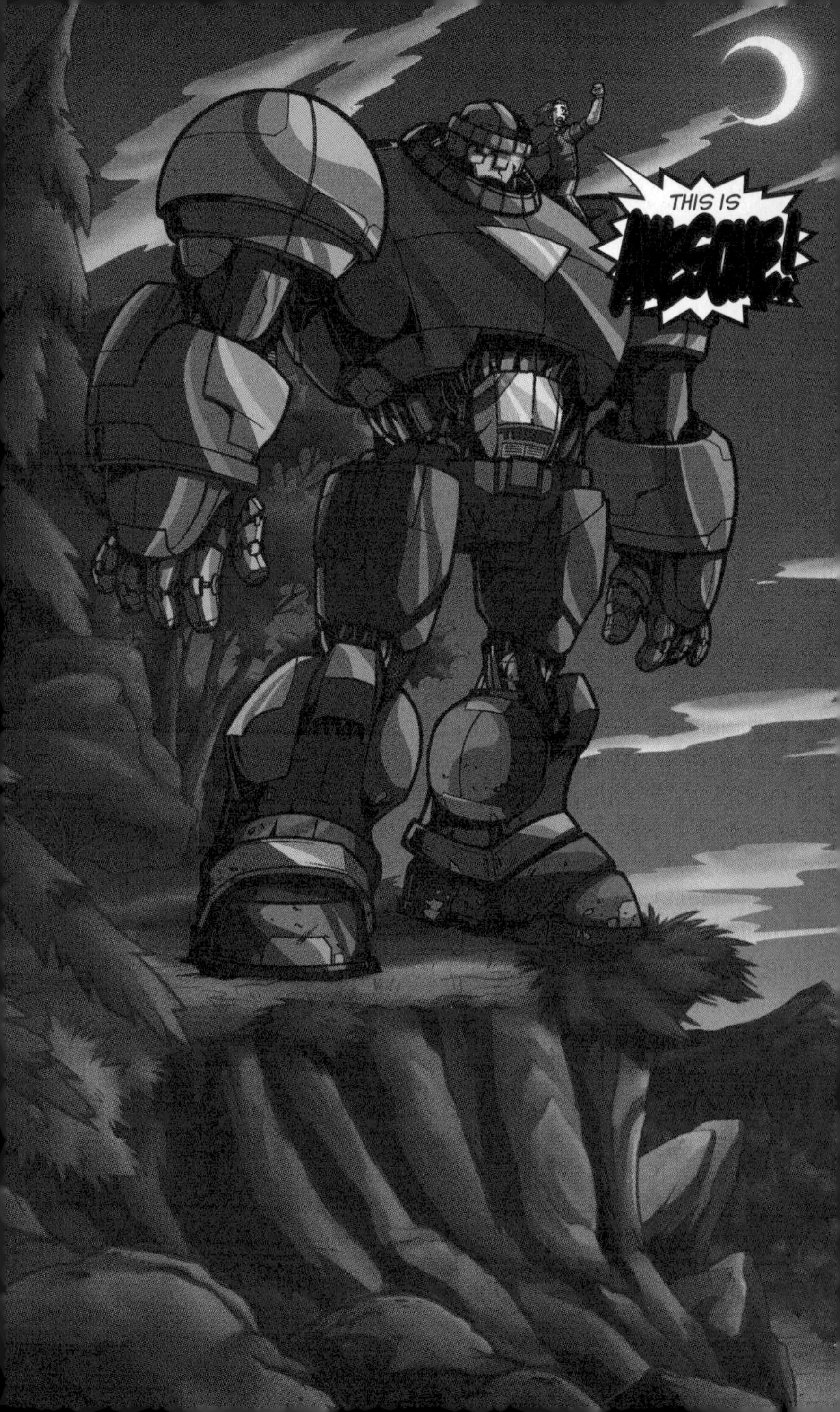
THIS IS AWESOME!!

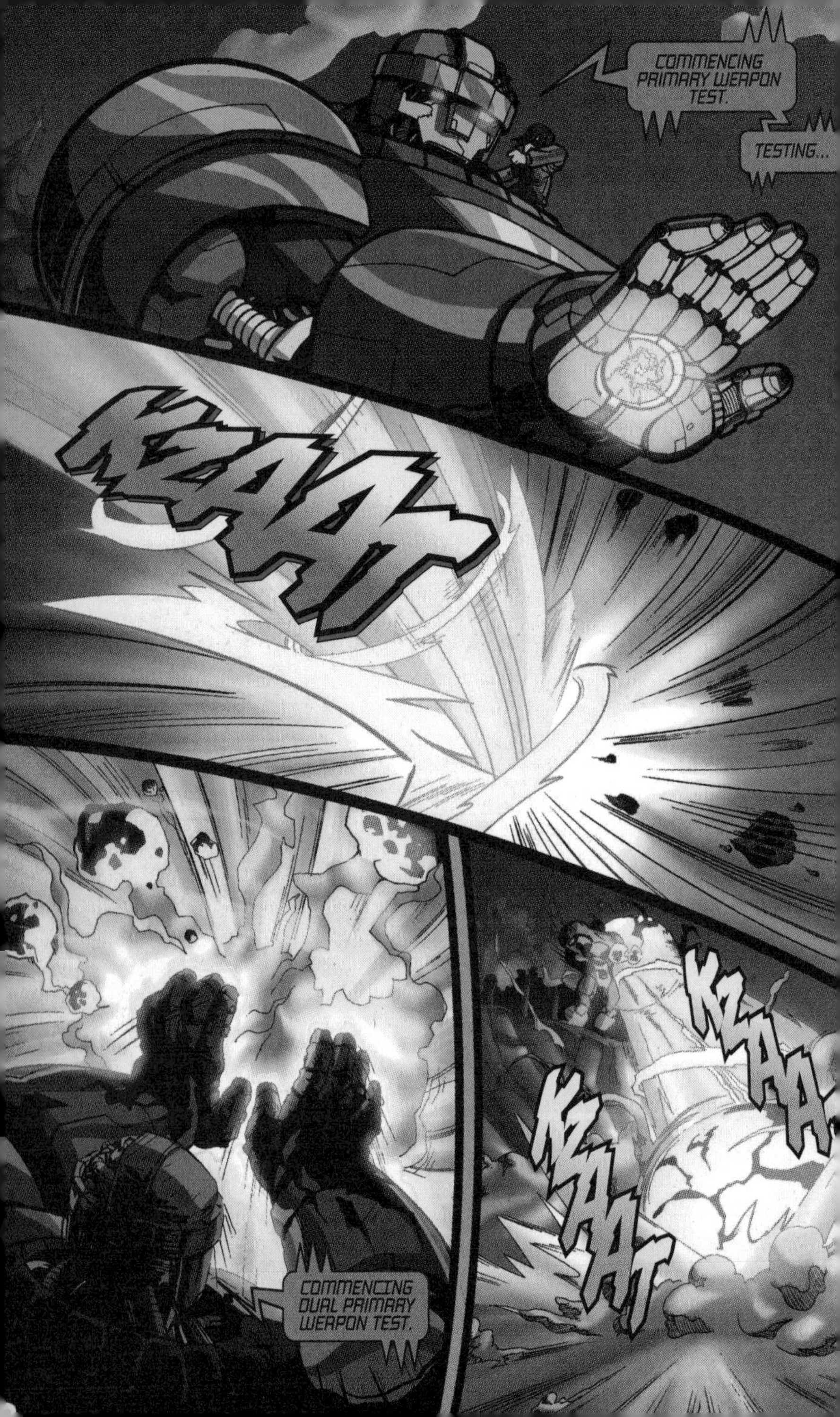
COMMENCING PRIMARY WEAPON TEST.
TESTING...
KZAAT
COMMENCING DUAL PRIMARY WEAPON TEST.
KZAAAT
KZAAA

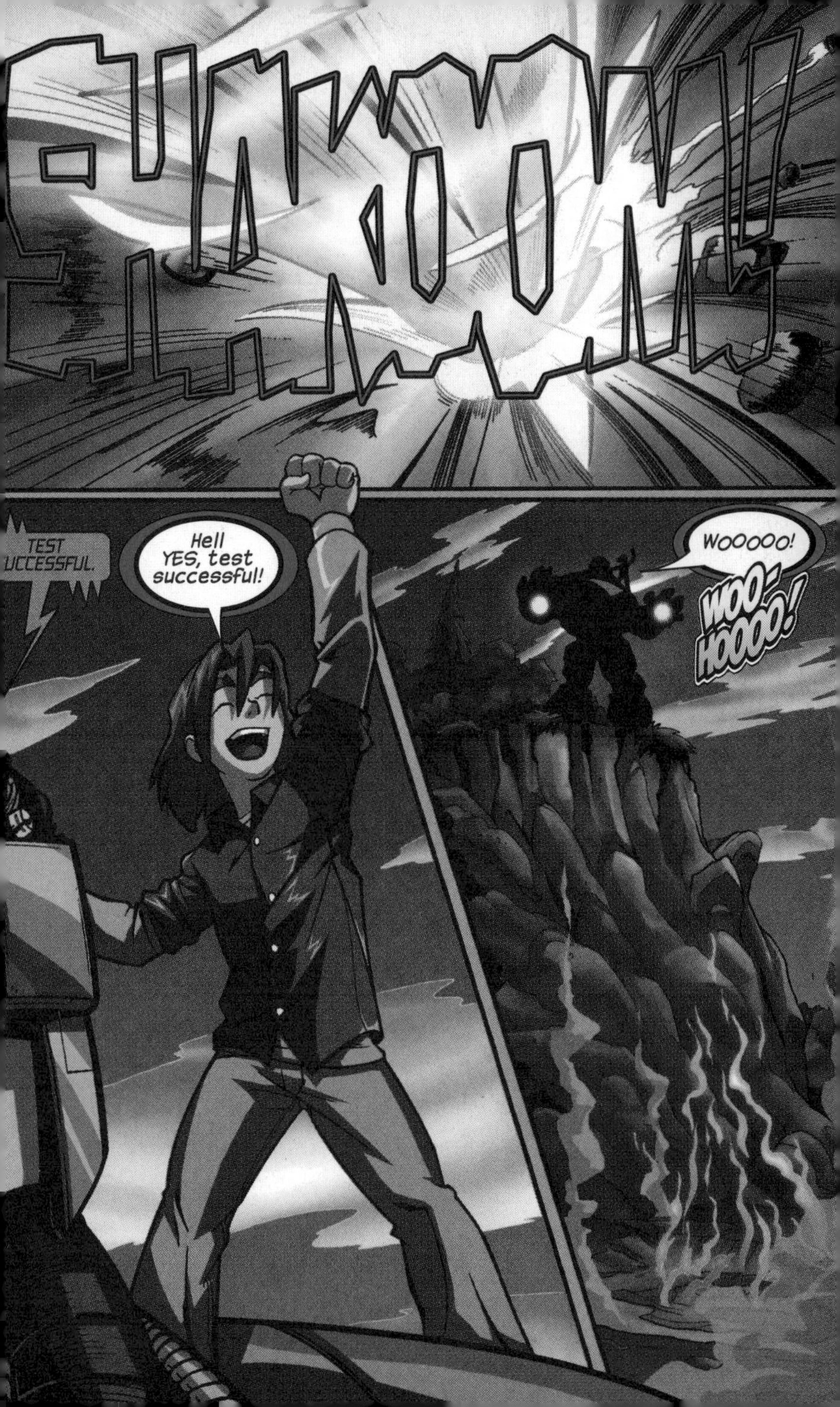
SHAKOOM!
TEST UCCESSFUL.
Hell YES, test successful!
WOOOOO!
WOO-HOOOO!

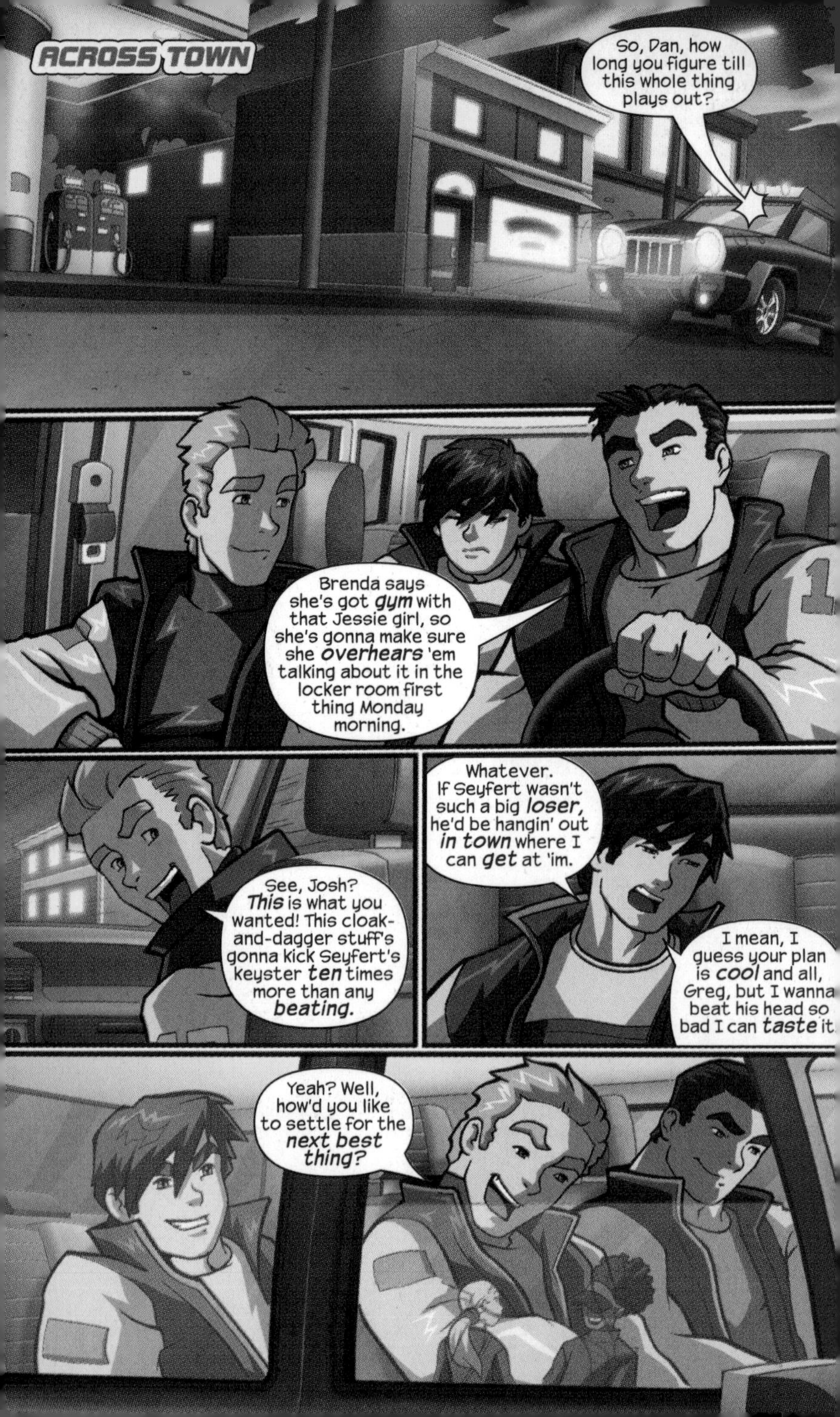
ACROSS TOWN
So, Dan, how long you figure till this whole thing plays out?
Brenda says she's got gym with that Jessie girl, so she's gonna make sure she overhears 'em talking about it in the locker room first thing Monday morning.
Whatever. If Seyfert wasn't such a big loser, he'd be hangin' out in town where I can get at 'im.
I mean, I guess your plan is cool and all, Greg, but I wanna beat his head so bad I can taste it.
See, Josh? This is what you wanted! This cloak-and-dagger stuff's gonna kick Seyfert's keyster ten times more than any beating.
Yeah? Well, how'd you like to settle for the next best thing?

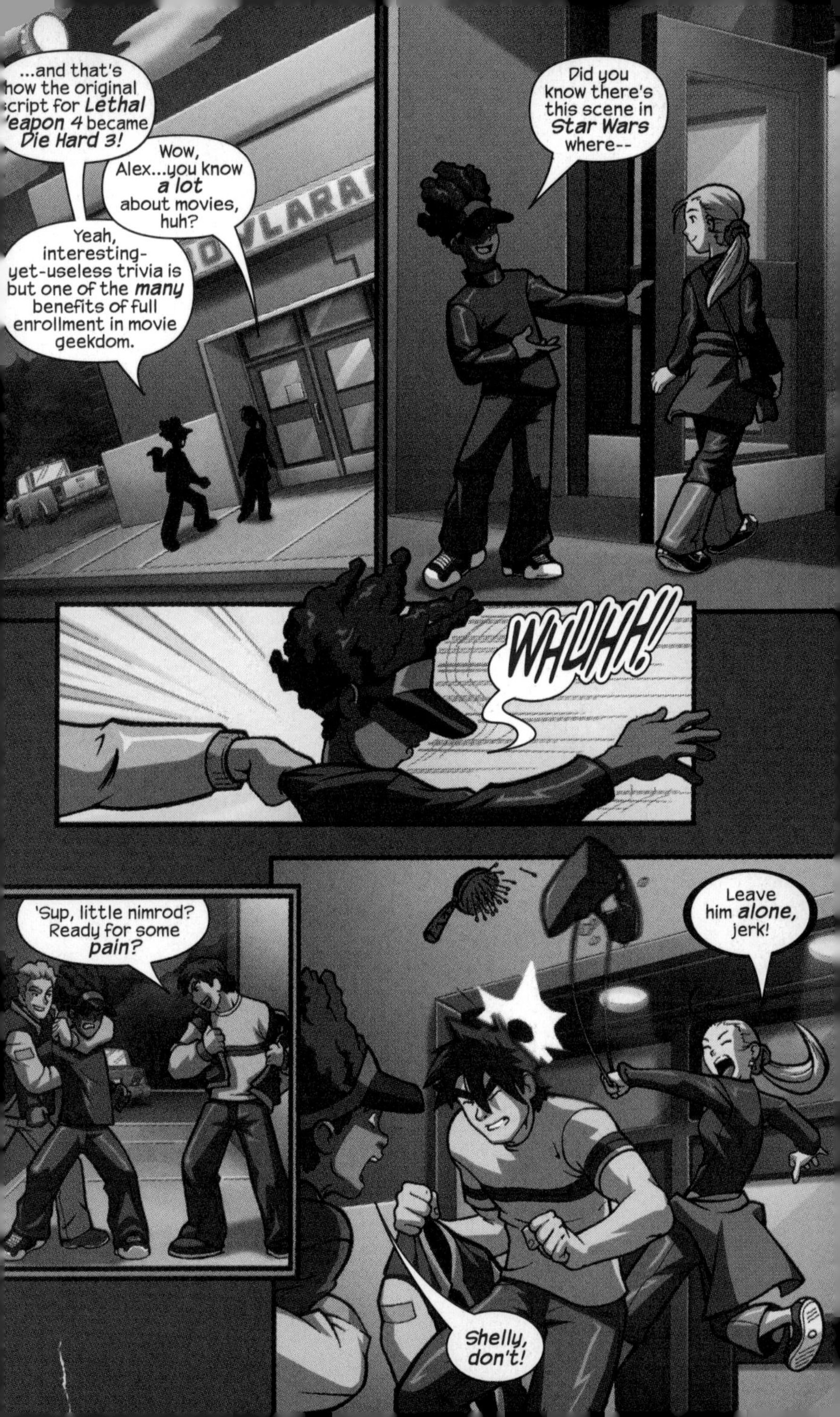
...and that's how the original script for Lethal Weapon 4 became Die Hard 3!
Wow, Alex...you know a lot about movies, huh?
Yeah, interesting-yet-useless trivia is but one of the many benefits of full enrollment in movie geekdom.
Did you know there's this scene in Star Wars where--
WHUHH!
'Sup, little nimrod? Ready for some pain?
Leave him alone, jerk!
Shelly, don't!

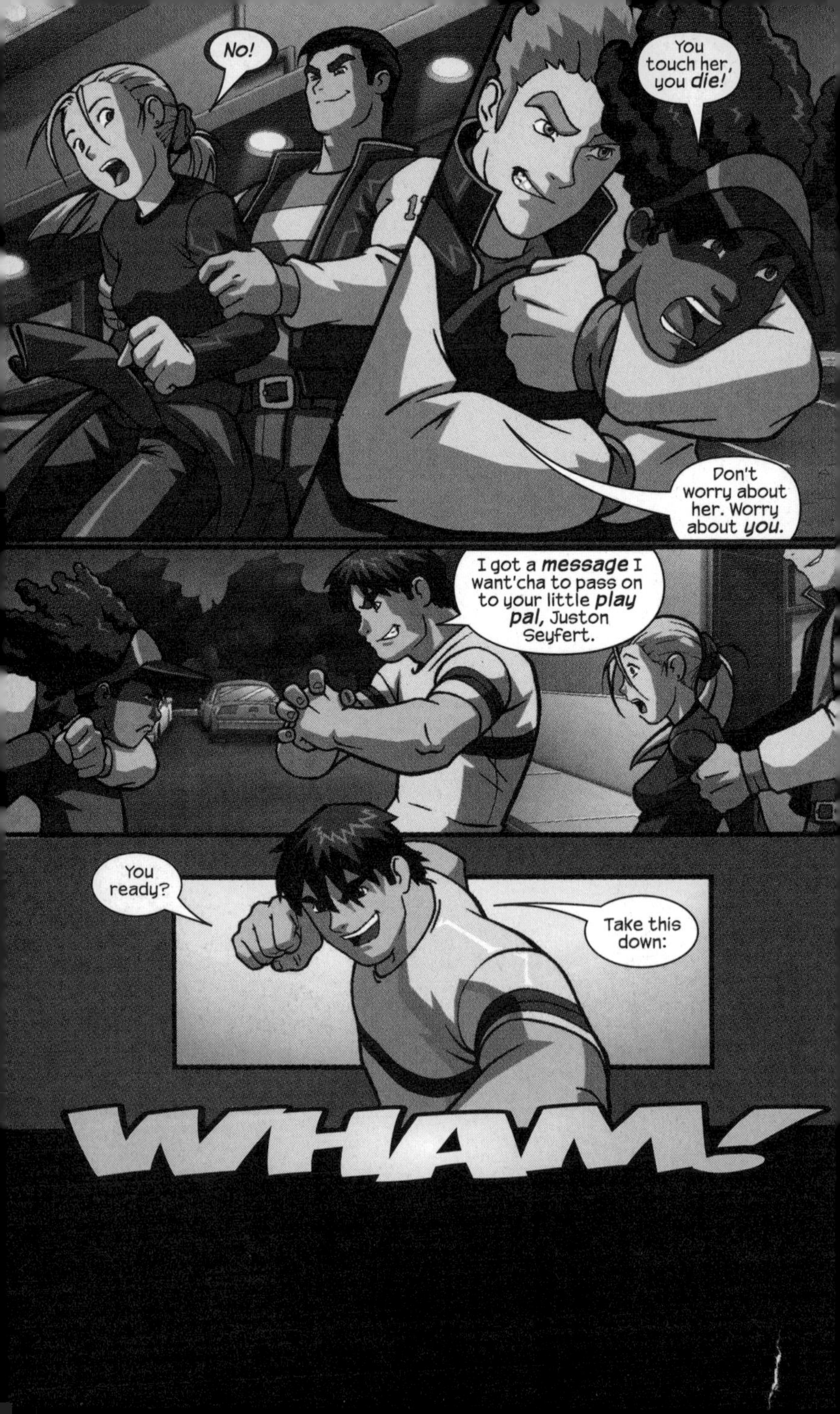
No!
You touch her, you *die!*
Don't worry about her. Worry about *you.*
I got a *message* I want'cha to pass on to your little *play pal,* Juston Seyfert.
You ready?
Take this down:
WHAM!

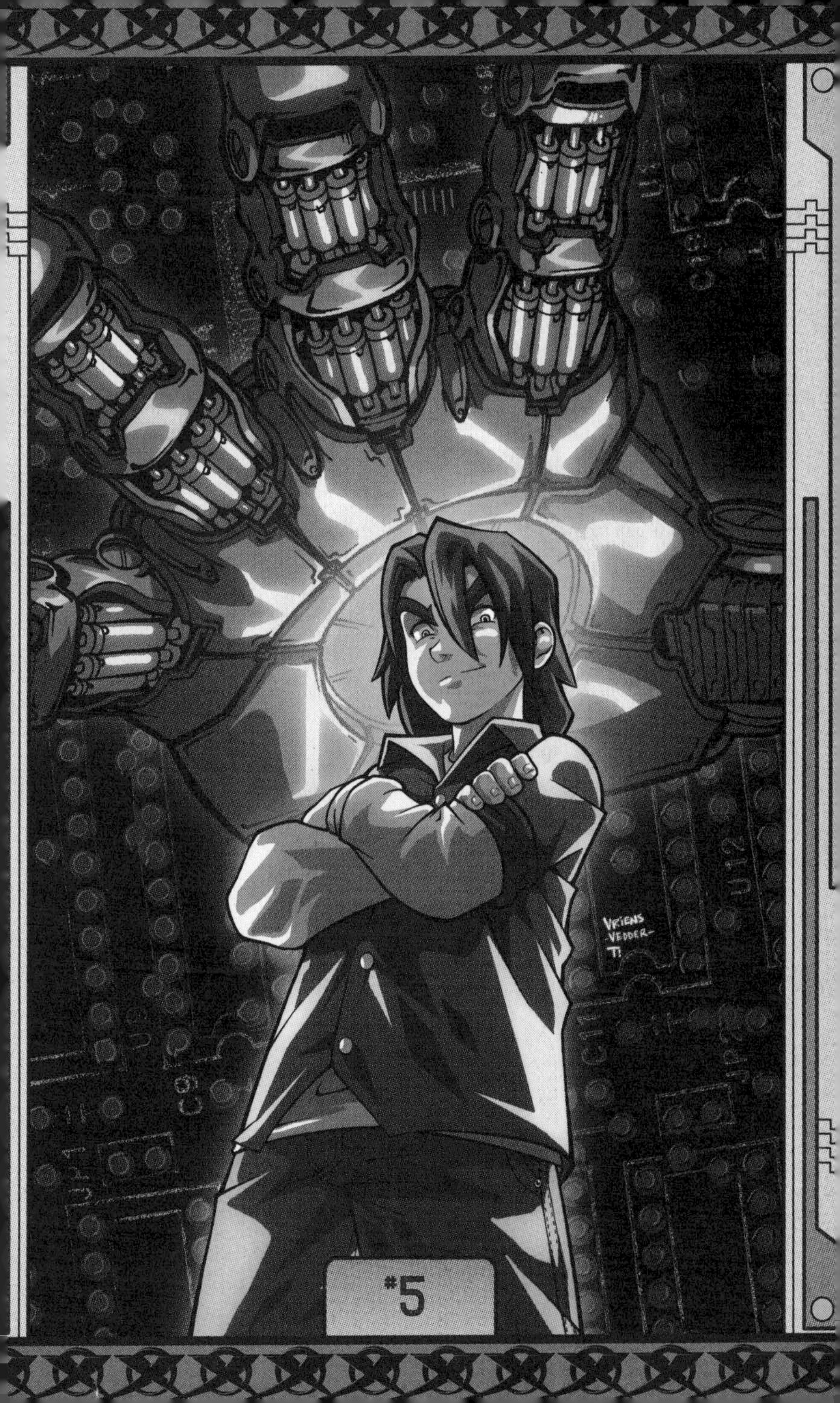
VRIENS -VEDDER- TI
#5

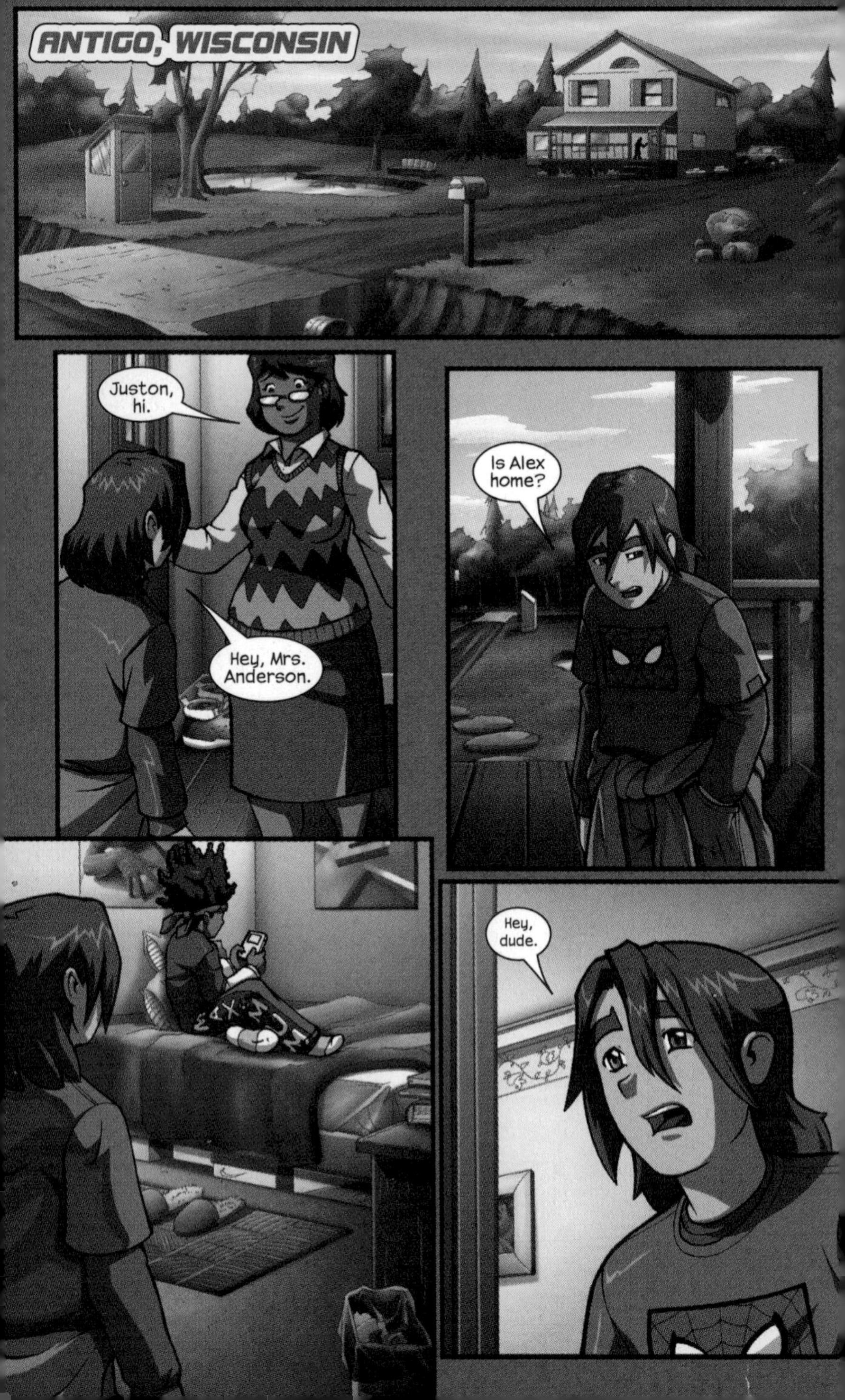
ANTIGO, WISCONSIN
Juston, hi.
Hey, Mrs. Anderson.
Is Alex home?
Hey, dude.

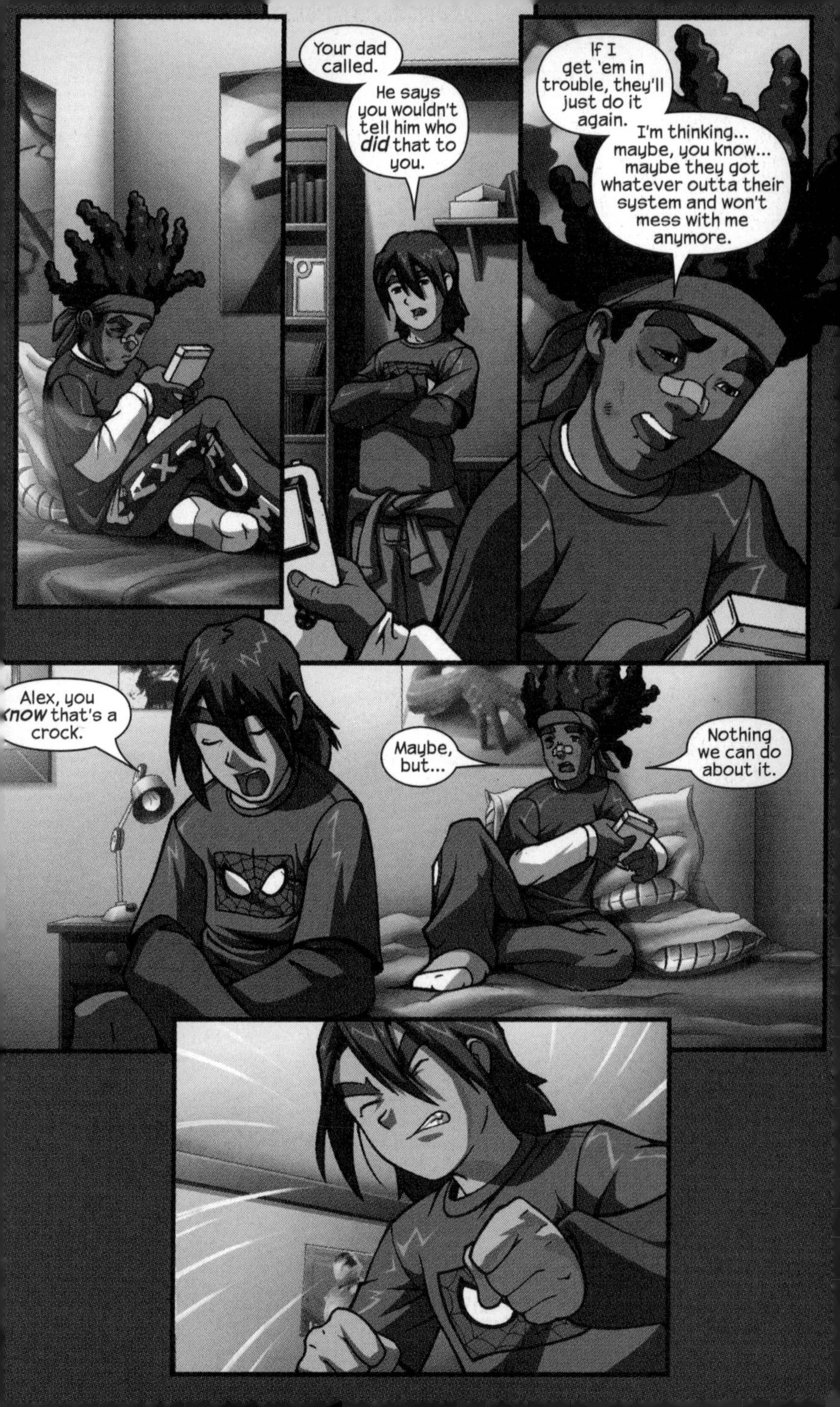

Your dad called.
He says you wouldn't tell him who *did* that to you.
If I get 'em in trouble, they'll just do it again.
I'm thinking... maybe, you know... maybe they got whatever outta their system and won't mess with me anymore.
Alex, you *know* that's a crock.
Maybe, but...
Nothing we can do about it.

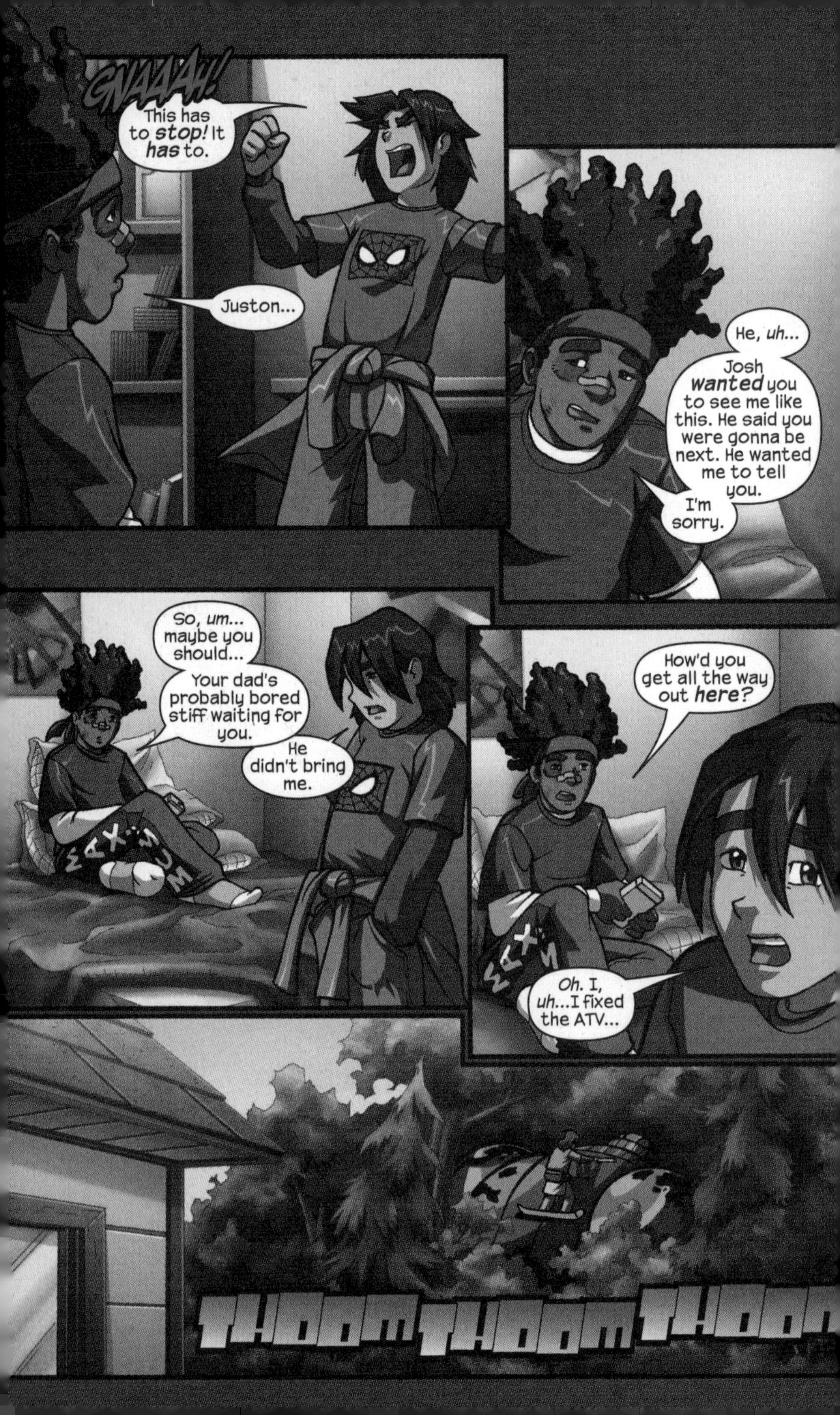
GNAAAH!
This has to *stop!* It *has* to.
Juston...
He, *uh*...
Josh ***wanted*** you to see me like this. He said you were gonna be next. He wanted me to tell you.
I'm sorry.
So, *um*... maybe you should...
Your dad's probably bored stiff waiting for you.
He didn't bring me.
How'd you get all the way out *here?*
Oh. I, *uh*...I fixed the ATV...
THOOM THOOM THOOM

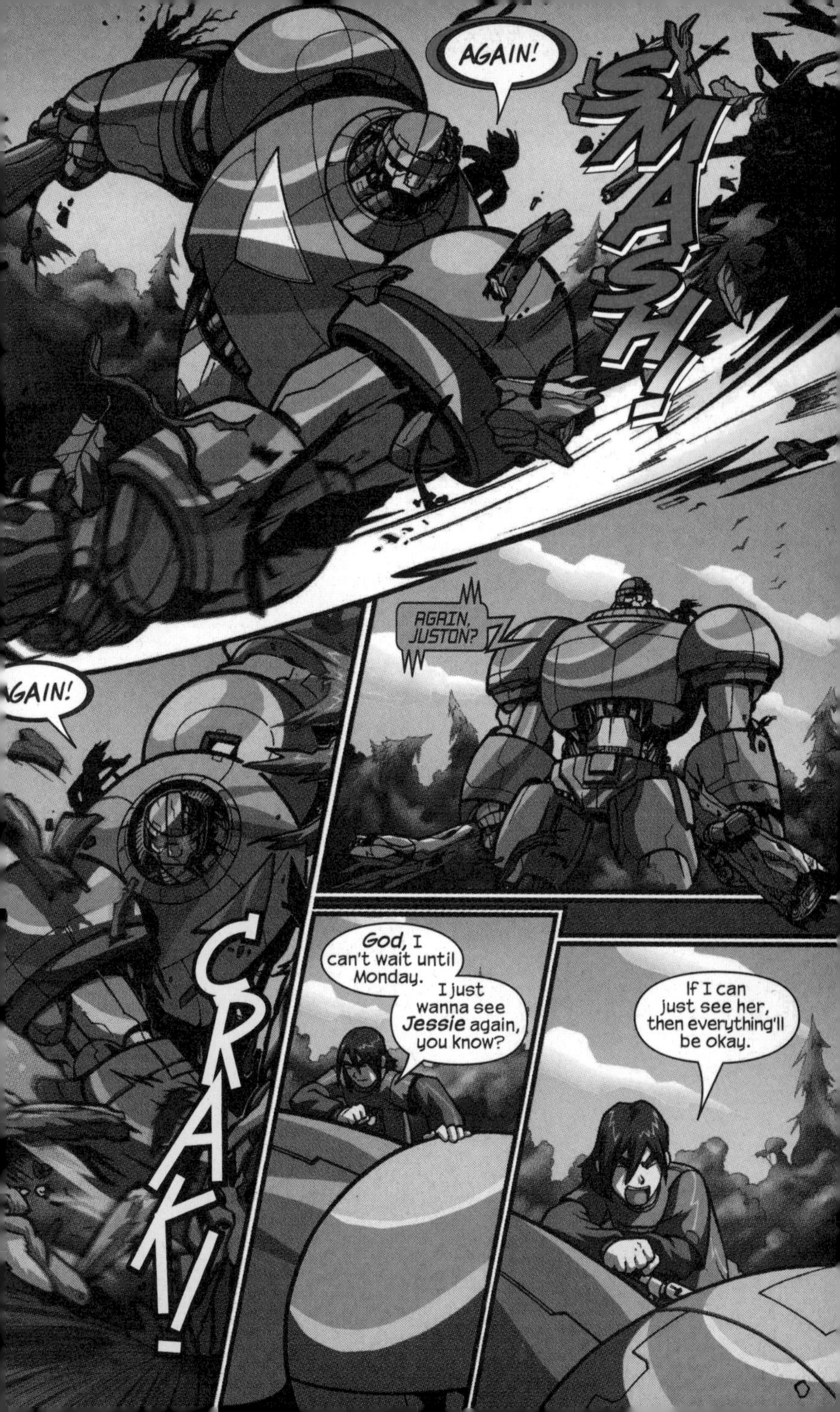

AGAIN!
SMASH!
AGAIN!
CRAK!
AGAIN, JUSTON?
God, I can't wait until Monday.
I just wanna see Jessie again, you know?
If I can just see her, then everything'll be okay.

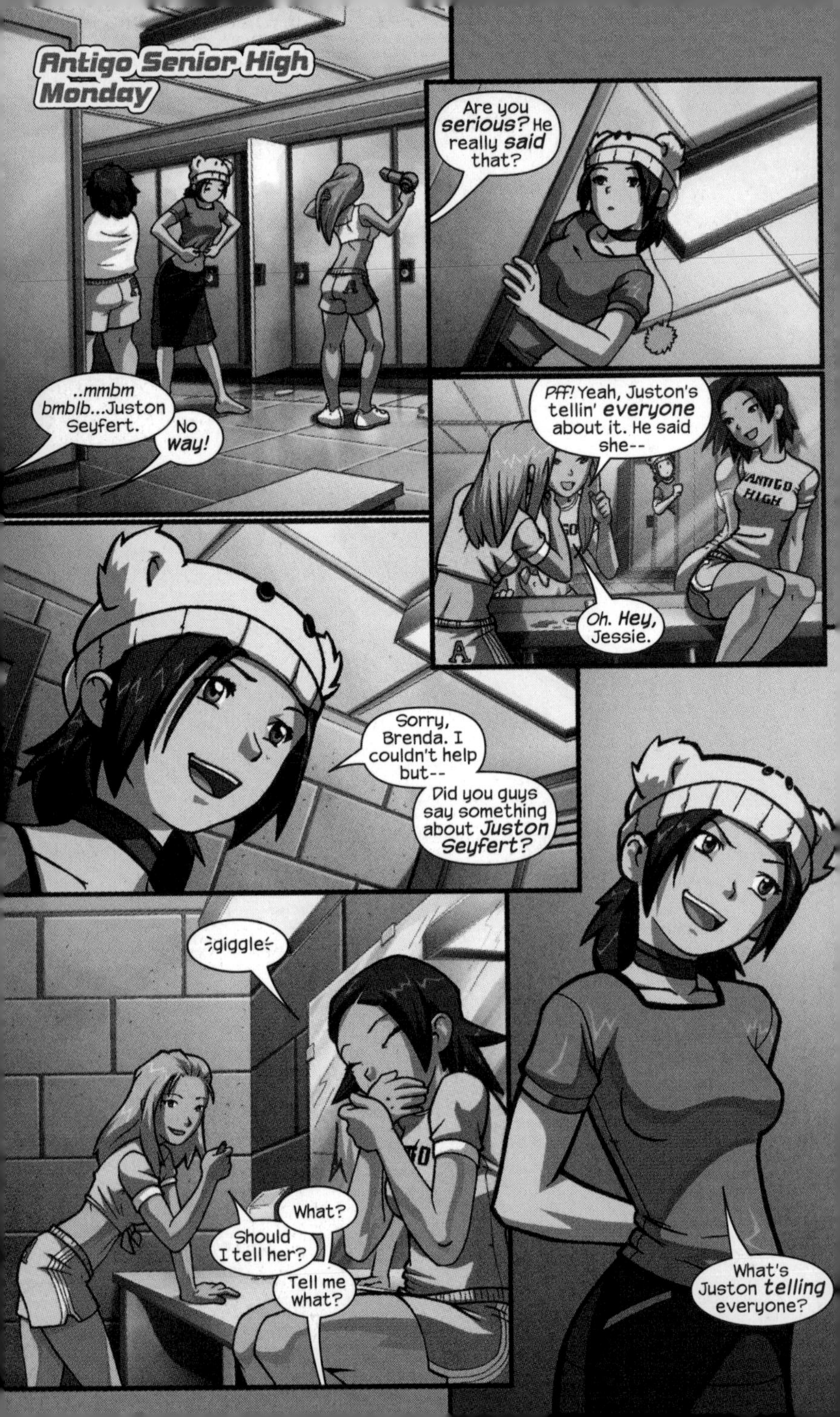

Antigo Senior High
Monday
..mmbm bmblb...Juston Seyfert.
No way!
Are you serious? He really said that?
Pff! Yeah, Juston's tellin' everyone about it. He said she--
Oh. Hey, Jessie.
Sorry, Brenda. I couldn't help but--
Did you guys say something about Juston Seyfert?
giggle
What?
Should I tell her?
Tell me what?
What's Juston telling everyone?

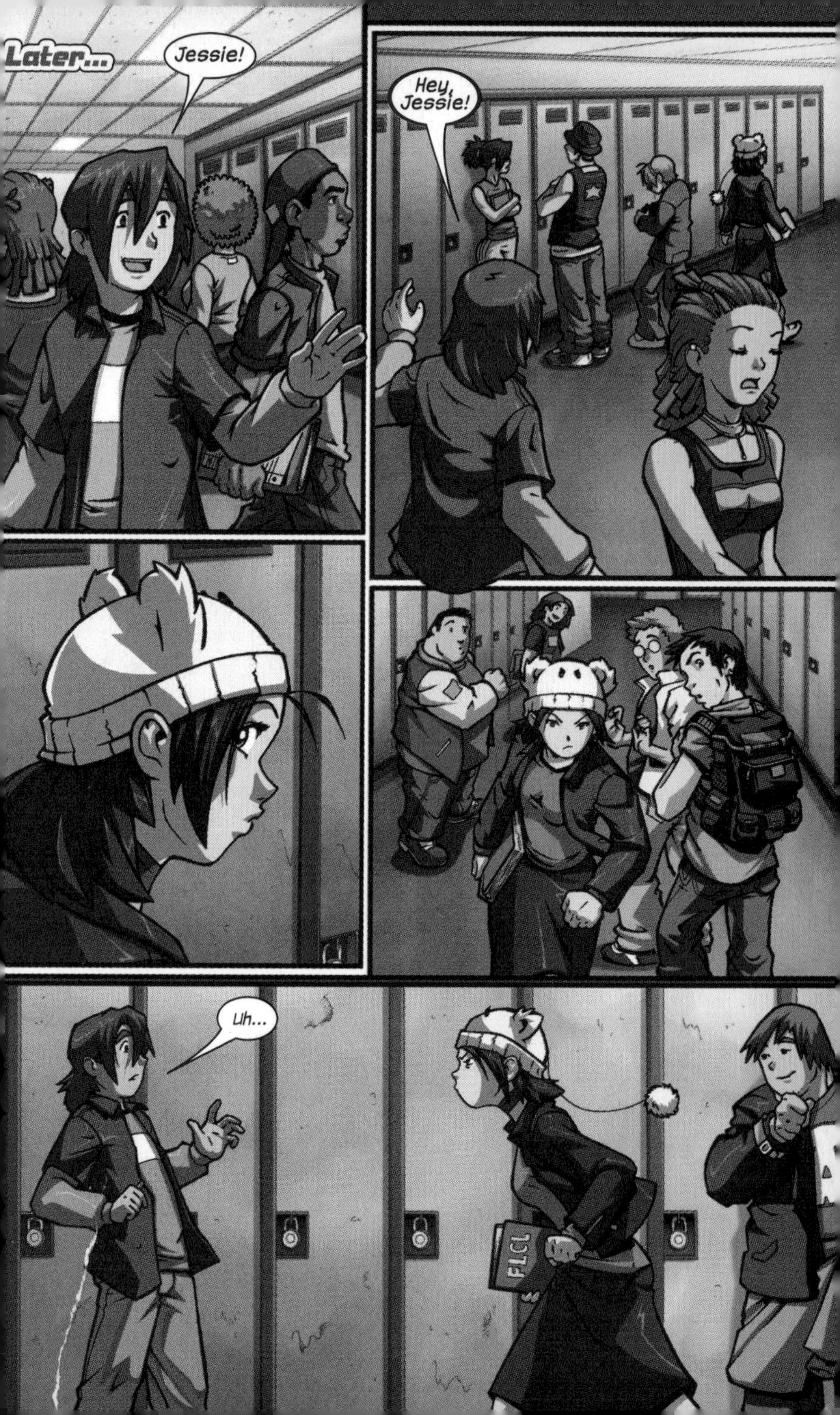
Later...
Jessie!
Hey, Jessie!
Uh...
FLCL

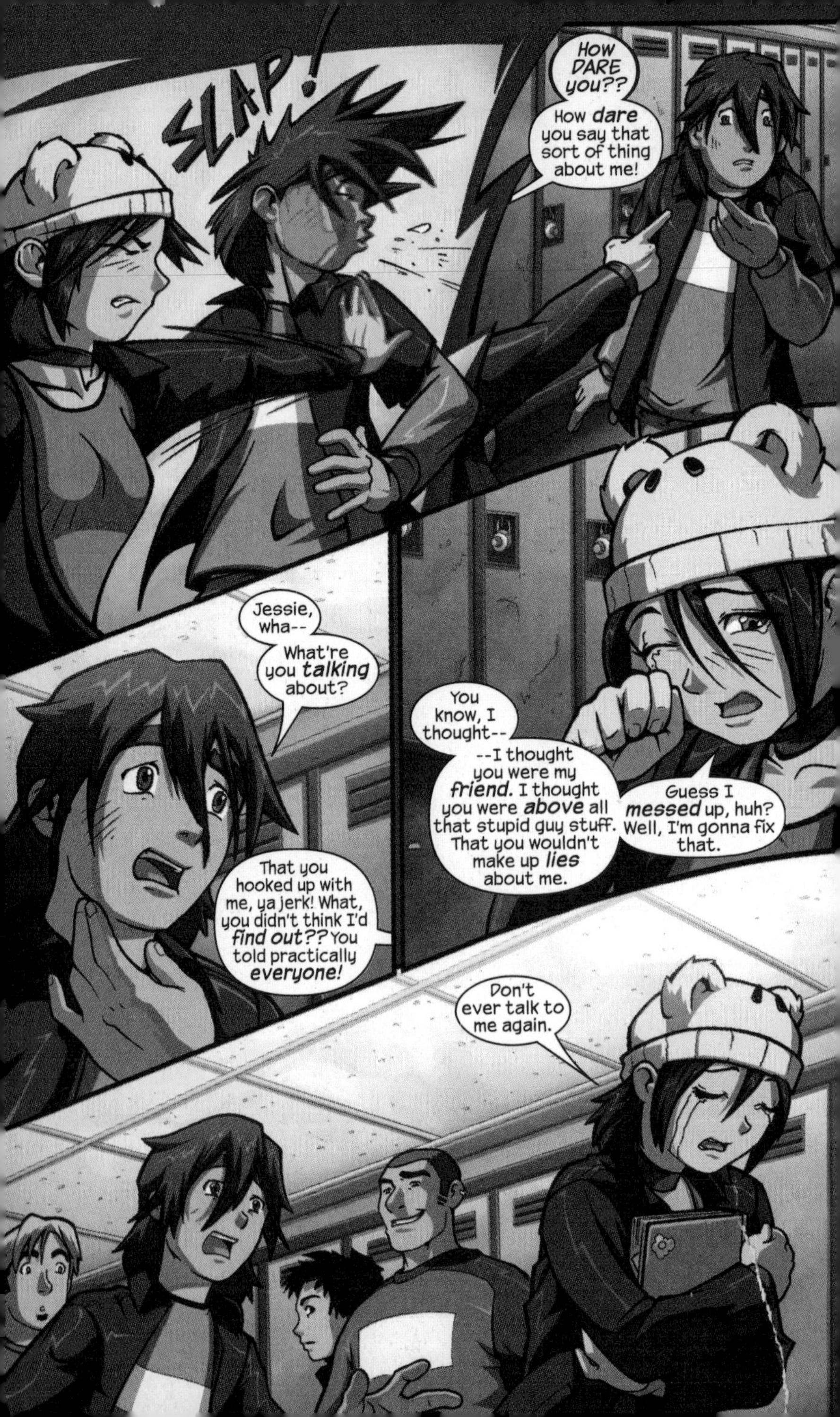
SLAP!
HOW DARE you??
How dare you say that sort of thing about me!
Jessie, wha--
What're you talking about?
That you hooked up with me, ya jerk! What, you didn't think I'd find out?? You told practically everyone!
You know, I thought--
--I thought you were my friend. I thought you were above all that stupid guy stuff. That you wouldn't make up lies about me.
Guess I messed up, huh? Well, I'm gonna fix that.
Don't ever talk to me again.

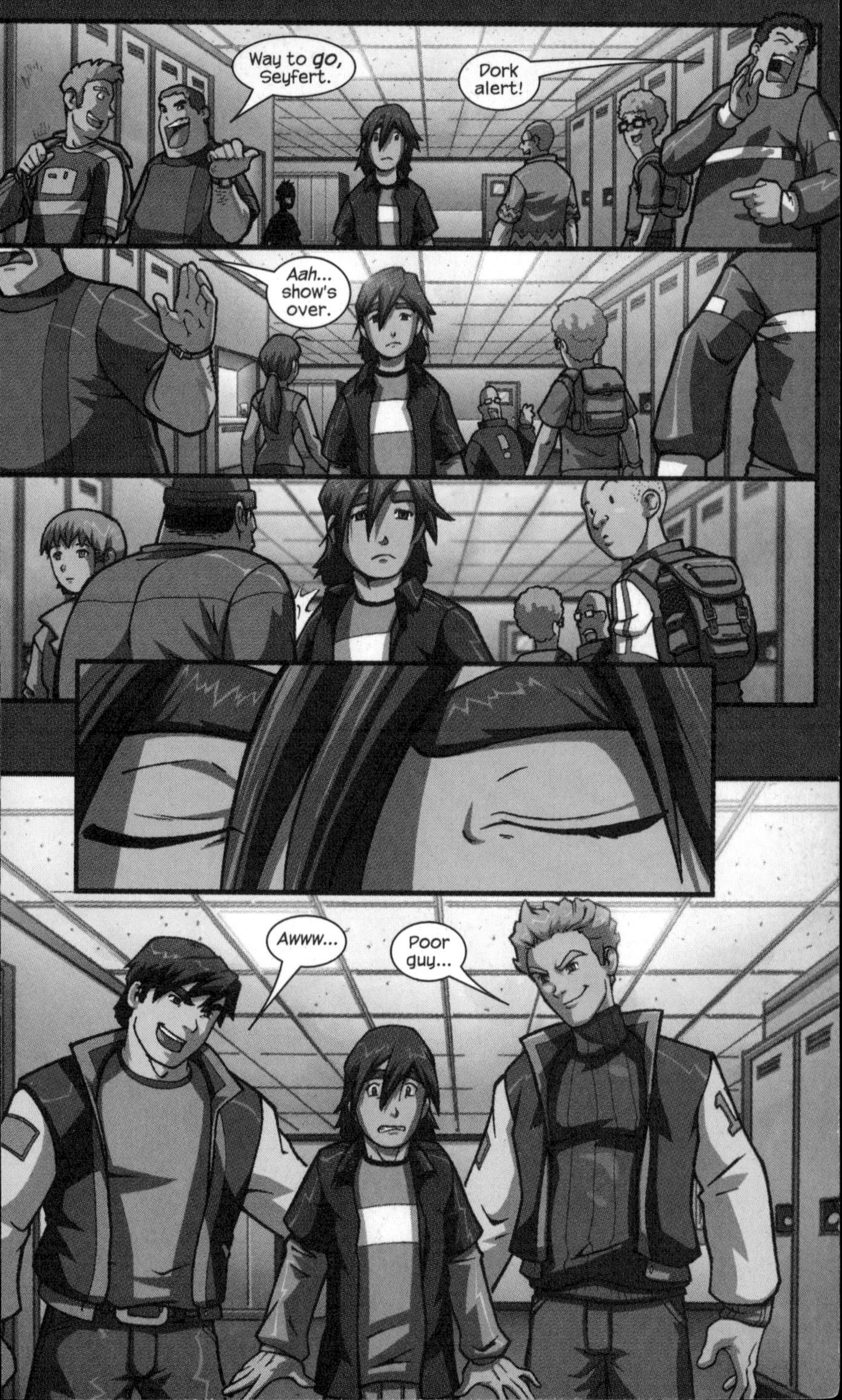
Way to go, Seyfert.
Dork alert!
Aah... show's over.
Awww...
Poor guy...

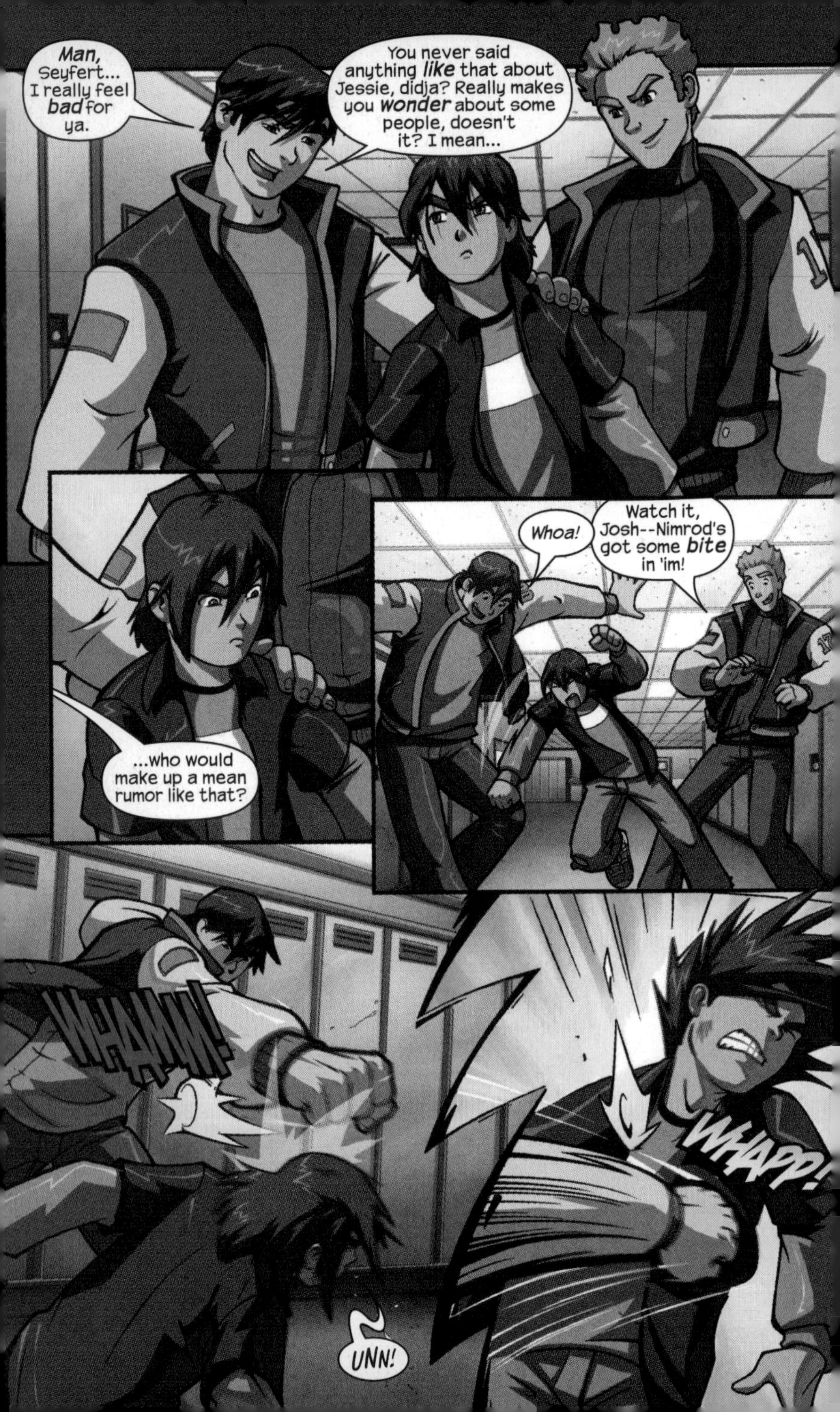
Man, Seyfert... I really feel bad for ya.
You never said anything like that about Jessie, didja? Really makes you wonder about some people, doesn't it? I mean...
...who would make up a mean rumor like that?
Whoa!
Watch it, Josh--Nimrod's got some bite in 'im!
WHAMM!
WHAPP!
UNN!

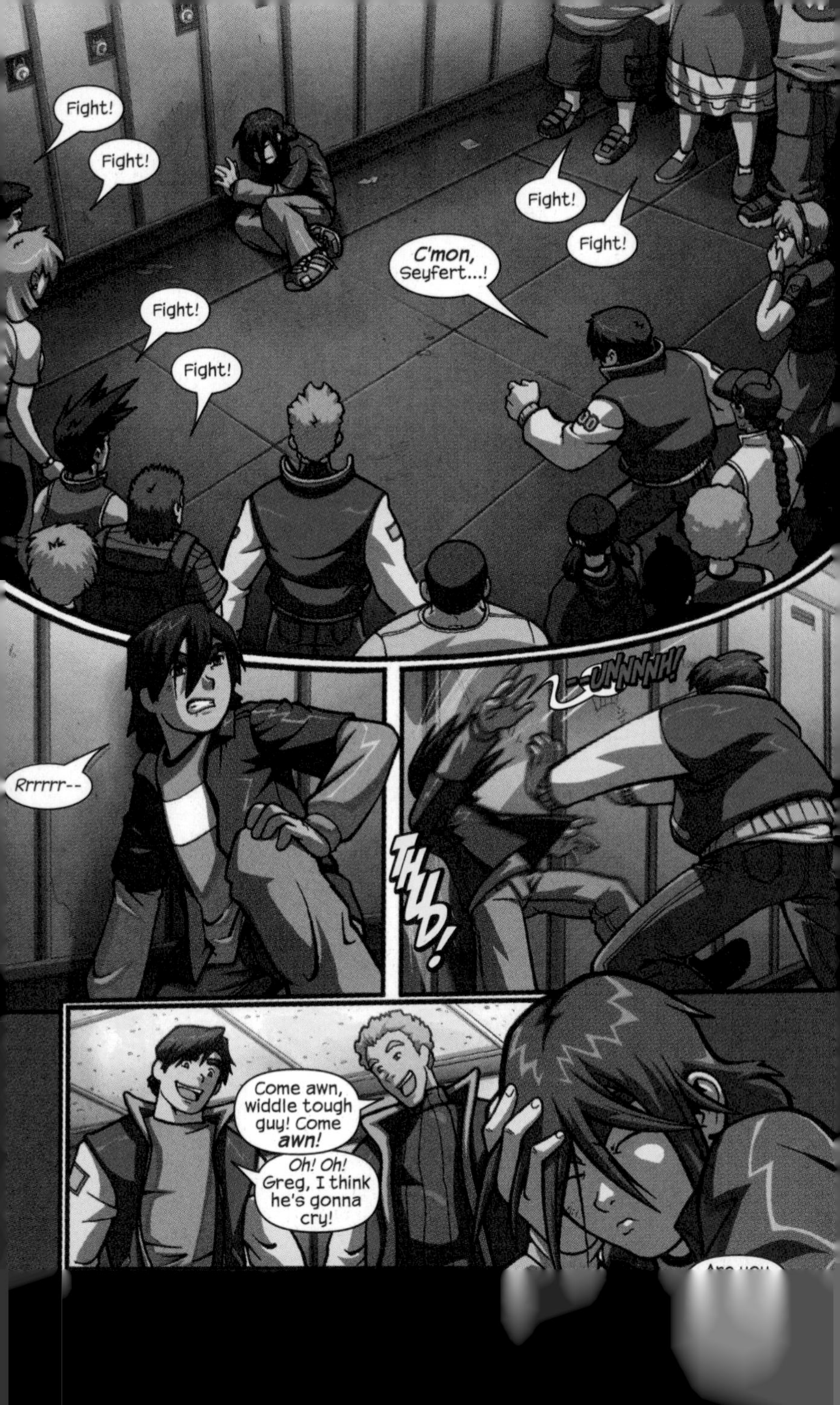

Fight!
Fight!
Fight!
Fight!
C'mon, Seyfert...!
Fight!
Fight!
Rrrrrr--
--UNNNNH!
THUD!
Come awn, widdle tough guy! Come awn!
Oh! Oh! Greg, I think he's gonna cry!

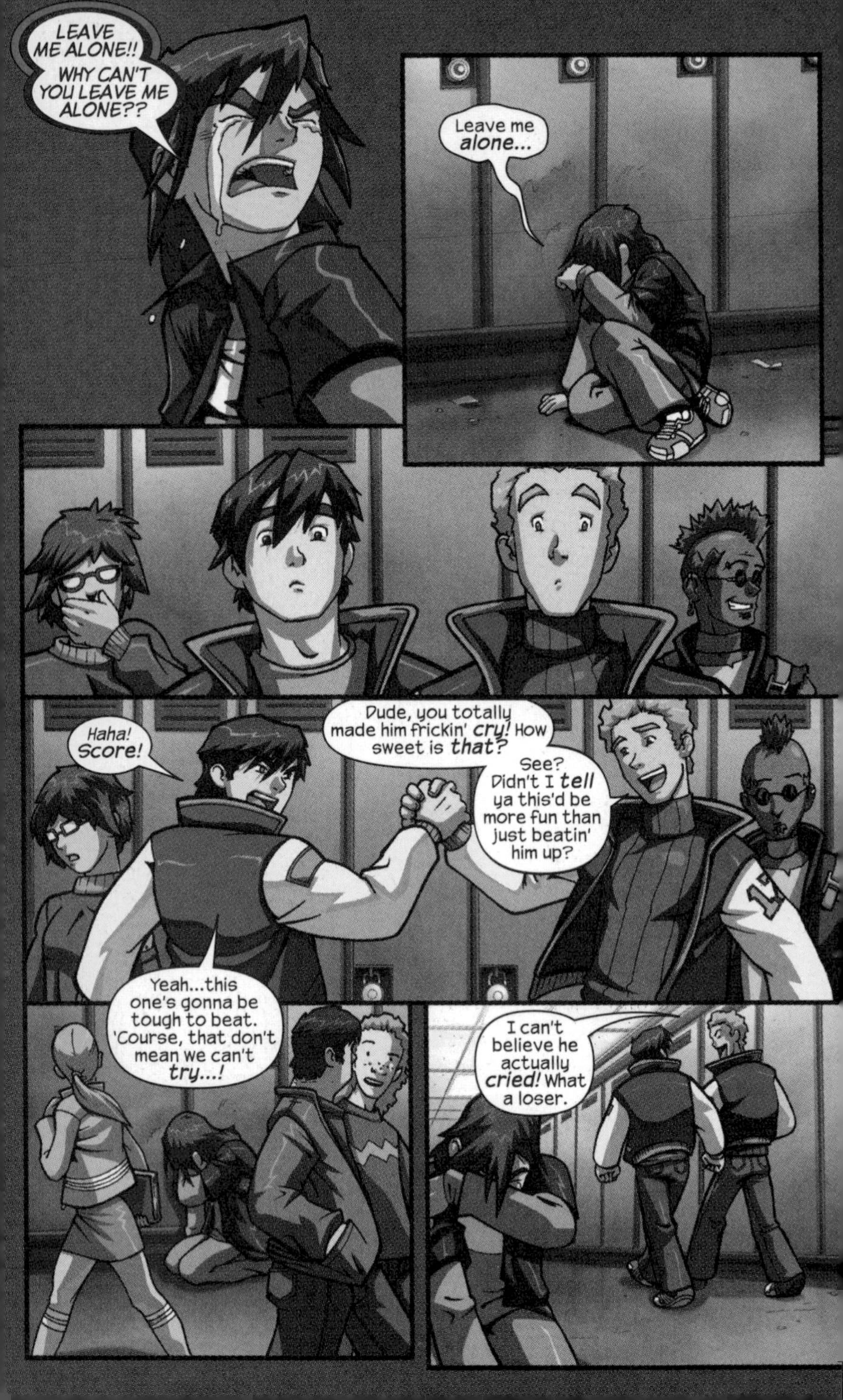
LEAVE ME ALONE!! WHY CAN'T YOU LEAVE ME ALONE??
Leave me alone...
Haha! Score!
Dude, you totally made him frickin' cry! How sweet is that?
See? Didn't I tell ya this'd be more fun than just beatin' him up?
Yeah...this one's gonna be tough to beat. 'Course, that don't mean we can't try...!
I can't believe he actually cried! What a loser.

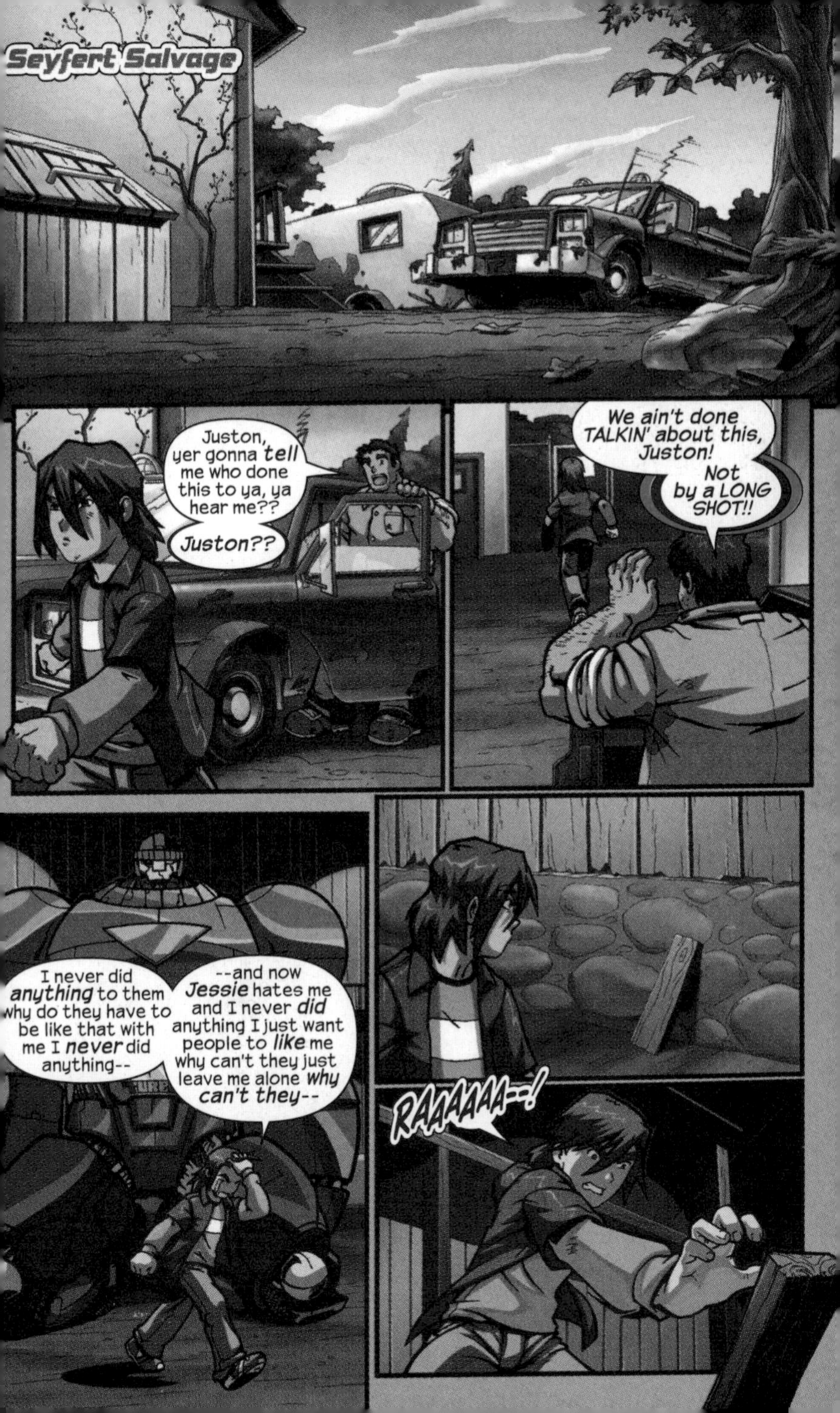
Seyfert Salvage
Juston, yer gonna tell me who done this to ya, ya hear me??
Juston??
We ain't done TALKIN' about this, Juston!
Not by a LONG SHOT!!
I never did anything to them why do they have to be like that with me I never did anything--
--and now Jessie hates me and I never did anything I just want people to like me why can't they just leave me alone why can't they--
RAAAAAA--!

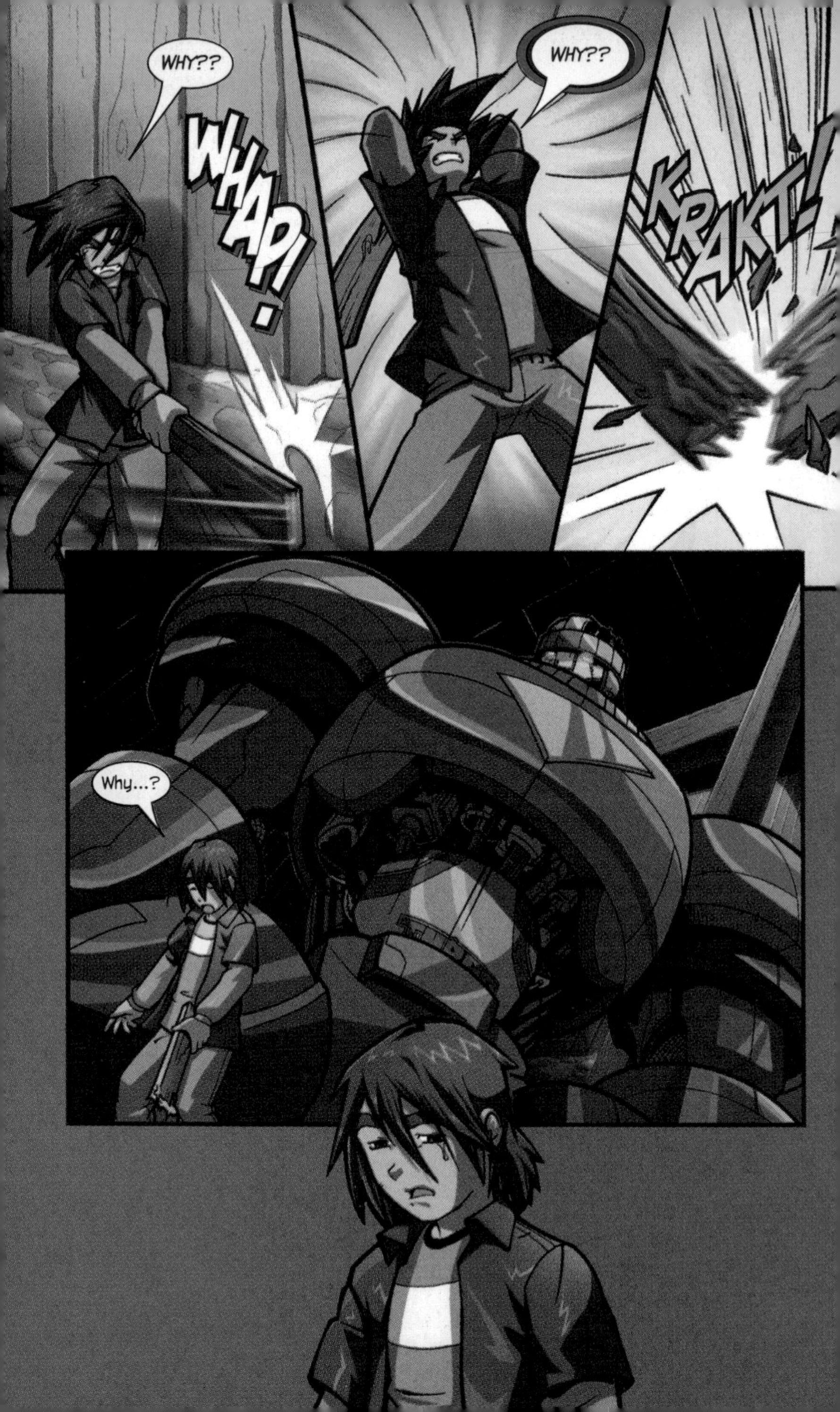
WHY??
WHAP!!
WHY??
KRAKT!
Why...?

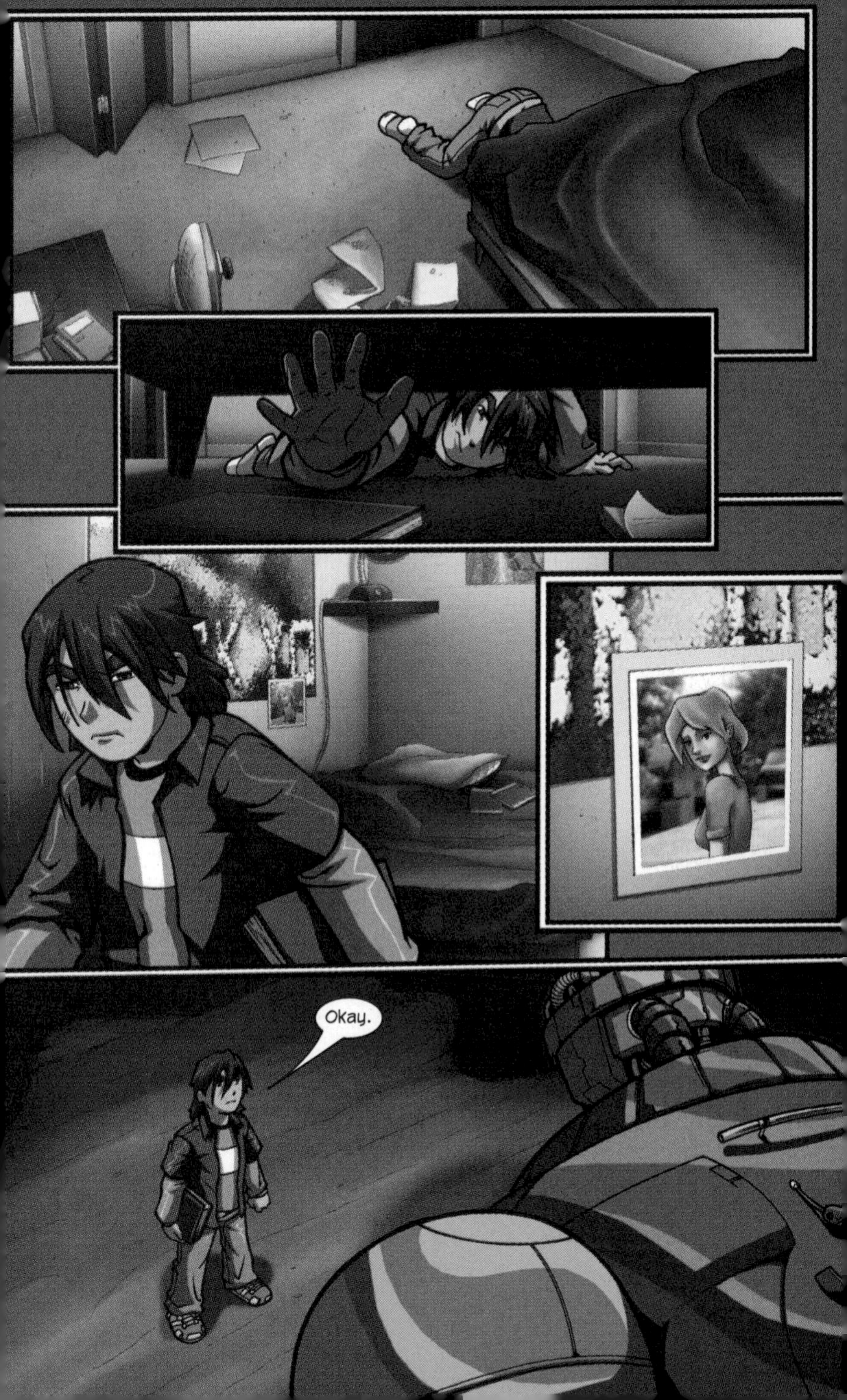
Okay.

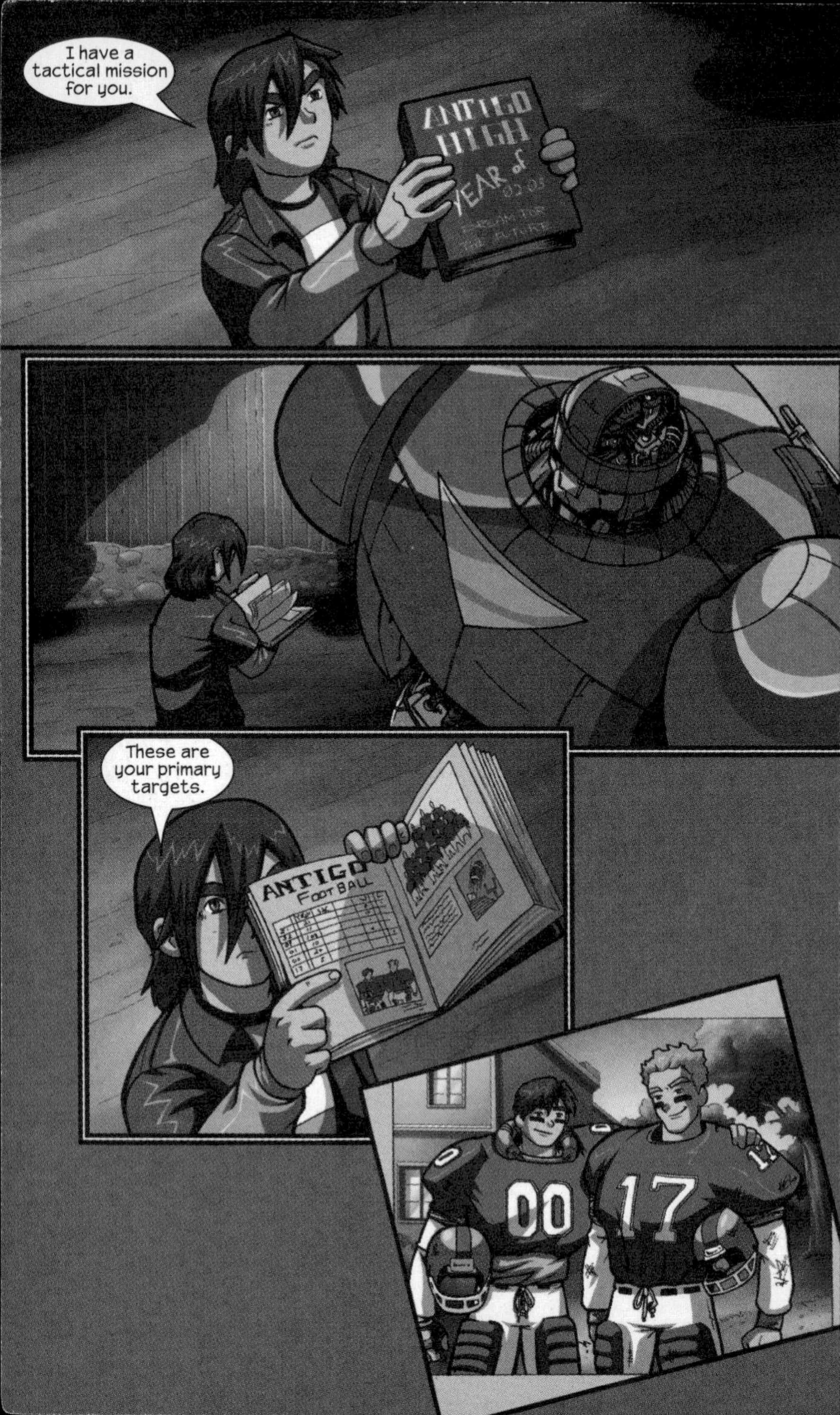
I have a tactical mission for you.
ANTIGO HIGH
YEAR of 02-03
These are your primary targets.
ANTIGO FOOTBALL
00
17

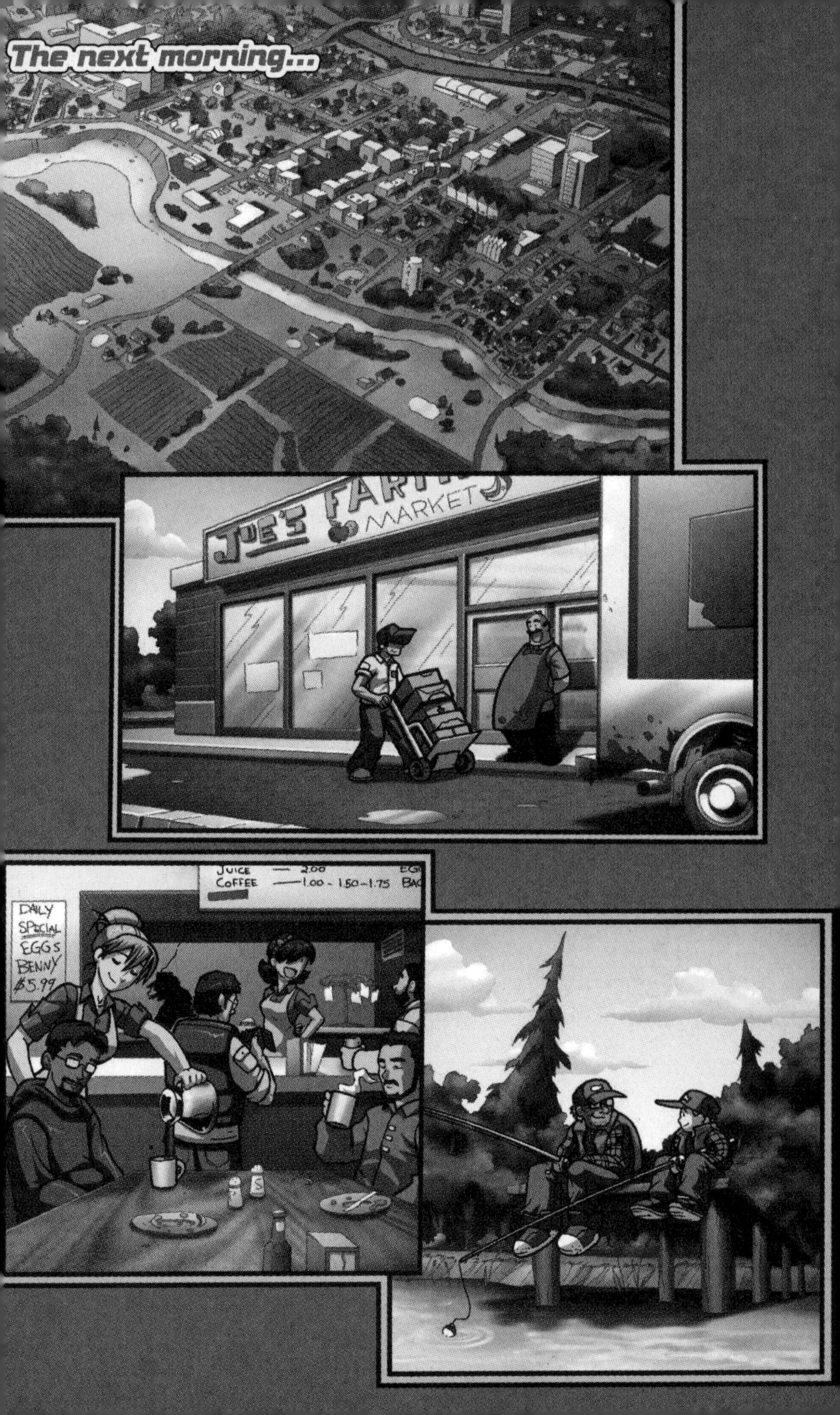
The next morning...
MARKET
JUICE — 2.00
COFFEE —1.00 - 1.50 - 1.75
DAILY
SPECIAL
EGGS
BENNY
$5.99

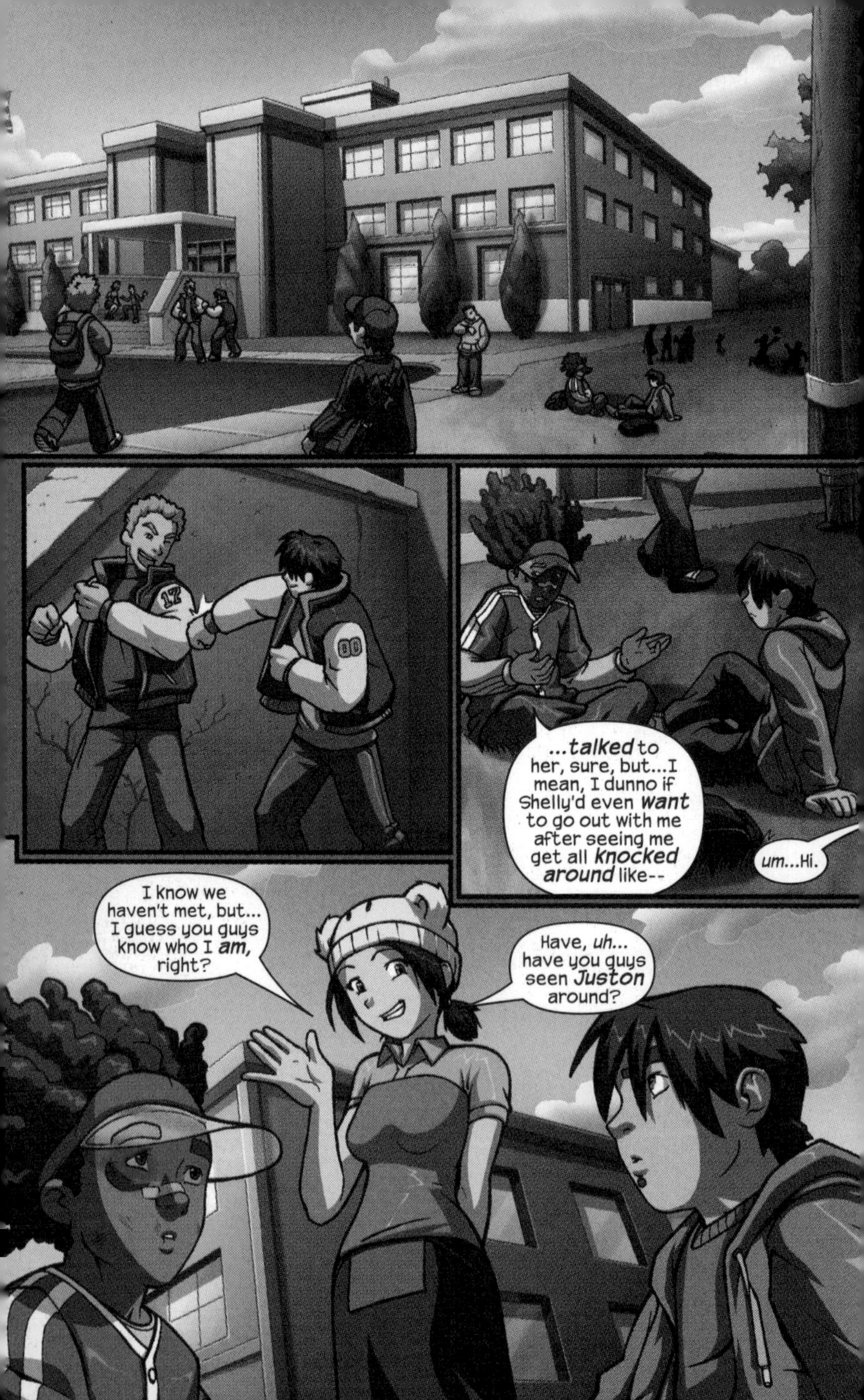
...talked to her, sure, but...I mean, I dunno if Shelly'd even want to go out with me after seeing me get all knocked around like--
um...Hi.
I know we haven't met, but... I guess you guys know who I am, right?
Have, uh... have you guys seen Juston around?

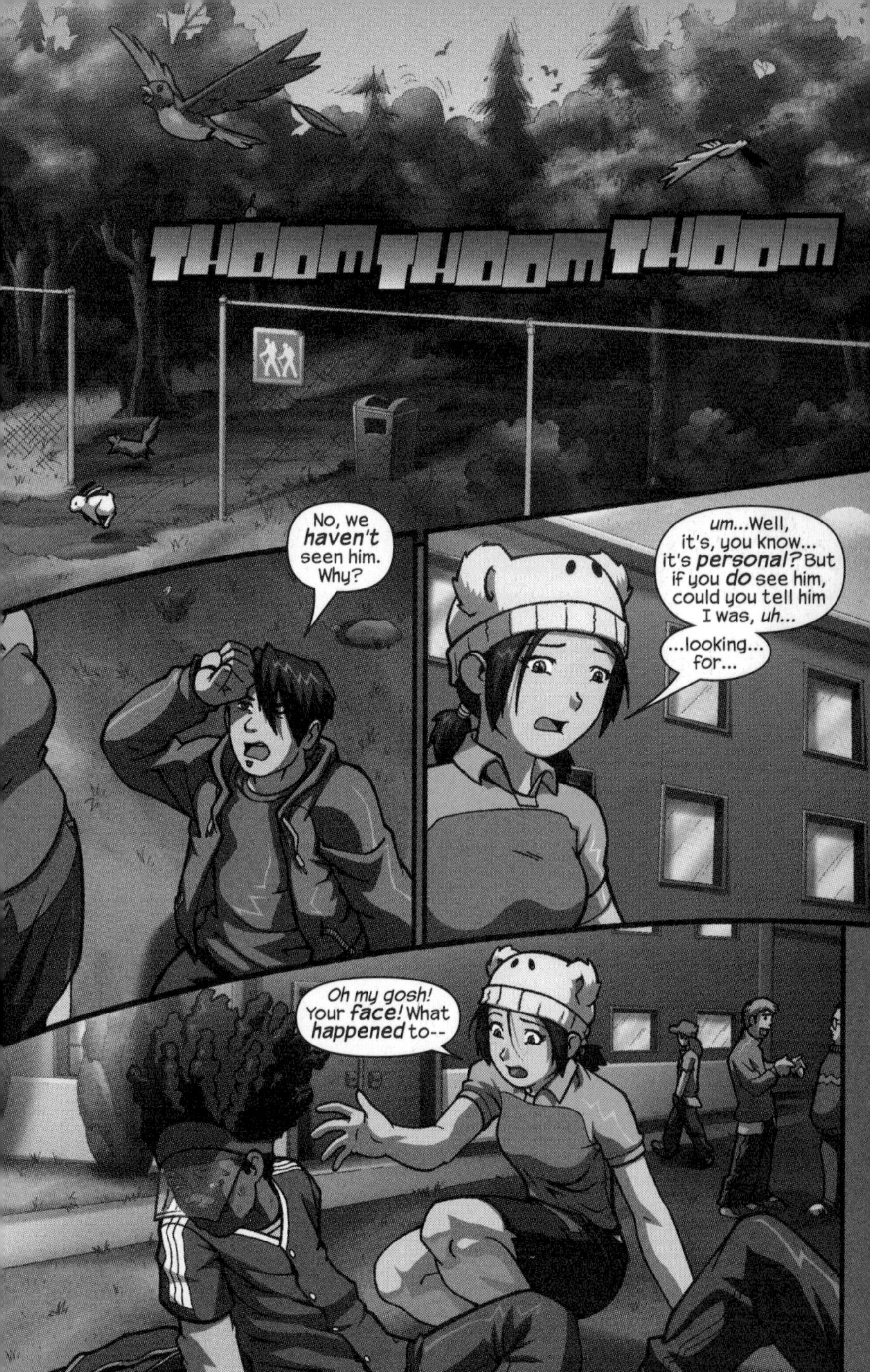
THOOM THOOM THOOM
No, we *haven't* seen him. Why?
um...Well, it's, you know... it's ***personal?*** But if you ***do*** see him, could you tell him I was, *uh*...
...looking... for...
*Oh my gosh! Your **face!** What **happened** to--*

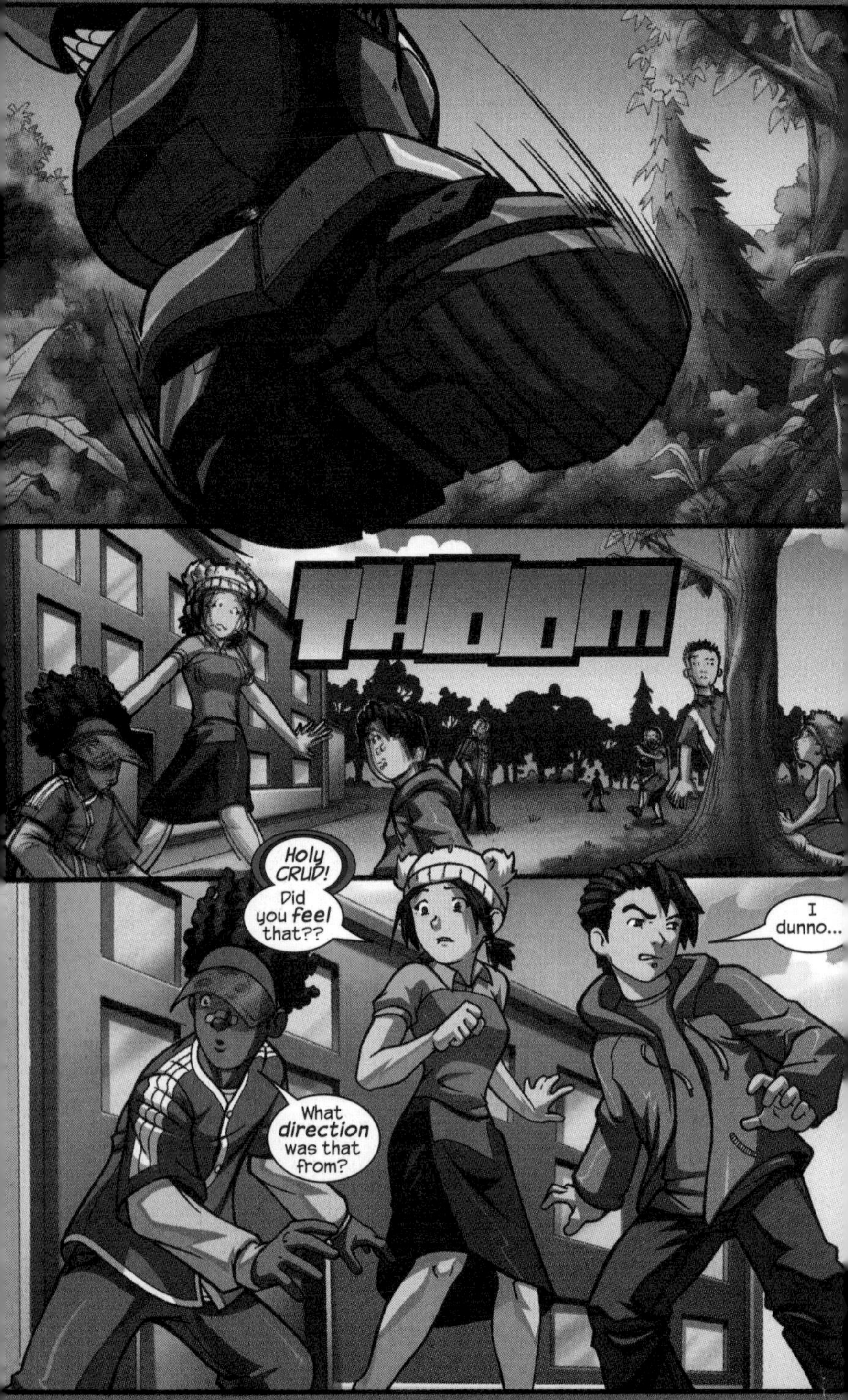
THOOM
Holy CRUD! Did you feel that??
I dunno...
What direction was that from?

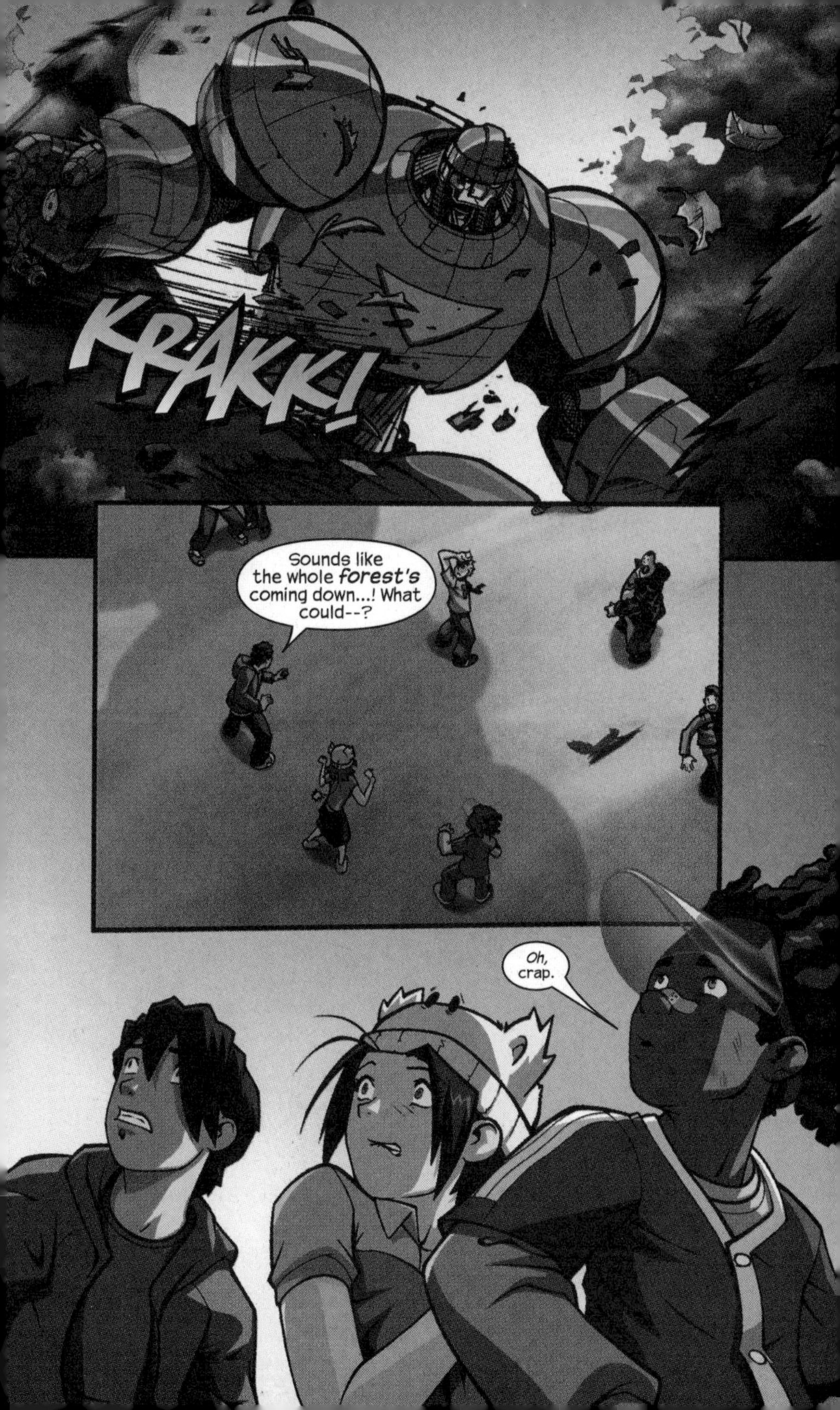
KRAKK!
Sounds like the whole *forest's* coming down...! What could--?
Oh, crap.

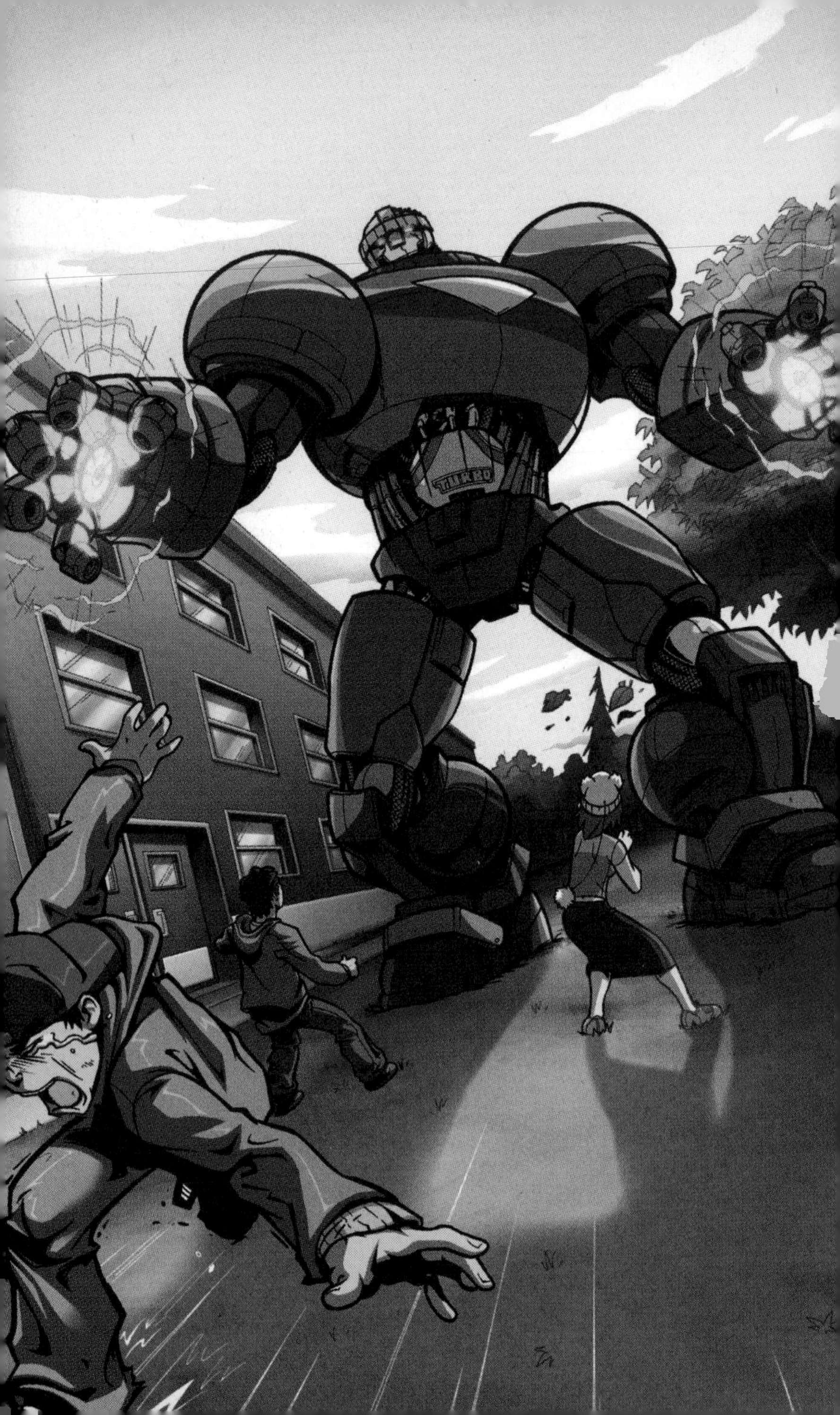

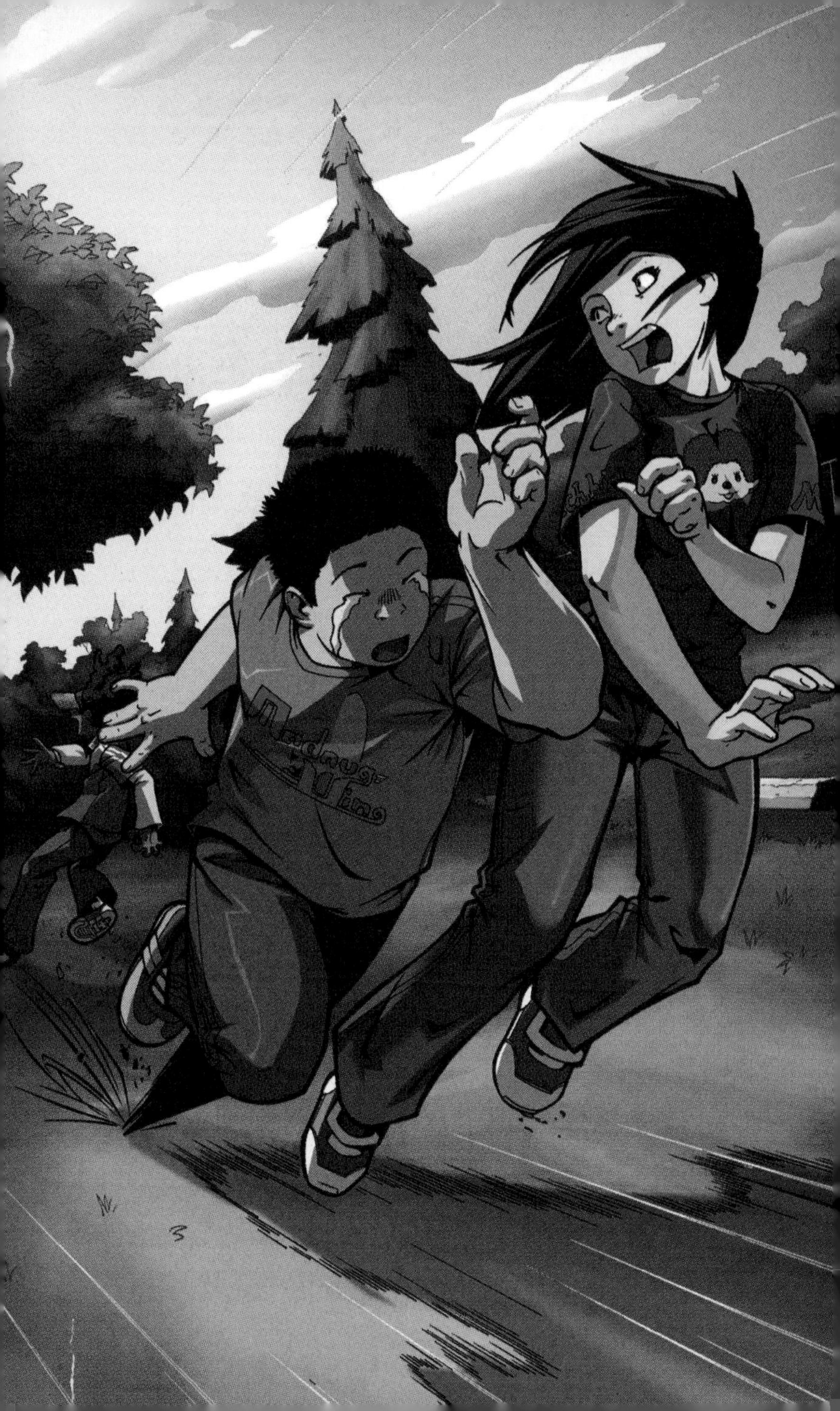

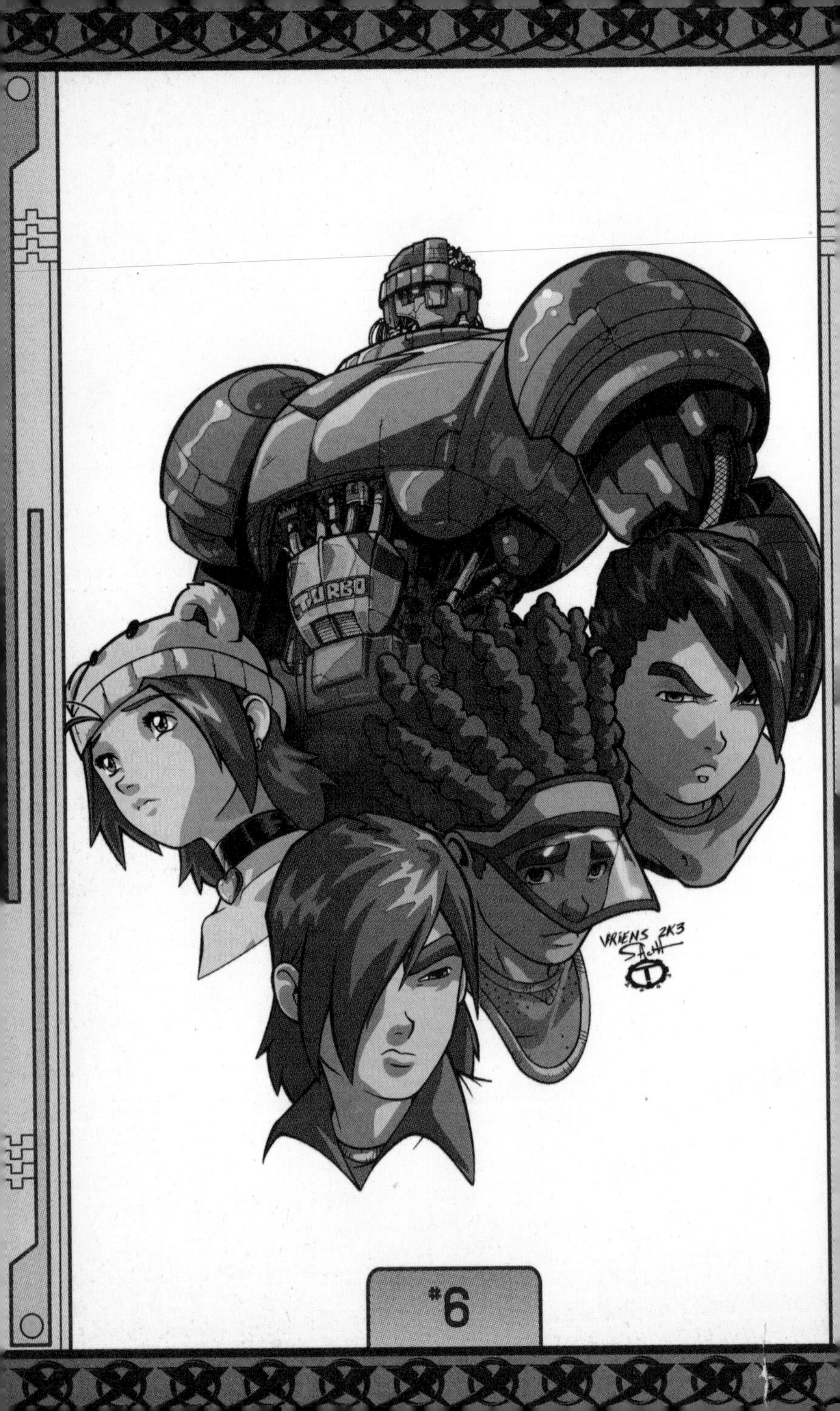
TURBO
VRIENS 2K3
#6

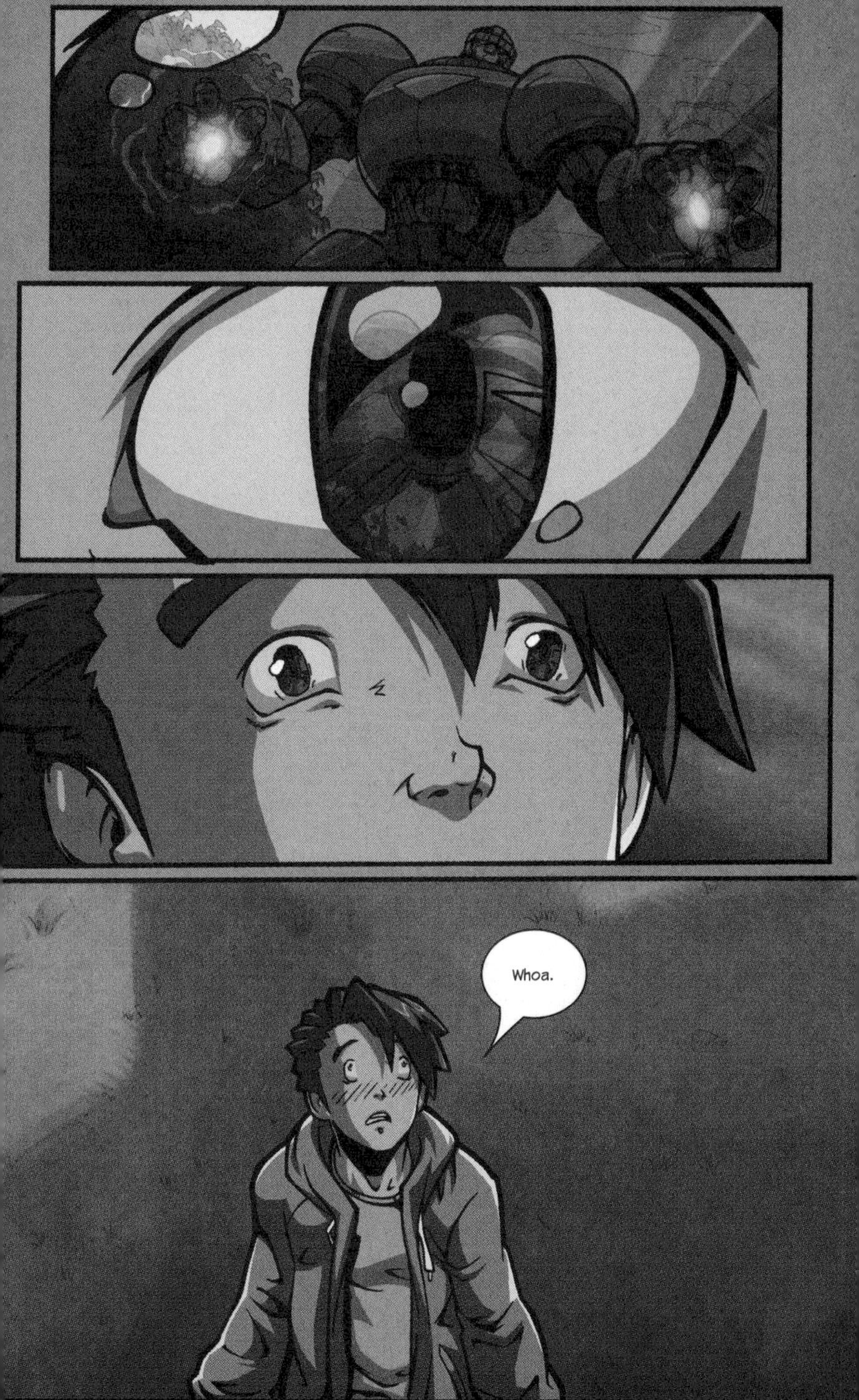
Whoa.

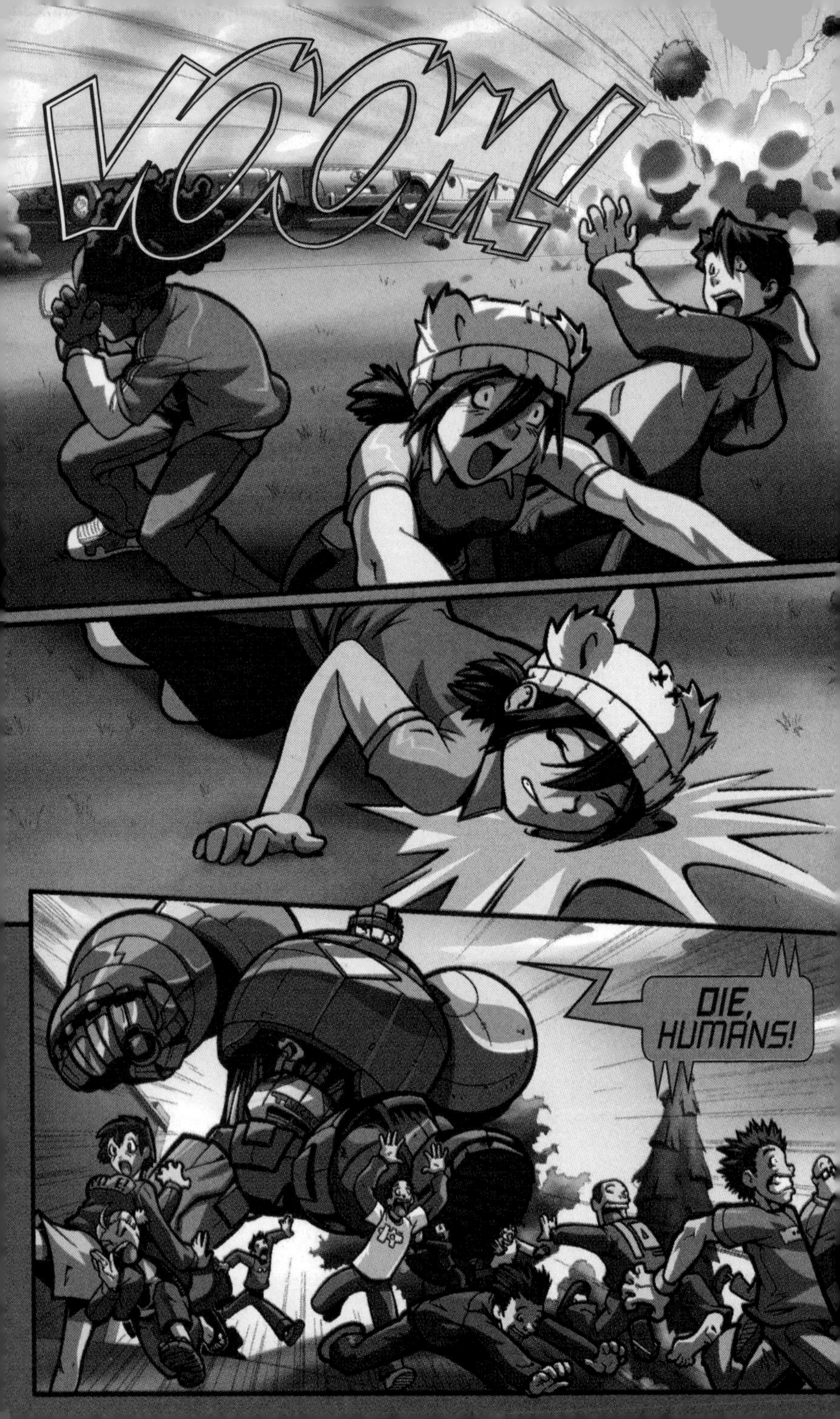
VOOM!
DIE, HUMANS!

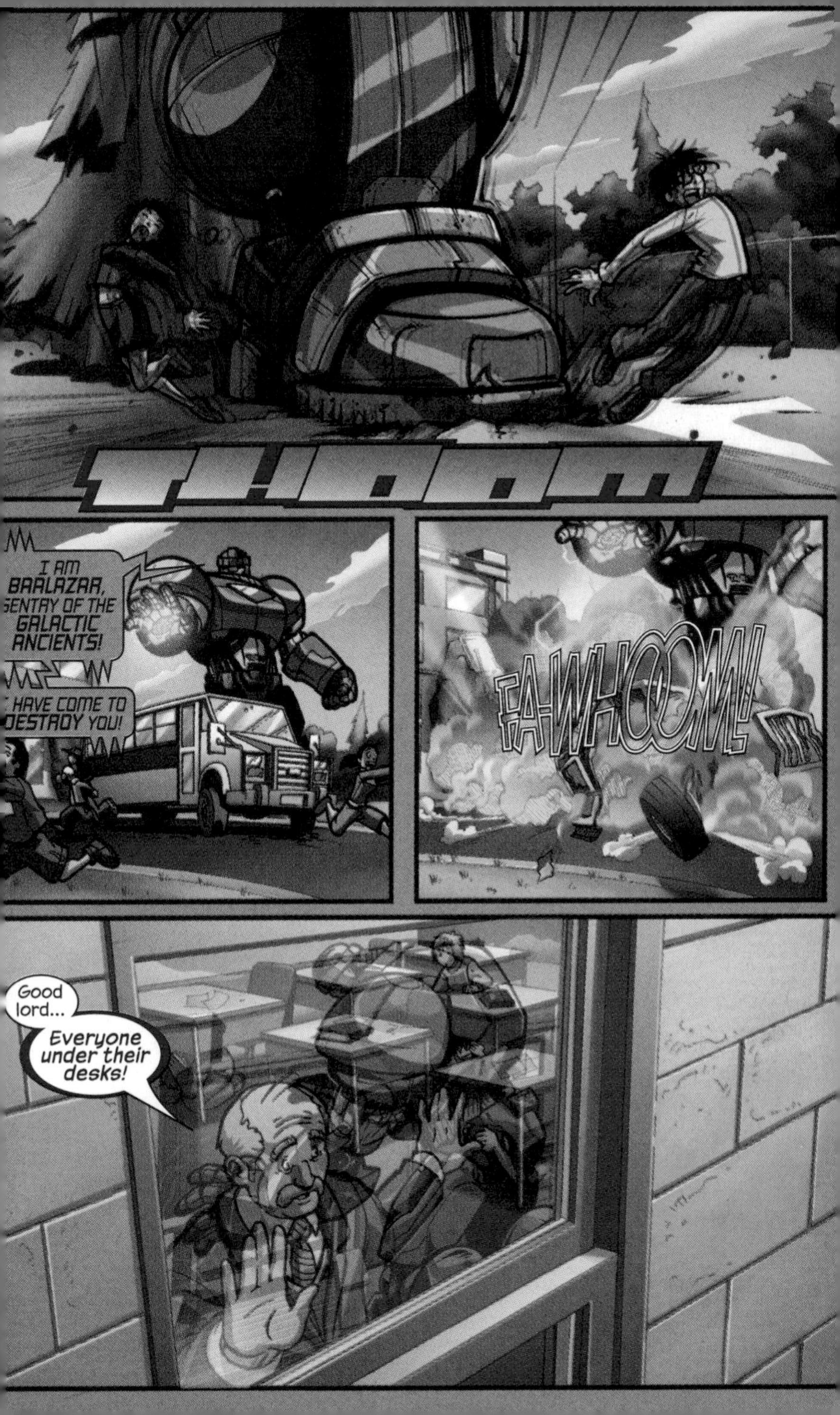
THOOM
I AM BAALAZAR, SENTRY OF THE GALACTIC ANCIENTS!
I HAVE COME TO DESTROY YOU!
FA-WHOOOM!
Good lord...
Everyone under their desks!

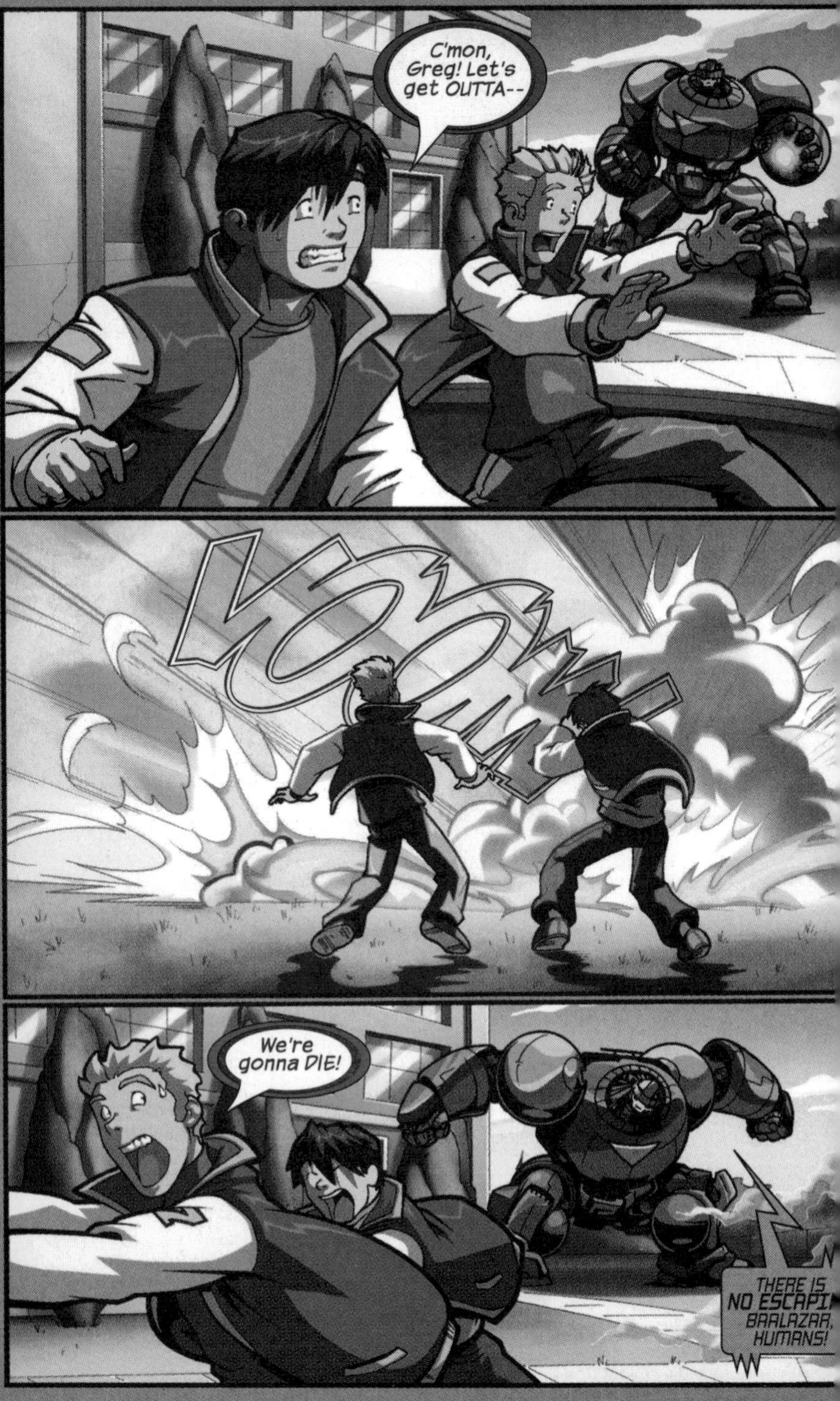

C'mon, Greg! Let's get OUTTA--
We're gonna DIE!
THERE IS NO ESCAPI
BAALAZAR, HUMANS!

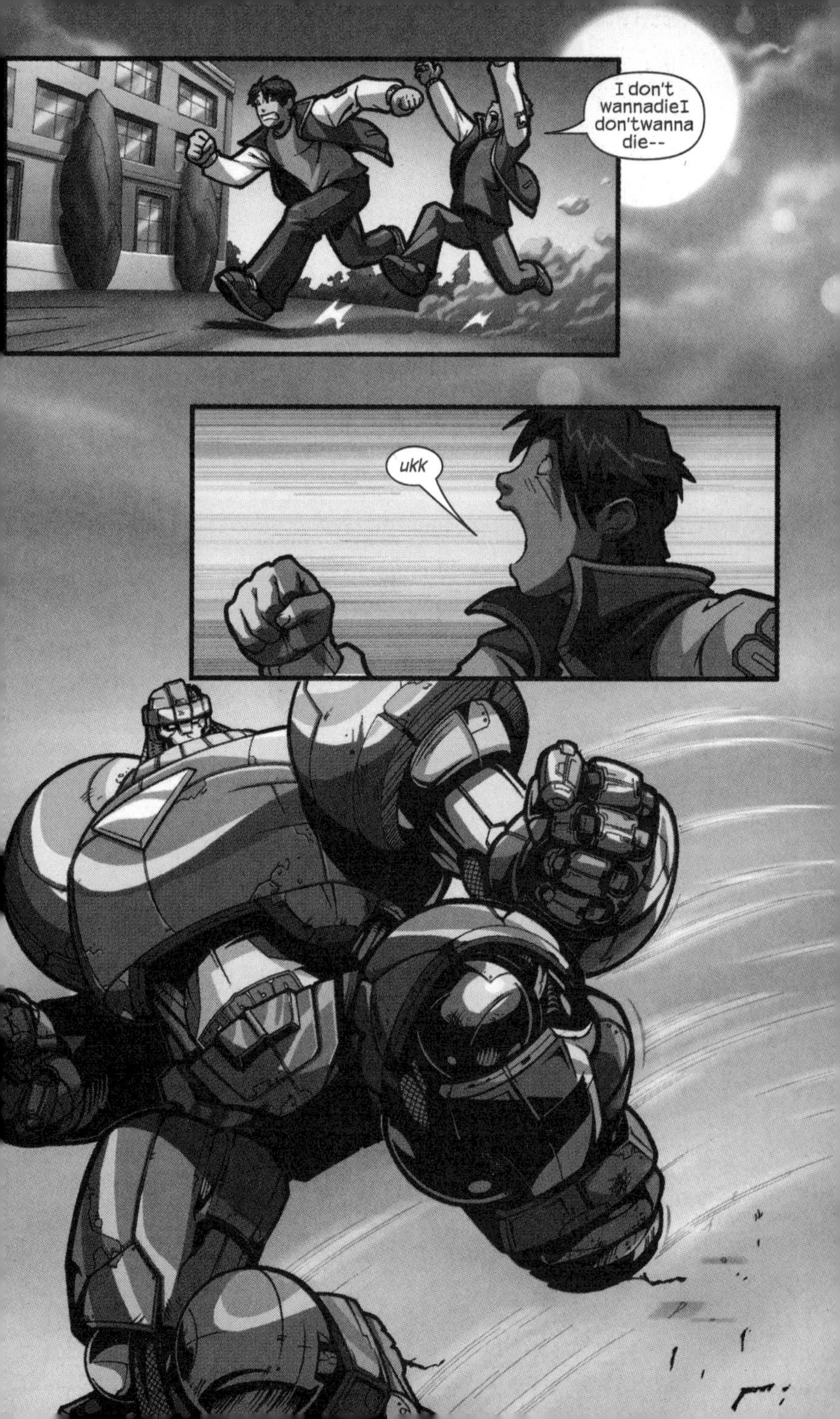
I don't wannadieI don'twanna die--
ukk

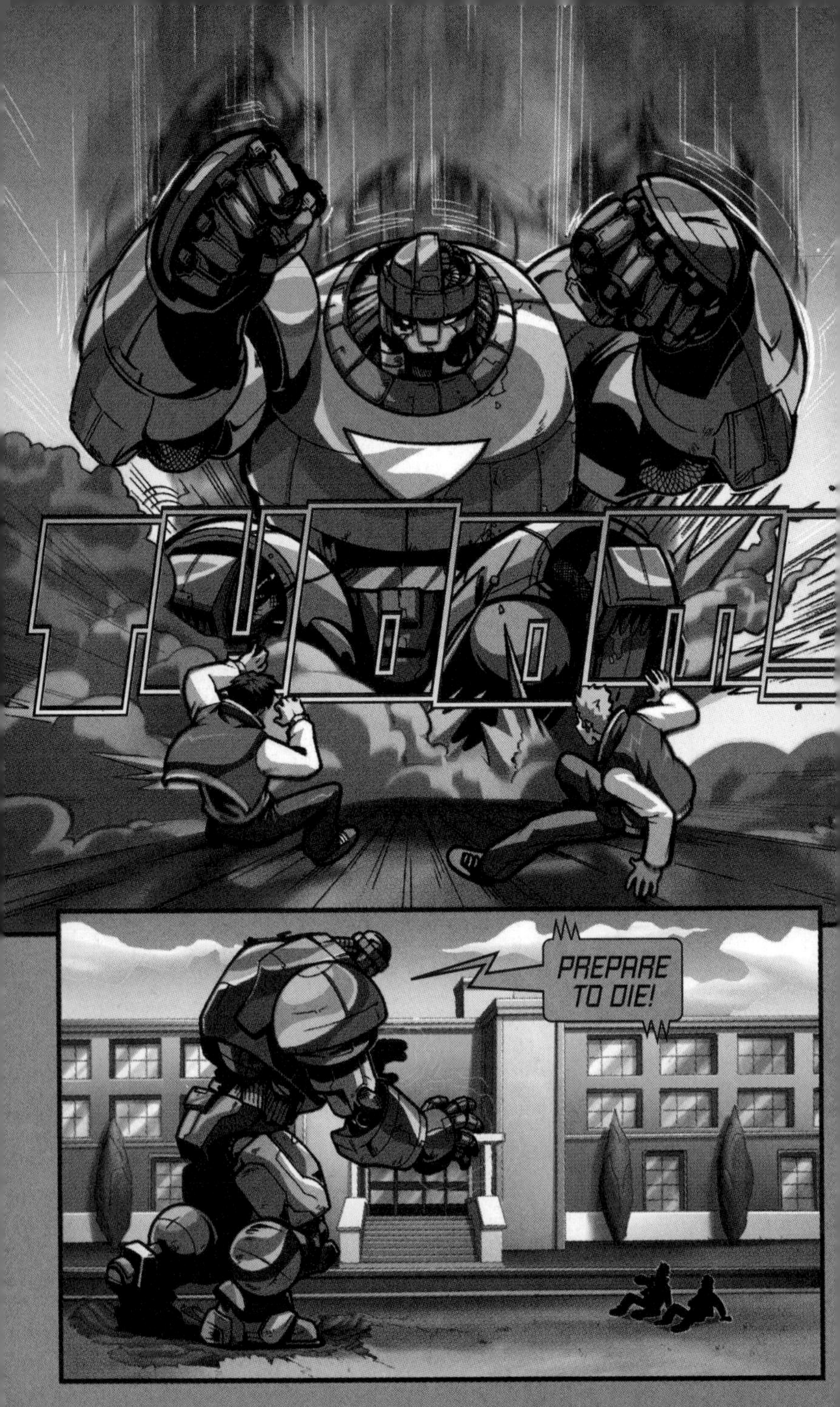
PREPARE TO DIE!

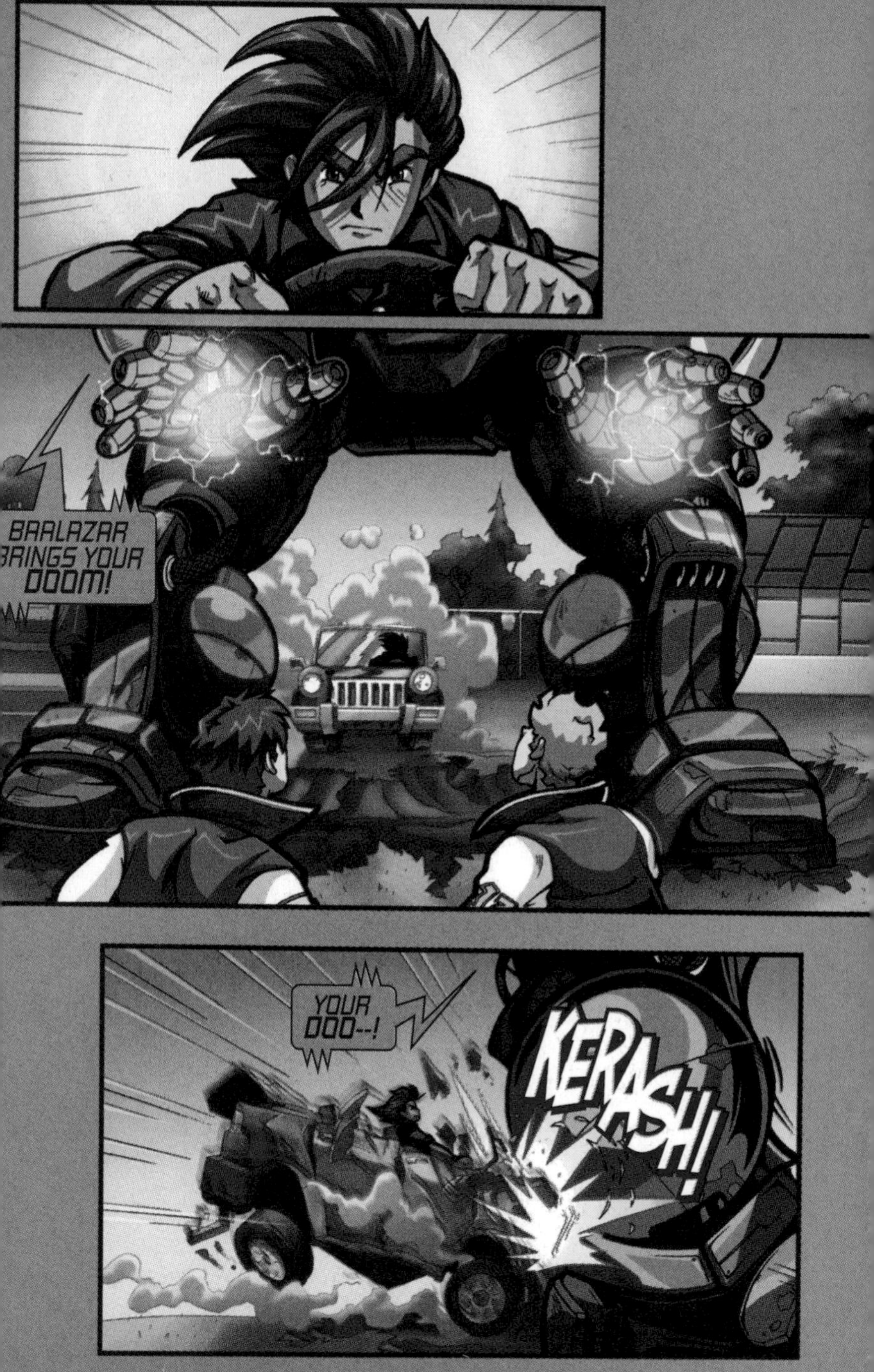
BAALAZAR BRINGS YOUR DOOM!
YOUR DOO--!
KERASH!!

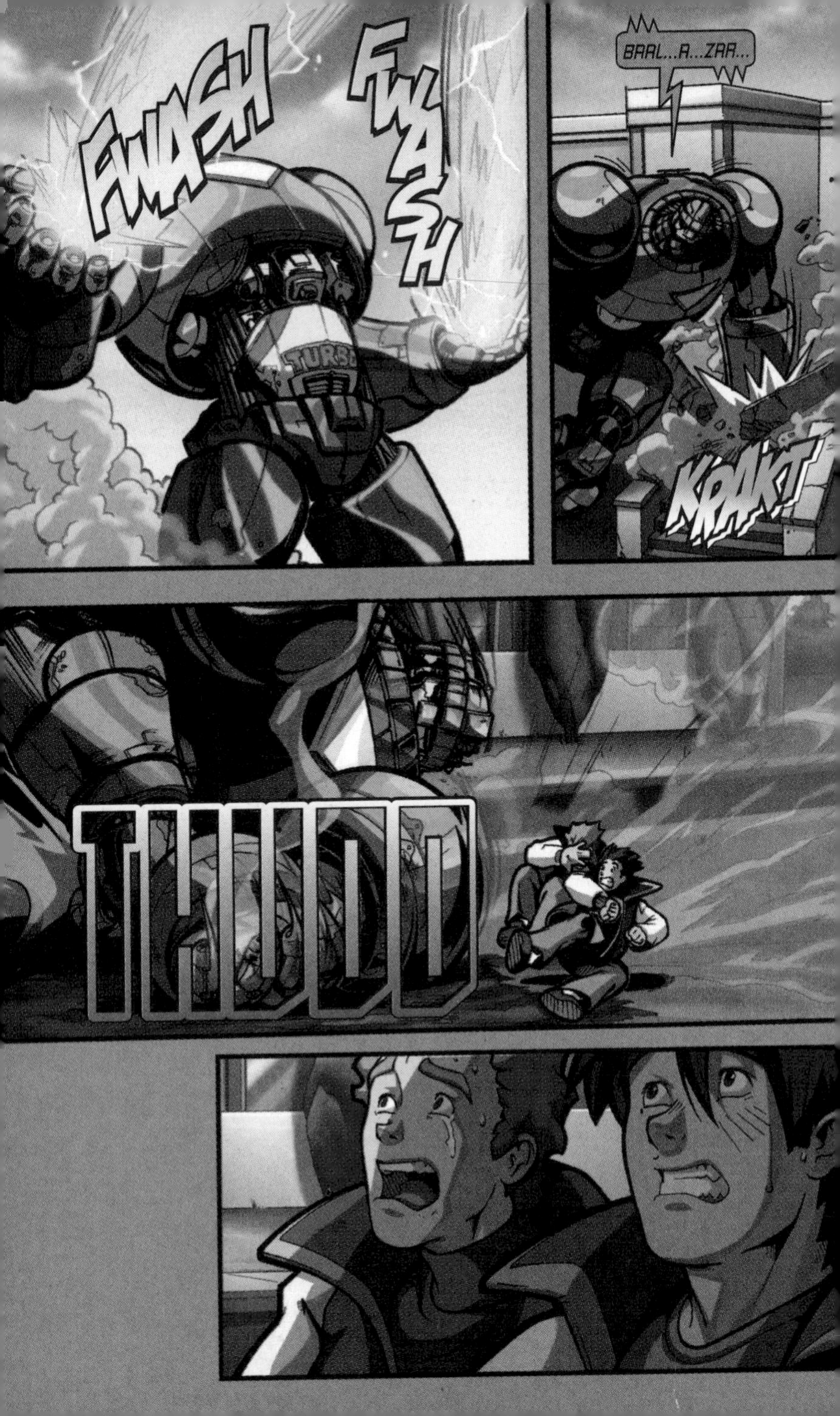
FWASH
FWASH
TURBO
BAAL...A...ZAA...
KRAKT!
THUDD

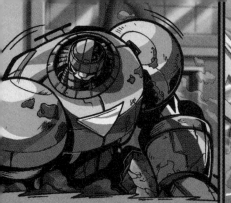

ROR! ERROR! ERROR! ERROR! ERROR! ERROR!
ROR! ERROR! ERROR! ERROR! ERROR! ERROR!
ROR! ERROR! ERROR! ERROR! ERROR! ERROR!
ROR! ERROR! ERROR! ERROR! ERROR! ERROR!
ROR! ERROR! ERROR! ERROR! ERROR!

SKREEE!

SKREEEE-EEEE!

He stopped it!

Juston Seyfert stopped it!

Hnnn...

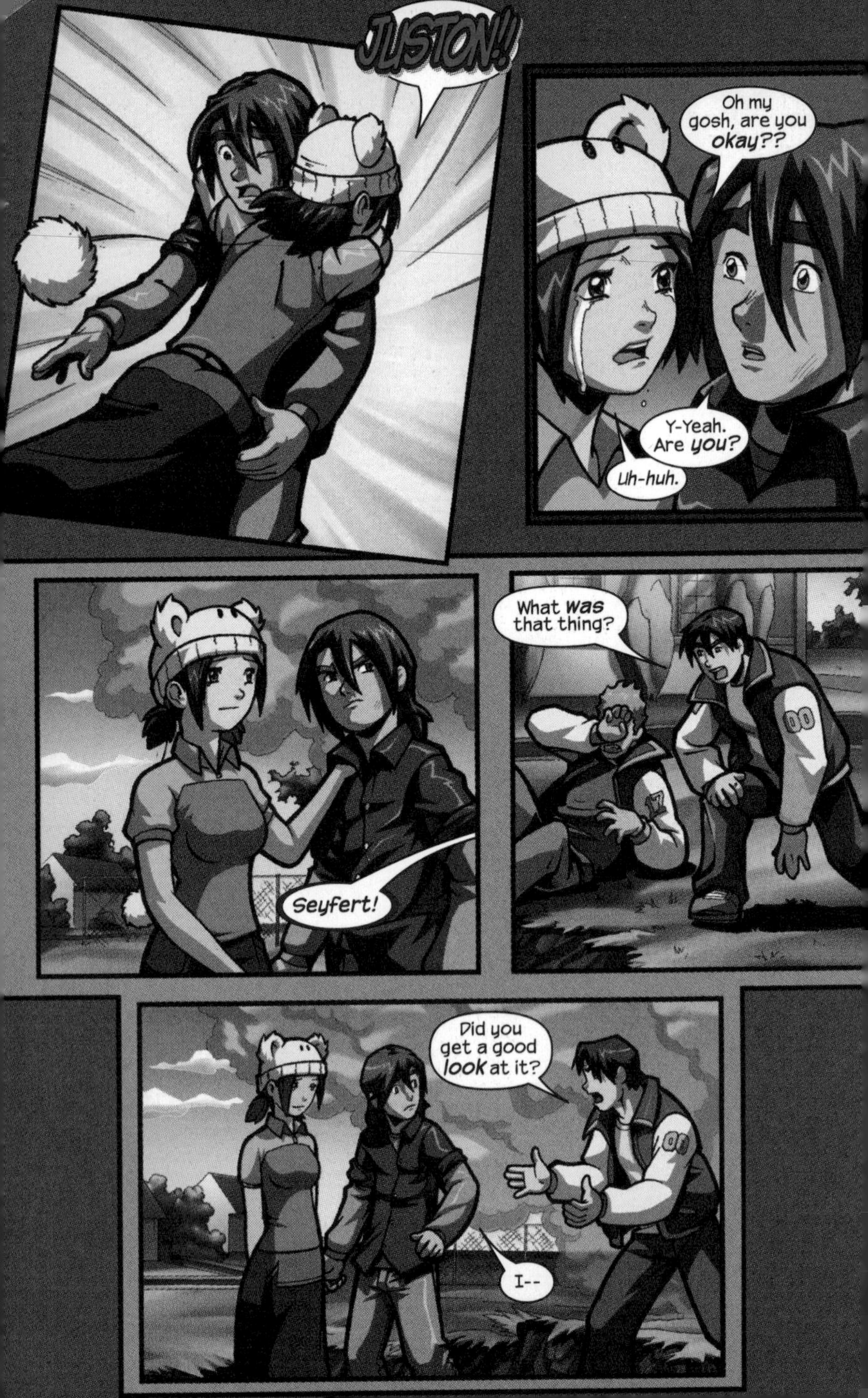
JUSTON!!
Oh my gosh, are you okay??
Y-Yeah. Are you?
Uh-huh.
Seyfert!
What was that thing?
Did you get a good look at it?
I--

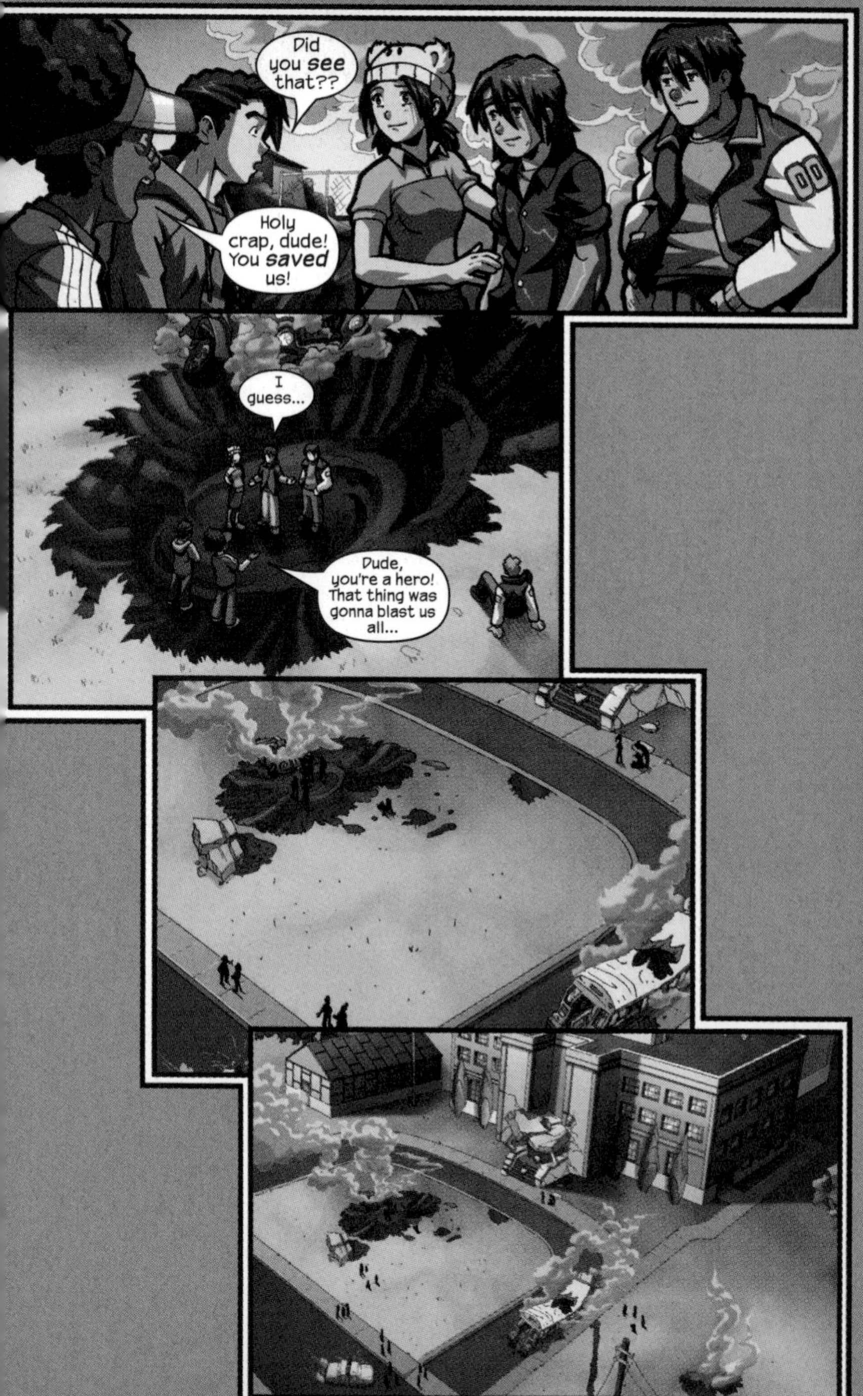
Did you see that??
Holy crap, dude! You saved us!
I guess...
Dude, you're a hero! That thing was gonna blast us all...

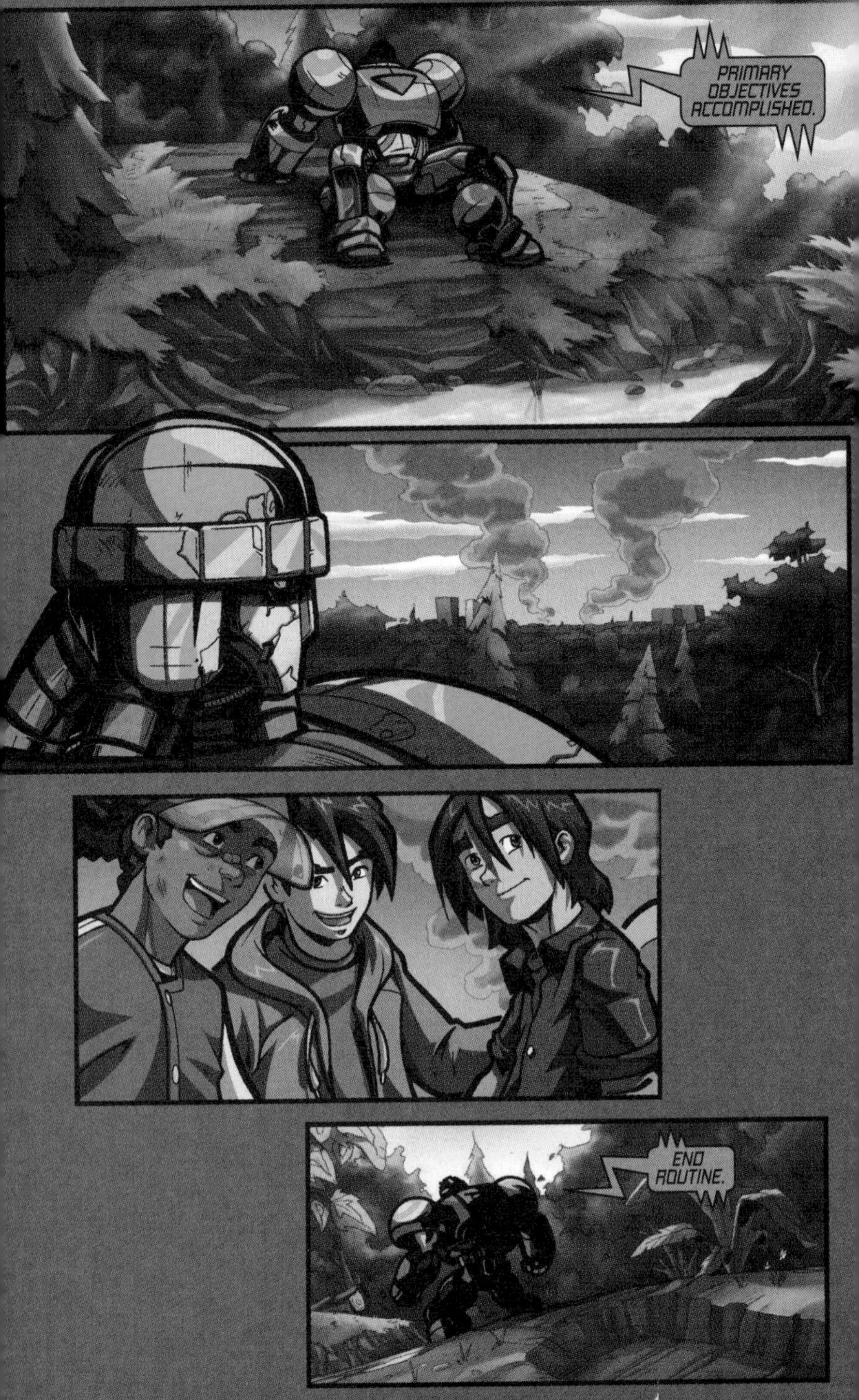
PRIMARY OBJECTIVES ACCOMPLISHED.
END ROUTINE.

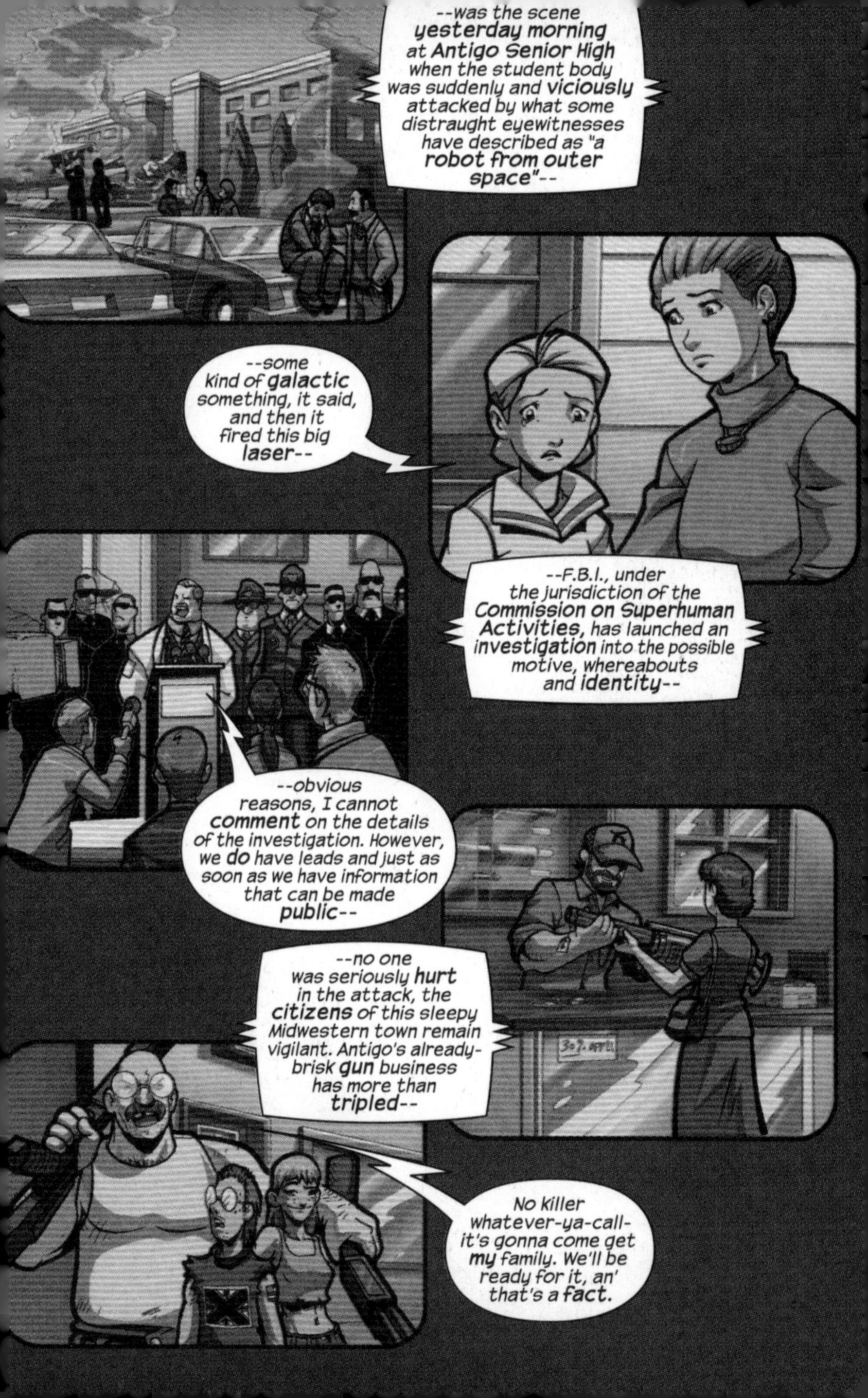
--was the scene yesterday morning at Antigo Senior High when the student body was suddenly and viciously attacked by what some distraught eyewitnesses have described as "a robot from outer space"--
--some kind of galactic something, it said, and then it fired this big laser--
--F.B.I., under the jurisdiction of the Commission on Superhuman Activities, has launched an investigation into the possible motive, whereabouts and identity--
--obvious reasons, I cannot comment on the details of the investigation. However, we do have leads and just as soon as we have information that can be made public--
--no one was seriously hurt in the attack, the citizens of this sleepy Midwestern town remain vigilant. Antigo's already-brisk gun business has more than tripled--
No killer whatever-ya-call-it's gonna come get my family. We'll be ready for it, an' that's a fact.

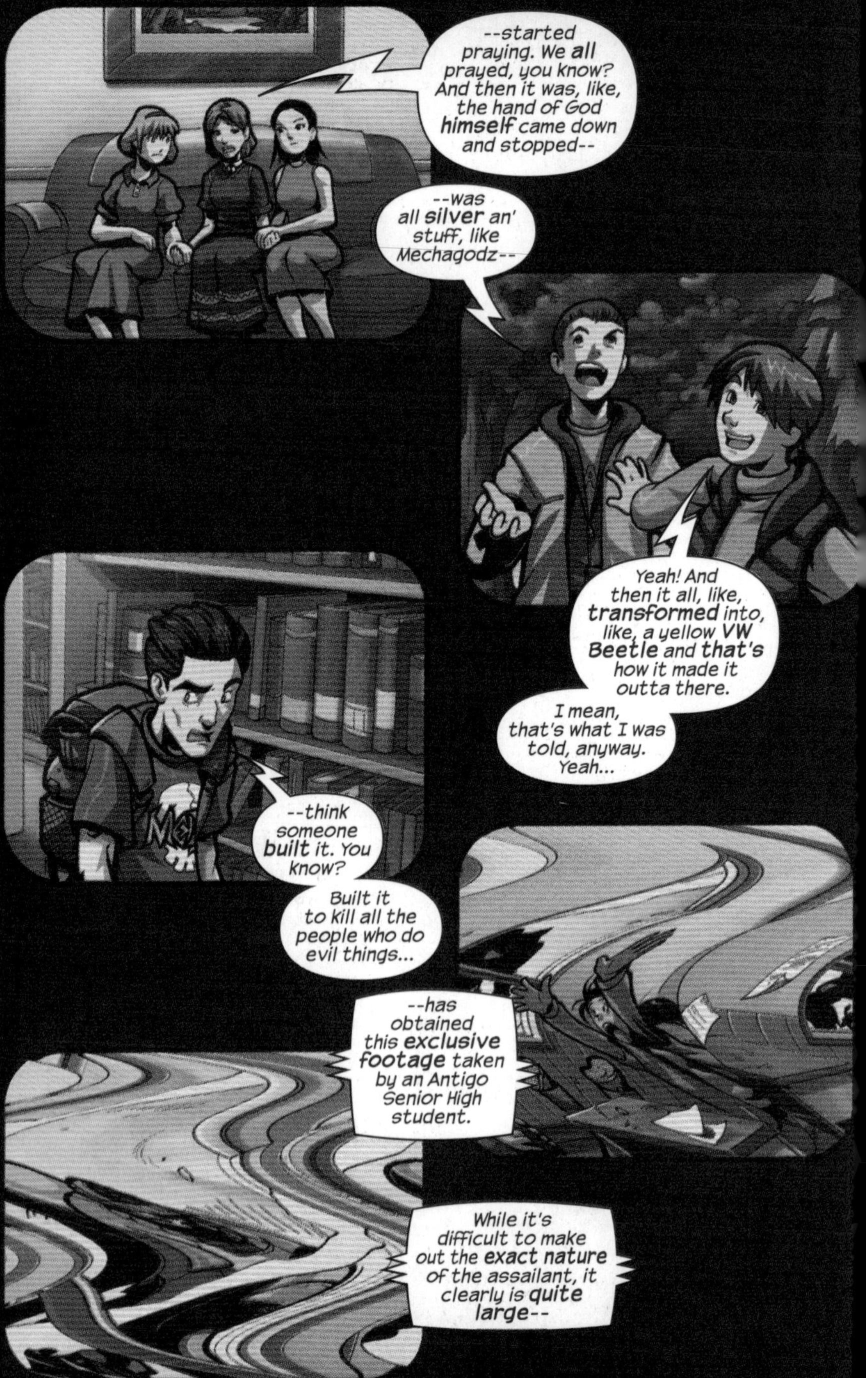
--started praying. We all prayed, you know? And then it was, like, the hand of God himself came down and stopped--
--was all silver an' stuff, like Mechagodz--
Yeah! And then it all, like, transformed into, like, a yellow VW Beetle and that's how it made it outta there.
I mean, that's what I was told, anyway. Yeah...
--think someone built it. You know?
Built it to kill all the people who do evil things...
--has obtained this exclusive footage taken by an Antigo Senior High student.
While it's difficult to make out the exact nature of the assailant, it clearly is quite large--

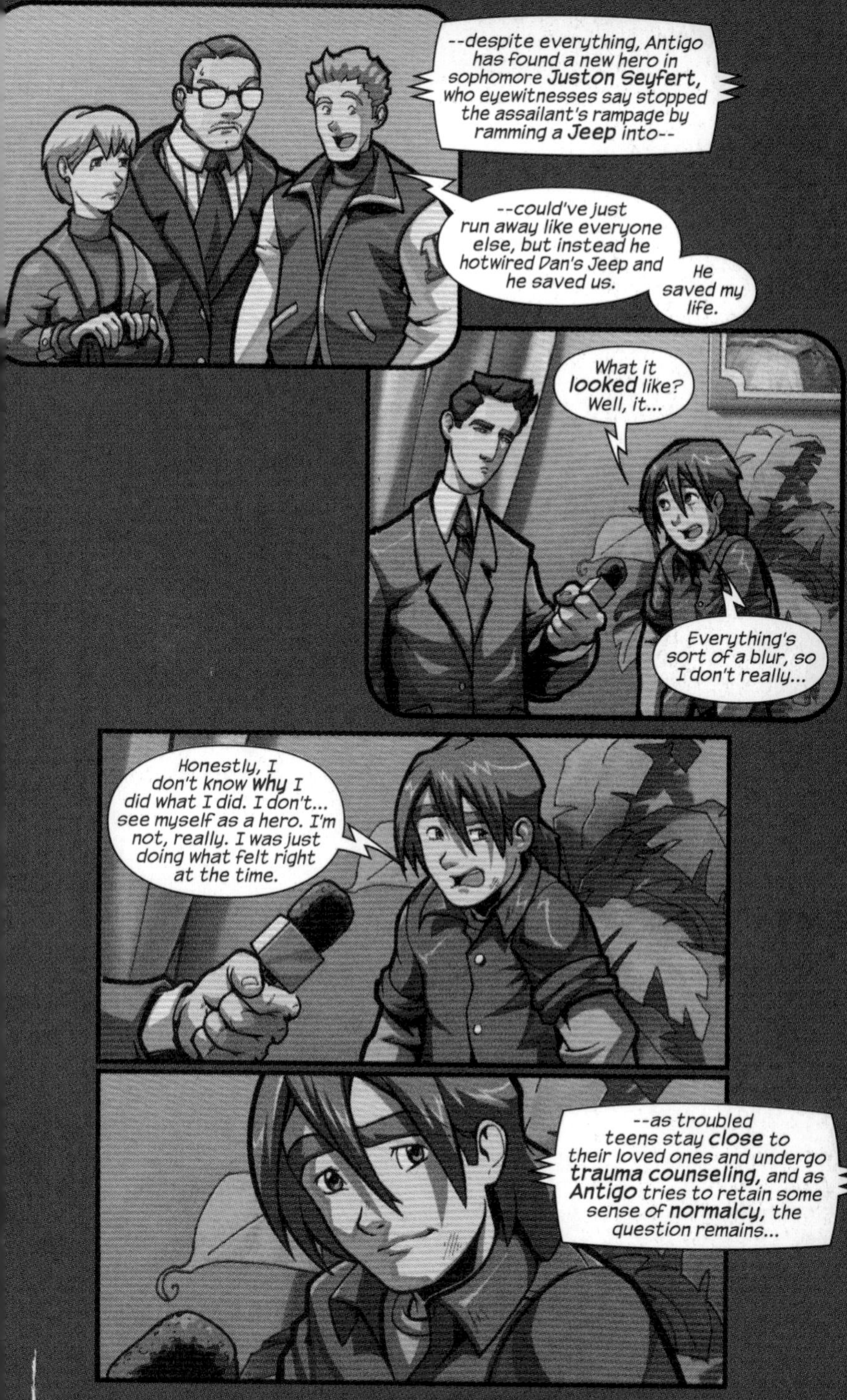
--despite everything, Antigo has found a new hero in sophomore Juston Seyfert, who eyewitnesses say stopped the assailant's rampage by ramming a Jeep into--
--could've just run away like everyone else, but instead he hotwired Dan's Jeep and he saved us.
He saved my life.
What it looked like? Well, it...
Everything's sort of a blur, so I don't really...
Honestly, I don't know why I did what I did. I don't... see myself as a hero. I'm not, really. I was just doing what felt right at the time.
--as troubled teens stay close to their loved ones and undergo trauma counseling, and as Antigo tries to retain some sense of normalcy, the question remains...

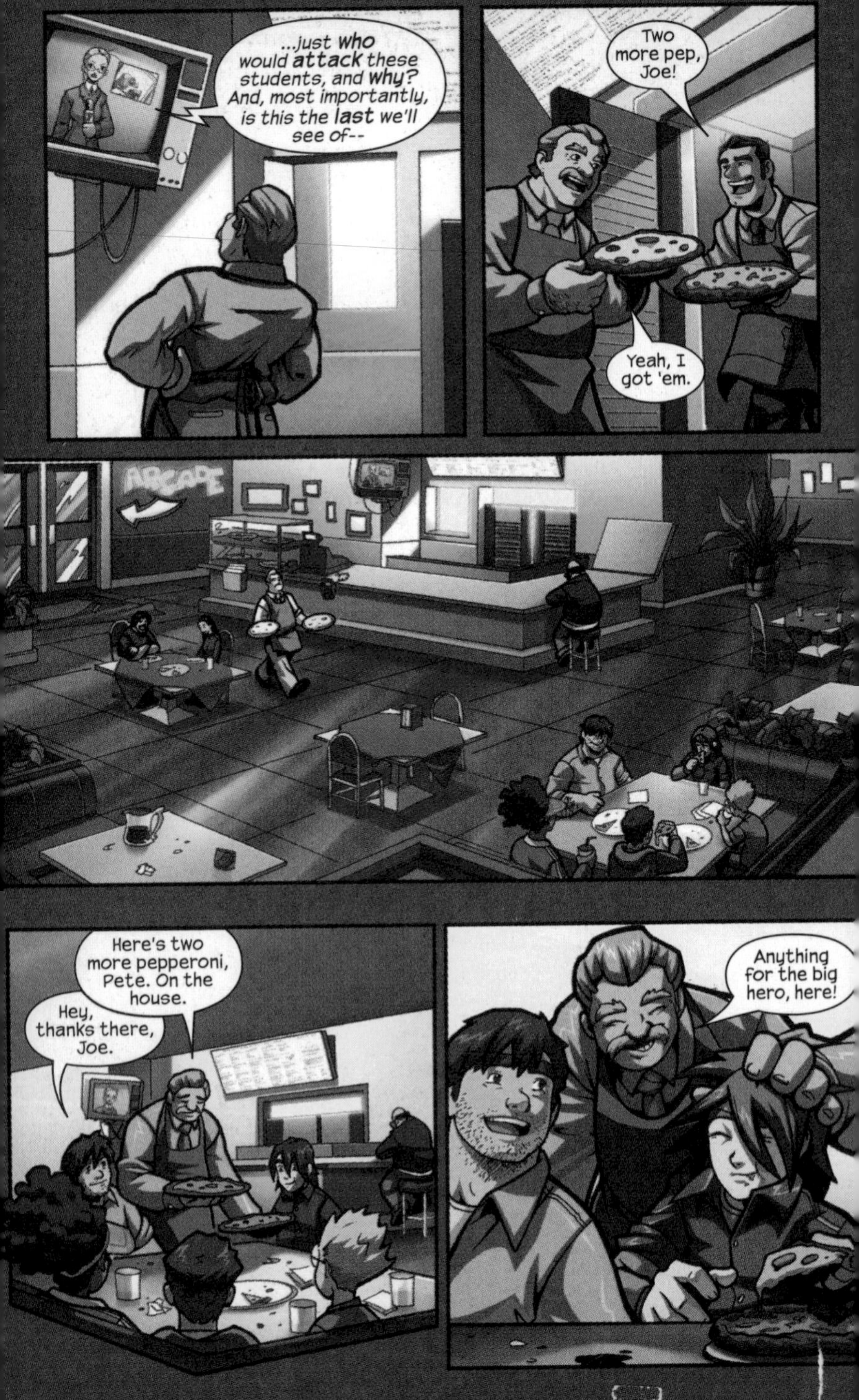
...just who would attack these students, and why? And, most importantly, is this the last we'll see of--
Two more pep, Joe!
Yeah, I got 'em.
ARCADE
Here's two more pepperoni, Pete. On the house.
Hey, thanks there, Joe.
Anything for the big hero, here!

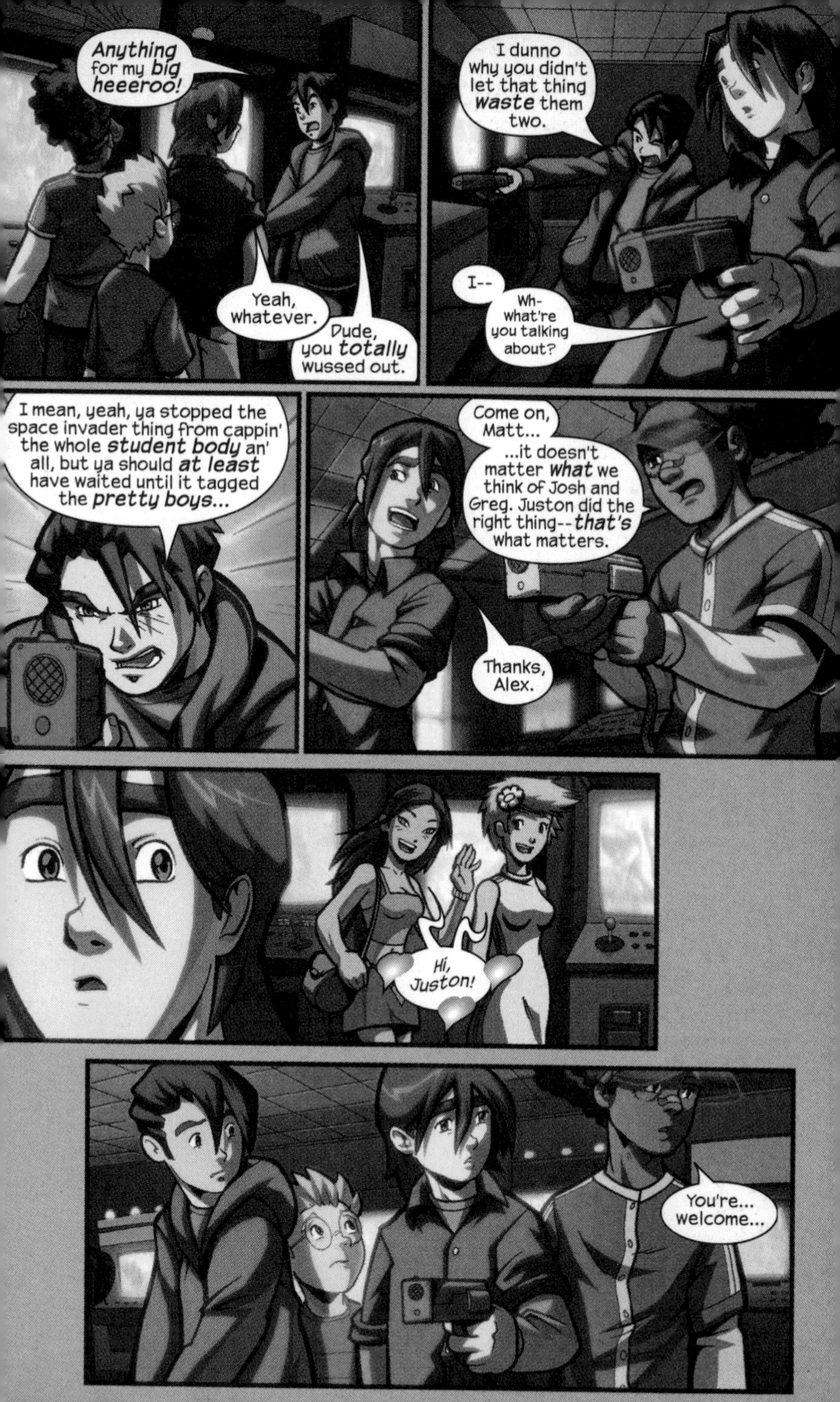
Anything for my big heeeroo!
Yeah, whatever.
Dude, you totally wussed out.
I dunno why you didn't let that thing waste them two.
I--
Wh- what're you talking about?
I mean, yeah, ya stopped the space invader thing from cappin' the whole student body an' all, but ya should at least have waited until it tagged the pretty boys...
Come on, Matt...
...it doesn't matter what we think of Josh and Greg. Juston did the right thing--that's what matters.
Thanks, Alex.
Hi, Juston!
You're... welcome...

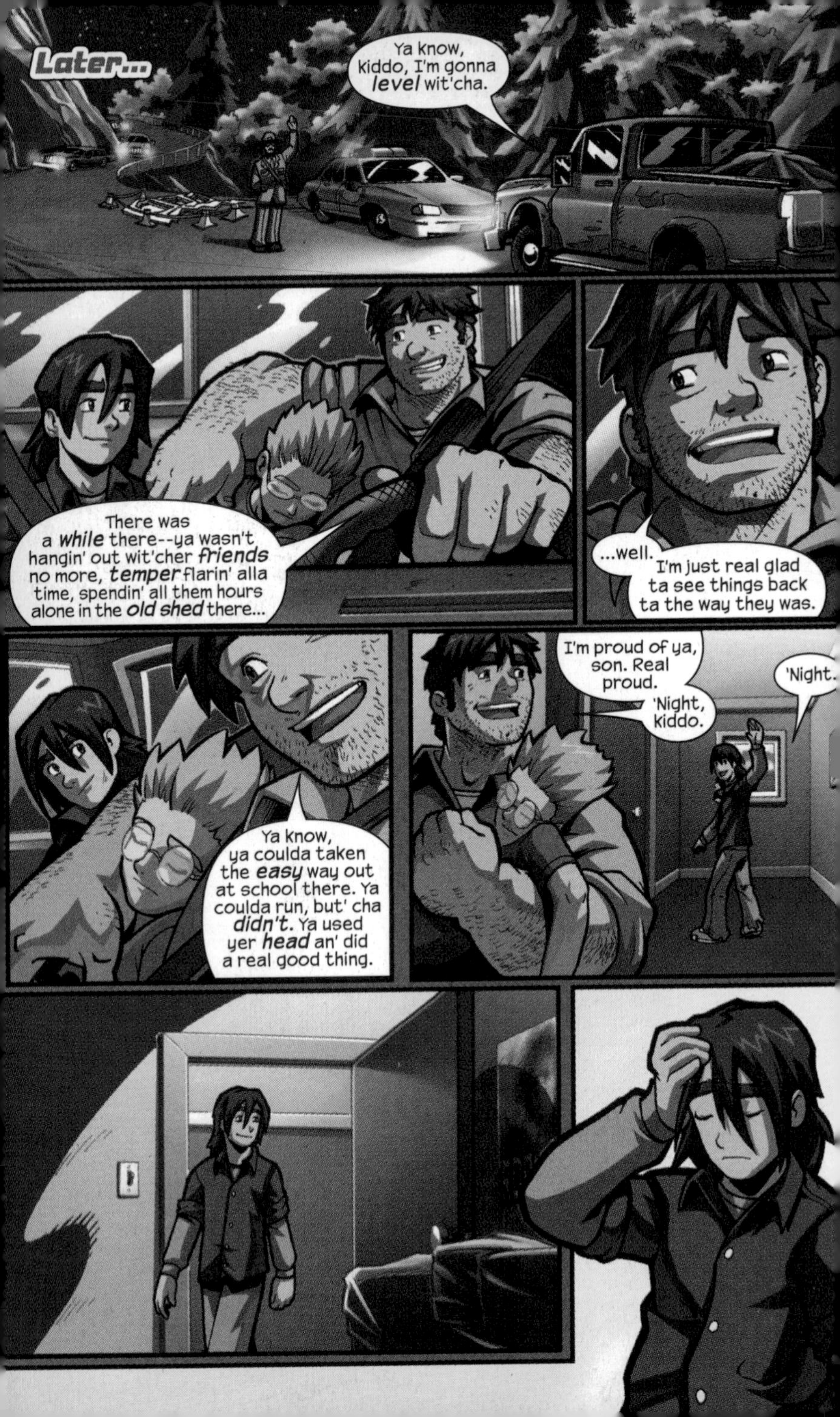
Later...
Ya know, kiddo, I'm gonna *level* wit'cha.
There was a *while* there--ya wasn't hangin' out wit'cher *friends* no more, *temper* flarin' alla time, spendin' all them hours alone in the *old shed* there...
...well.
I'm just real glad ta see things back ta the way they was.
Ya know, ya coulda taken the *easy* way out at school there. Ya coulda run, but' cha *didn't*. Ya used yer *head* an' did a real good thing.
I'm proud of ya, son. Real proud.
'Night, kiddo.
'Night.

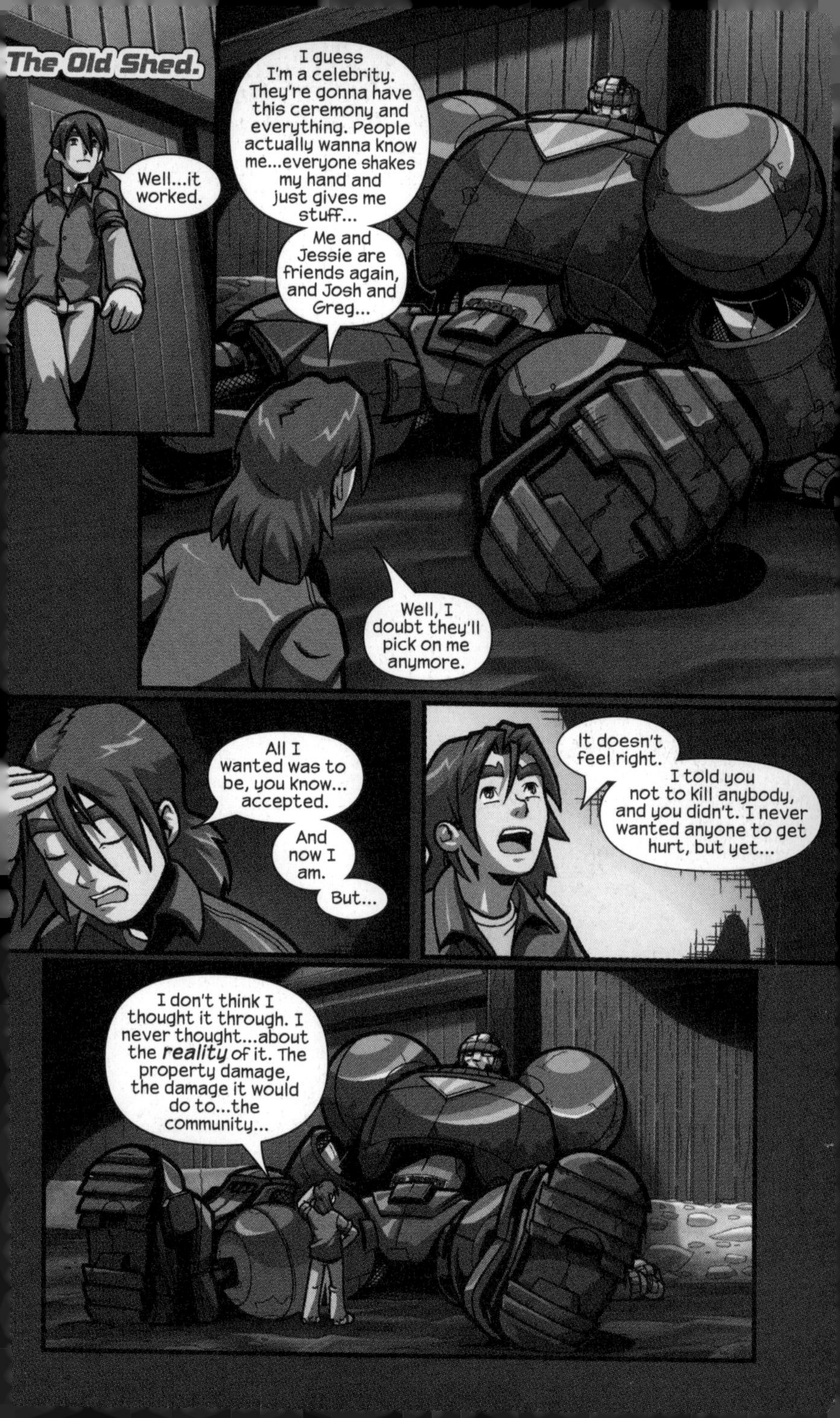
The Old Shed.
Well...it worked.
I guess I'm a celebrity. They're gonna have this ceremony and everything. People actually wanna know me...everyone shakes my hand and just gives me stuff...
Me and Jessie are friends again, and Josh and Greg...
Well, I doubt they'll pick on me anymore.
All I wanted was to be, you know... accepted.
And now I am.
But...
It doesn't feel right.
I told you not to kill anybody, and you didn't. I never wanted anyone to get hurt, but yet...
I don't think I thought it through. I never thought...about the *reality* of it. The property damage, the damage it would do to...the community...

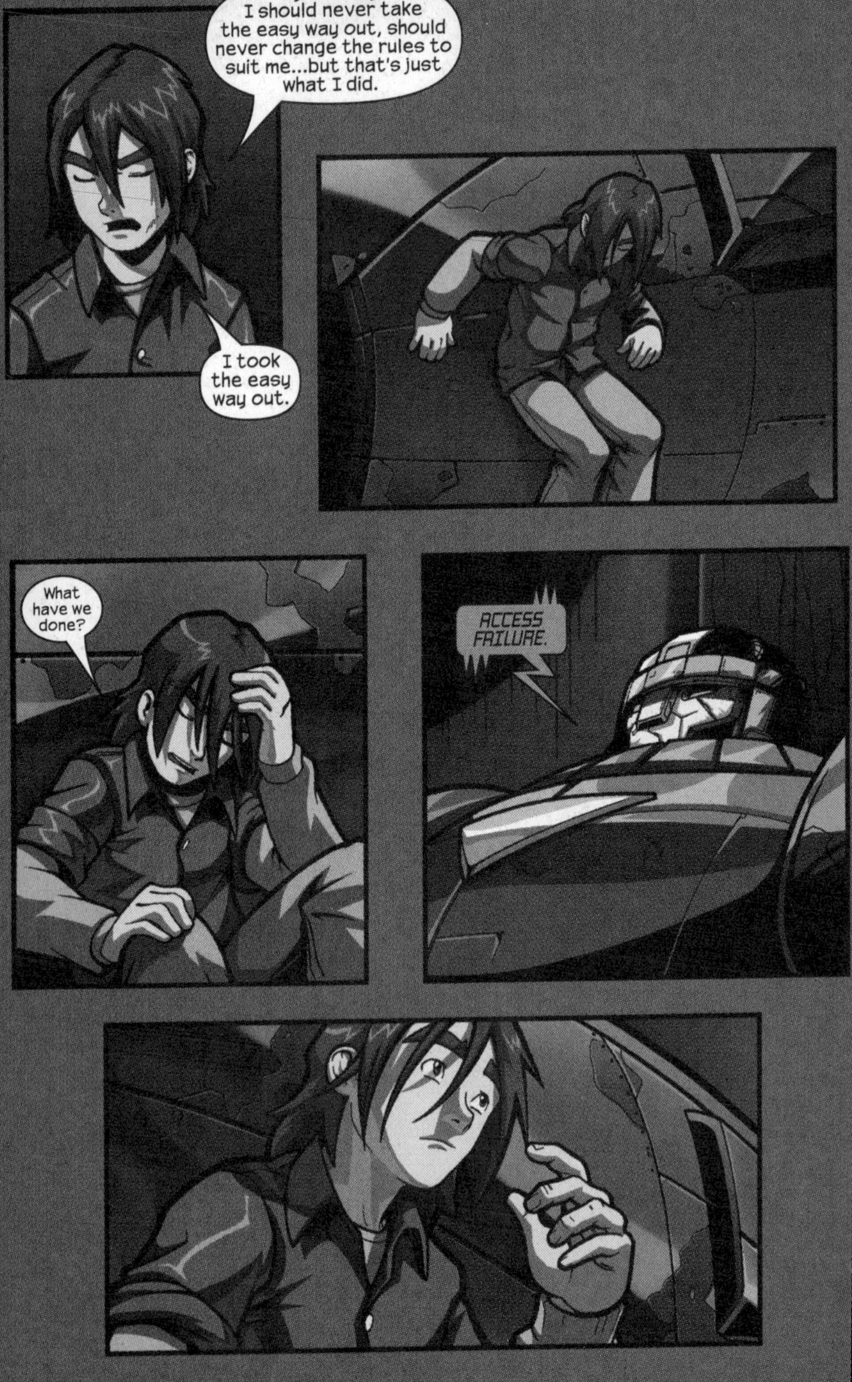
My dad says I should never take the easy way out, should never change the rules to suit me...but that's just what I did.
I took the easy way out.
What have we done?
ACCESS FAILURE.

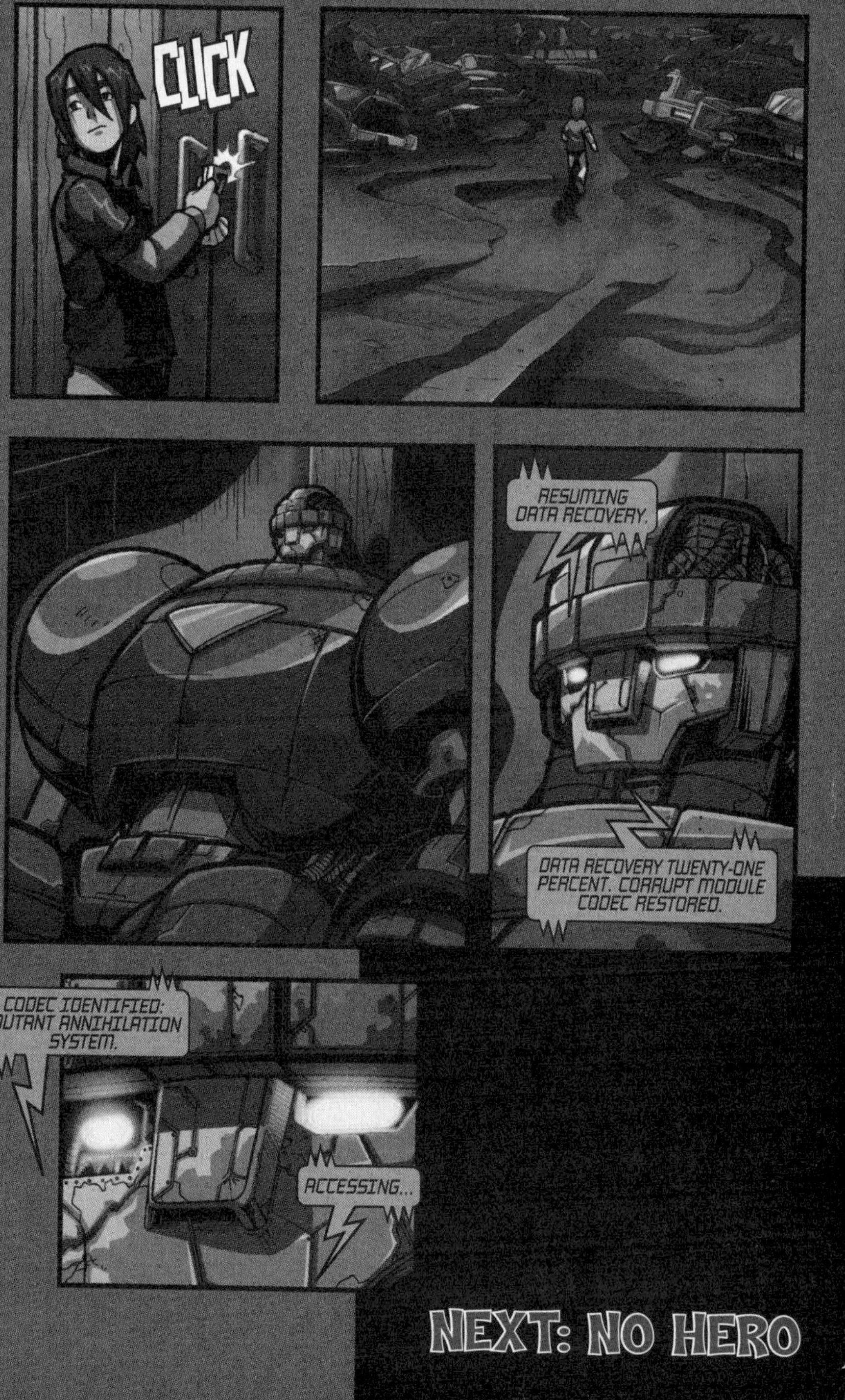
CLICK
RESUMING DATA RECOVERY.
DATA RECOVERY TWENTY-ONE PERCENT. CORRUPT MODULE CODEC RESTORED.
CODEC IDENTIFIED: MUTANT ANNIHILATION SYSTEM.
ACCESSING...
NEXT: NO HERO

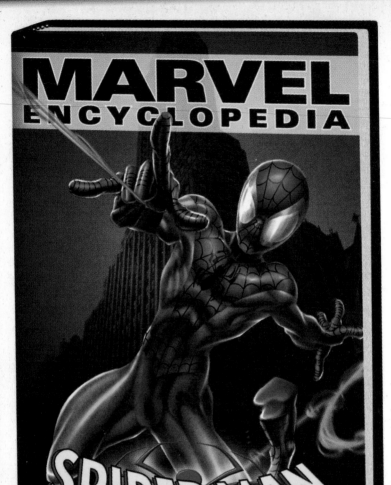

MARVEL®

EVERYTHING You Ever Wanted to Know About Spider-Man
And Weren't Afraid to Ask!